Library of
Davidson College

PEOPLE AND PLACES

Also by P.J. Kavanagh

POEMS
Presences: New and Selected Poems (1987)

MEMOIR
The Perfect Stranger (1966)

NOVELS
A Song and Dance (1968)
A Happy Man (1972)
People and Weather (1978)
Scarf Jack (1978)
Rebel for Good (1980)
Only By Mistake (1986)

EDITED
Collected Poems of Ivor Gurney (1982)
The Bodley Head G.K. Chesterton (1985) /
The Essential G.K. Chesterton (1987)
The Oxford Book of Short Poems, with James Michie (1985)

P. J. KAVANAGH

People and Places

A SELECTION 1975-1987

CARCANET

First published in Great Britain 1988 by
Carcanet Press Limited
208-212 Corn Exchange Buildings
Manchester M4 3BQ

Copyright © 1988 P.J. Kavanagh
All rights reserved

British Library Cataloguing in Publication Data

Kavanagh, P.J.
  People and places : a selection 1975-1987.
  I. Title
  824'.914   PR6061.A9

ISBN 0-85635-747-2

The publisher acknowledges the financial
assistance of the Arts Council of Great Britain

Typeset in 10½pt Bembo by Bryan Williamson, Manchester
Printed in England by SRP Ltd, Exeter

For Cornelius and Bruno

Acknowledgements

———— o ————

I am grateful to the editors of the journals and the publishers of the books in which the pieces here collected appeared for the first time: *Grand Street*, the *Guardian*, *The Listener*, *PN Review*, the *Spectator*, the *Telegraph Sunday Magazine*, *Theology; The Essential G.K. Chesterton* (Oxford University Press, 1987; previously *The Bodley Head G.K. Chesterton*, 1985), *In Pursuit of Spring:* Edward Thomas (Wildwood House, 1981), *In Ruins: the once great houses of Ireland* (Collins, 1980), *The ITMA Years:* Scripts by Ted Kavanagh (The Woburn Press, 1974), *People: essays and poems,* edited by Susan Hill (Chatto and Windus / The Hogarth Press, 1983), *Summer Days: writers on cricket,* edited by Michael Meyer (Eyre Methuen, 1981).

Thanks are also due to the BBC for permission to print talks originally broadcast.

I would particularly like to record my gratitude to W.L. Webb of the *Guardian* and John Anstey of the *Telegraph Sunday Magazine* who first pushed me in the direction of this kind of writing, and to Alexander Chancellor and Charles Moore of the *Spectator* who encouraged me to continue.

Contents

―――○―――

NAMING NAMES *Telegraph Sunday Magazine*	page 9
BANKSIDE *Spectator*	17
MARGIAD EVANS *Listener*	24
BIRDLIP MIRROR *Spectator*	32
THE GREEN AND THE GREY *Telegraph Sunday Magazine*	34
THE SOFT SIDE *Spectator*	40
A WALK *Spectator*	42
BY THE LIGHT OF THE POACHER'S MOON *Telegraph Sunday Magazine*	45
CATARACTS AND CREEKS *Radio 3*	52
FATHER TIME *Spectator*	60
GREEN SHADES *Spectator*	62
LABYRINTHINE WAYS *Spectator*	64
MR HORNBY AND BARLOW *Spectator*	67
THE MYSTERY OF CRICKET *Summer Days*	70
A BOOK IN MY LIFE *Spectator*	80
A GLASTONBURY ROMANCE *Theology*	83
TRUE STORY *Spectator*	91
ICELAND *Telegraph Sunday Magazine*	93
IS IT ALAS, YORICK? *People*	99
ITMA *Introduction*	104
FEAR OF AN ODD SORT *Guardian*	109
SEPTEMBER SONG *Spectator*	114
OTHER MEN'S TROUSERS *Spectator*	117
A WAY OF ESCAPE *Telegraph Sunday Magazine*	123
LIQUID LIGHT *Spectator*	133
RUINED IRISH HOUSES *Introduction*	135
SHEEP'S LIB *Spectator*	139
FINDING A VOICE *Radio 3*	141

TRIFLES *Spectator*	149
THE REAL THING *Spectator*	151
AN APPETITIVE DECORUM *Grand Street*	153
ORTHODOXIES *PN Review*	163
DUN ROAMIN' *Spectator*	172
IMAGES OF HEAVEN AND HELL *Radio 3*	174
SOAME JENYNS *Spectator*	180
DIS-CONGLOBATED *Spectator*	182
AESTHETE *Spectator*	185
EDWARD THOMAS AND RICHARD JEFFERIES *Radio 3*	188
IN PURSUIT OF SPRING *Introduction*	194
A TRAVELLER IN LITTLE THINGS *Radio 3*	199
STILL COMPANION OF THE DEW *Spectator*	207
GONE BEFORE *Spectator*	209
BROTHERHOOD *Spectator*	216
A DRY TIME *Spectator*	219
THE FENCE *Spectator*	221
COPPER *Spectator*	223
UNPOMPOUS CIRCUMSTANCE *Spectator*	225
ZEN *Spectator*	227
G.K.C., THE MOB *Introduction*	230
BEYOND HAGIOGRAPHY *Spectator*	244
CREDIT WHERE CREDIT IS DUE *Spectator*	246
SEPTEMBER 1984 *Spectator*	249
MENTIONED IN DISPATCHES *Spectator*	251
LOOKING FOR A LANE *Telegraph Sunday Magazine*	253
THE SECRET PEOPLE *Spectator*	262
Index	265

Naming Names

I

THERE IS a special power in names. There must be, because here we are standing at the edge of a tiny cornfield, staring with special interest at a red-brick barn in a tiny undistinguished hamlet in northern France called Riez Bailleul, because a poet, long dead, mentioned the place.

Dogs bark round us, a woman stands, suspicious, in her doorway – but how can we explain to her what we barely understand ourselves, why we are there? That we are here because Ivor Gurney, musician and poet, who died in 1937, wrote of this place, remembering when he was here with the Gloucestershire Regiment, in 1916? Yet the barn he may well have stayed in, as we stare at it, takes on an extra significance, even a personality.

Primitive societies have always believed in the magical properties of names. Ivor Gurney certainly did. Born in Gloucester in 1890, he recited in his poems written in France, like a litany, the names of the villages along the Severn – Ashleworth, Maisemore, Framilode, Minsterworth... After the war he did the same for the places he knew as a private soldier in northern France, until the syllables of the names start to re-echo in the mind – Aveluy, Laventie, Robecq, Riez Bailleul.... The good thing about good writers is that they refuse to die; he has made us follow in his tracks, and we feel his presence.

Gurney, amid all the horror of the war, clearly loved northern France – 'the clarity, amiability of North French air'. He loved the rare estaminets where he and his comrades drank coffee, remembered the kindnesses they received from French people, and celebrated, above all, the wide Somme skies glimpsed from a trench. His pictures of that part of France are so clear and excited they make the war seem even more wasteful and detestable than poems of direct complaint, though he wrote those too.

It has much to do with the sense he gives of a specific time and place. He knew this. During the war, censorship did not allow such precision – 'forbidden names or dates without which the poets / Are done for' – and it is only after the war, when he could specify place and weather, that his war poems come fully alive.

> Riez Bailleul in blue tea-time...
> There's dusk here; west hedgerows show thin;
> In billets there's sound of packs reset,
> Tea finished; the dixies dried of the wet.
> Some walk, some write, and the cards begin.
> Stars gather in heaven and the pools drown in.

It is the name 'Riez Bailleul' that catches the attention first, gives authenticity. Though, with all our knowledge of Somme mud, we might not have thought of the stars 'drowning' in soup-like shell-crater pools.

Riez Bailleul is still a hamlet, barely even that. Six or seven red-brick farm buildings, at least one dating from Gurney's time. It may well be the one in which Gurney and his platoon sheltered, snug in straw, withdrawn a mile or so from the line. He enjoyed watching the shadows their candles cast on the roof. Like so many soldiers returned from the war, desolate from their experience, Gurney in his poems seems to miss the comradeship, the shared simplicity:

> Never more delight comes of the roof dark lit
> With under-candle flicker nor rich gloom on it,
> The limned faces and moving hands shuffling the cards,
> The clear conscience, the free mind...

The barn stands in a small orchard, next to cropped meadows, their surfaces still uneven with the traces of old trenches: 'A hundred things of age, of carefulness / Spoiling: a farmer's treasure perhaps soon a wilderness.' Along the road, once the front line, are other villages, really strings of houses – 'Tilleloy, Fauquissart, Neuve Chapelle, and mud like glue.' (Now along the road are signs directing you to the 'Poney Club'.) 'But Laventie, most of all, I think is to soldiers / The town itself with plane trees, and small-spa air'. It is at this point that one feels like clapping Gurney on the back because no phrase, still, could capture that town better than 'small-spa air'. 'Neat French market-town look so clean, / And the clarity, amiability of North French air.' One is conscious of that air, among the wide, sweeping cornfields of the Somme, and among 'the mere cabbage fields and potato plants lovely to see'. (Gurney is fond of the practical and familiar, it is one of the sources of his power.)

In another part of the Somme is one building that Gurney and his fellow-soldiers certainly did use: the mausoleum at Caulaincourt. It was the only building standing so they crawled inside. It still stands and I found it by asking a roadside workman where the English soldiers had hidden during the First World War. He knew at once and grinned widely: 'The Boche never found them out.' I wanted to tell him that I knew of it because one of those soldiers had had diarrhoea:

> Half dead with sheer tiredness, wakened quick at night
> With dysentery pangs, going blind among dim sleepers
> And dazed into half dark...

It is an odd construction, built for the dead of the local noble family, cruciform like a Greek church; hard to imagine that more than a hundred Gloucesters crammed into it, grateful to be there. But Gurney did not only write about his dysentery and 'ill body-creepers', but about what met his eyes when sick, lousy, he stumbled outside – 'the cold bringing me sane.' To him it was a scene of remembered Gloucestershire, 'Witcombe Steep as it were, but no beeches there' and the stars 'Mysterious glowing on the cloths of heaven'. He wrote about it years later, sick in mind and body, bewildered by his memories.

Dark was the billet after that seeing of rare
Gold stars, stumbling among the still forms to my lair.
Still were the stars bright – my sick mind hung on them even.

But long after, in solitary day walking, I recalled
Caulaincourt's Mausoleum and the stars March midnight called...

And I was there because he had told of it, straining to see as he saw, imaging him stumbling out 'through the difficult door'. It is an exercise in humility and continuity, this attempt to reconstruct the past, and one is grateful to a poet for making it possible. Other places are mentioned, many of them. La Gorgue 'with a mill, and still canal, and like – Stroudway bridges' (still there) and Aveluy at New Year's Eve, and Robecq with its comfortable tavern. A landscape is evoked and it is easy to follow him through it.

But all the time, slowly at first, then with increasing speed and force, it is borne in upon one that something has happened since he was there, something almost as enormous as what he experienced. At Aveluy there is a small graveyard of soldiers, surprisingly pretty; at Laventie there is another, and then you realize that at almost every bend in the road, hidden in cornfields, in orchards, in copses, are these small cemeteries each prettier than the last – *two thousand nine hundred and thirty-seven of them in France alone* – and in each is the row of identical, well-designed headstones, sometimes no more than twenty and never too many, so that the mind is not overwhelmed, and on each of these headstones is a *name*.

All the time Gurney was in England, ill (he spent his last fifteen years in an asylum), naming names of people and places, this business of naming had been going on, unknown to him, in the places he knew.

To someone who has not come across these little cemeteries before the effect is almost indescribable; they are intimate, personal, the way Gurney's poems are. Of course I knew there were war cemeteries on the Somme but I imagined them terrible, impersonal places, with monuments. But the whole of this part of France is subtly and almost unnoticeably a graveyard and the graveyards are all English gardens, with roses and dogwood and prunus trees. That is, the Commonwealth cemeteries are. The German ones, with their tens of thousands of black iron crosses in long rows, and no flowers, give a different impression. It could be argued that they are more appropriate to the carnage they mark. What is sure is that the little British ones have become places of beauty and peace. As a reassertion of the value of the individual, after the indiscriminate blood-letting, they could hardly be bettered. They have the same insistence on the significance of each separate human personality that is in Gurney's

Naming Names

poetry. Possibly he never knew of them.

They are so well and expensively kept, by hundreds of gardeners, that they are a story in themselves. The hero is a man called Fabian Ware, who began recording individual, hastily dug graves during the war. He could have had little idea of the magnitude of the task ahead of him. After many fights with officialdom and public opinion ('Why spend money on the dead?' or 'Bring them back home', or, worst of all 'How could an Officer and a Private have the same design of headstone?'), he seems to have won all his battles and the Commonwealth War Graves Commission was set up, each member-country paying a share according to the number of their losses.

After the war, teams of specially trained gardeners, 'The Flying Circus', many of them ex-servicemen, toured the carnage, gathering scattered graveyards together, keeping them as near the place where the men had died as they could. Some of the ground had been fought over so often that identification was no longer possible. In which case 'Known unto God' is on the stone, a phrase contributed by Rudyard Kipling, whose own son had disappeared in this way. In some cases the sons of these original gardeners continue the work and, in the case of James MacDonald, whom we met tending the graves at Aveluy, looking entirely French in his beret, the son of one of the original gardeners (who himself fought on the Somme) is followed by *his* son: three generations.

In each cemetery is a book with the name of every soldier known to be there, his parents' names and his address; also a book for the remarks of visitors. The French comments are oddly French – 'Très bien entretenu', 'Endroit reposant et sage'. The British ones vary from the eloquent 'Humbled' and the conventional, though doubtless deeply felt 'They shall not be forgotten' to 'The Old Lie, Dulce et Decorum est pro Patria mori' (itself a quotation from Gurney's fellow war poet Wilfred Owen). Well – yes. But these beautifully tended English gardens do not fill one with indignation, not exactly. Who is there to blame? The politicians, the generals, seem pitifully small when compared to this vast fact, made so human and particular here. God? It was not God that invented the machine-gun. And in his only reported appearance among men he recommended love. These cemeteries seem a humble, and almost infinitely laborious, attempt to put a known face on a nightmare. Which is what Gurney tried to do in his poems. He wrote about one of those hasty wayside burials that were to be brought together after the war, calling it 'Butchers and Tombs'.

> After so much battering of fire and steel
> It had seemed well to cover them with Cotswold stone –
> And shortly praising their courage and quick skill
> Leave them buried, hidden till the slow, inevitable
> Change came should make them service of France alone.
> But the time's hurry, the commonness of the tale
> Made it a thing not fitting ceremonial,
> And so the disregarders of blister on heel,
> Pack on shoulder, barrage and work at the wires,
> One wooden cross had for ensign of honour and life gone –
> Save when the Gloucesters turning sudden to tell to one
> Some joke, would remember and say – 'That joke is done,'
> Since he who would understand was so cold he could not feel,
> And clay binds hard, and sandbags get rotten and crumble.

Later, reminiscing in hospital, he says:

Don Hancocks, shall I no more see your face frore,
Gloucester-good, in the first light? (But you are dead!)
Shall I see no more Monger with india-rubber
Twisted face? (But machine-gun caught him and his grimace.)

A telephone call, sixty years later, and it took the War Graves Commission twenty minutes to find them. Corporal Leonard Dodd Hancocks, Lijssenthoek. Plot 18. Row B. 19a. L/Cpl J.E. Monger. St. Sever. Block P. Plot 6. Row K. 12b.

There is not much you can do for the dead, but that is one thing: to name them, and know where they are. It would not satisfy Gurney, or anyone, but he would have approved.

1982

Naming Names

II

We are shown to our places by black-dressed stewards, male and female, with silver insignia round their necks on broad ribbons. We wait, in that curious junk-collection of bust and plaque and bas-relief, Poets' Corner in Westminster Abbey. There are perhaps three hundred of us and we have all been invited. This fact, and something in the gentlemanly (and ladylike) demeanour of the stewards gives the occasion the atmosphere of a subdued party. It is evening, and we sit under ballroom chandeliers.

At the appointed time 'the Procession of the Collegiate Body' moves between us towards Poets' Corner. Most of its members are in gowns, over suits, and carry silver-topped sticks, like maces. It could be taking place in classical Rome; there are prayers but, although there is mention in them of Jesus Christ, it seems they could as well be addressed to Jove. I mention this to a young companion and he murmurs back: 'All prayers are to Jove.' There is just enough surprising truth in this to make the important distinctions sound finicking, on such an occasion.

A stone is being unveiled, on this 11 November, to sixteen 'War Poets' of the First World War. There is a hymn ('O God our help in ages past'), an address by the Regius Professor of Modern History at Oxford, the stone on the floor is unveiled by the Poet Laureate, there are more prayers, which contain some forgivably vague literary comment ('who, through their sensitivity of spirit and disciplined use of language, bore witness to the truth that was in them') and some of their poems are read; then it is Elgar's 'For the Fallen' on the organ, the maces and dignitaries make their way once more between us, and the audience greet one another, and mingle, like a drinkless party.

Many things come to mind: the strangeness of Poets' Corner itself: Dryden does well, on a plinth alone, which is just; Blake's head in bronze, larger than life, is perched on a pillar edge, a deserved prominence. The rest for the most part take their chance, in a variety of methods and periods; it is a delightful English muddle, or a mess, take your pick. The oddest thing is that it should exist. The ceremony was probably all right, given the proportion of people present who would have been embarrassed by stronger spiritual meat, who were there from *pietas*. The intention was to commemorate, in stately fashion, and the state church was lending its *gravitas* to the attempt.

More worrying was the fresh impetus it gave to the category 'war poet'. It was a label imposed on them, under which those who survived were left to writhe. It held back the recognition of Edward Thomas for years, because he hardly deigned to mention the war, although he fought and was killed in it. It is a pity that their names are surrounded by that famous quotation from Owen: 'My subject is war and the pity of war, the poetry is in the pity.' In so far as I have been able to discern any meaning in this it seems quite false. Whatever their subject Owen's poems are cunningly made; the poetry is in the poem.

That journalist's label 'war poet' had at least one curious side-effect. When I went through the manuscripts of Ivor Gurney, written in his mental hospital in the early 1920s, I thought some were signed 'Ivor Gurney. Was Poet.' This sounded heart-breaking, as well as heartbroken. But when I grew used to his handwriting and saw that he had written, not 'Was Poet' but 'War Poet', the pathos was even louder. He had heard of the new category and was crying out to be included; anything, to be heard. He was even induced to become competitive. Above one such poem he scribbled, 'To knock out Robert Graves' (and below it he put 'Unsuccessful'). He was not a 'war poet' – whatever that may be – he was moved by sights and skies and friends on the Western Front and wrote about them, as any poet might.

Perhaps it does not matter, except that it is lazy-minded, and defines poetry too closely by its subject, as though it is journalism. But Gurney would surely be pleased and honoured to find his name on the stone. Not everyone would be pleased to find himself there, perhaps; the Abbey is hospitable; they have recently unveiled a stone to David Herbert Lawrence, by Jove.

1985

Bankside

———— o ————

I

SOME TIME in the sixth century, before the battle of Dyrham settled the natives' hash, the British actually beat the Saxons, at a place called Fretherne. The Severn, still wide, describes a large curve at this point, creating a sort of peninsula that juts from Gloucestershire westwards, towards Wales. If the invaders are coming from the east, pushing you west, it is the last place for a last stand, the inhospitably wide river at your back.

The knowledge that for once it was the invaders who found themselves in the water, and not the locals, adds to a sense of strangeness there is in that part, a slight but unmistakable off-centredness.

We were walking round the peninsula at Easter, enjoying what my companion, James Michie, called 'the Gauguin-in-Brittany colours' – sullen skies of variegated slate, but in the trees and fields a luminosity, as though there was a light inside them – trying again to discover what it was that drew us to that place, for we had walked there before. One of the things, undoubtedly, is that you can walk round it in a day, always with the river for companion, and always in a state of slight surprise. There is a grassy rampart round most of it, built (originally by the Saxons) to keep the worst of the Severn floods from the fields, which gives you an exalted view.

The first surprise this time, apart from the sudden sense of space and sky that comes when you reach the river, was three Shakespearian villains crouched on the horrible bank below the rampart. They grinned wickedly up at us from their desolation. The Severn mud is pink and glutinous and recent flooding had thrown up a sad wrack of tins and plastic bottles and other objects of a vaguely poisonous appearance. Amid this rubbish, torn at by the wind, they were boiling a blackened kettle. They looked like the survivors of a nuclear disaster, or, perhaps, of a Saxon raid. What were they doing there? Pleased to be puzzled we strode on, soon to be engulfed in mud ourselves. It can be very wet, round the Severn.

In the evening, in Berkeley, we learned that they were probably poaching elvers, the small eels that appear in the river at this season. Elizabeth I had her yearly consignment of elvers from this stretch of it. At another pub the barmaid gave a small scream. In the morning we had bought petrol from her on the main road ten miles away, but much further in spiritual distance; at lunch-time in Arlingham, in the quiet heart of the peninsula and in a different world, we had walked past her house and now, in another small town in a different direction, we had appeared in her place of work. The coincidence reinforced the sense of a cohesive population, watchful of strangers, bunched against threat of invasion. The fact that the barmaid came from Dumfries we did not allow to damage this impression.

We learned also that another kind of invasion was expected. It was full moon, it was near the equinox, and next day a monster bore was expected to crash its way up from the estuary, fighting the river-flow, audible a mile away. We were warned to keep well back, it was a drowner. We decided to watch it from the other bank, opposite our peninsula, on the fringes of the Forest of Dean.

Innocent, as one always is away from home, we imagined our discovery of an imminent tidal wave to be almost private. Of course, at the appointed time, roads were lined for miles with cars, double-parked, and gumbooted crowds were clambering over fences and lining the bankside rampart in thin rain. The mood was like that of an Italian *festa*, part-religious, part-jamboree. 'Here she comes!' the cry went up, and we all craned forward as though at Cheltenham Races at the Off. It was not the mighty crested wave we had been promised. It was a smoothly motoring body of pink-brown force, pushing the river back to Gloucester. Like a playful giant it showed what it could do, with white teeth at the edges that tore and gouged the banks, scattering earth and spray. The mood of the crowd was affectionate and respectful, as though towards a local god. Part of Newnham – all blossom and daffodils and fine domestic architecture – was flooded by it, cut off. There, a shopkeeper told us that up the river some canoeists ride the crest of it. 'Only a matter of time till one is drowned,' he said, unable to keep a note of primitive satisfaction out of his voice.

1985

II

Let us not make too much of it. We were within inches of oozy death. Stuck on the crumbling cliff-face (the path had fallen into the river) torn by brambles thick as thumbs, water and mud twenty vertical feet below, there seemed no way out but up. Clinging to ash seedlings, looping our arms gratefully round larger trunks when there were any, we pulled ourselves upwards, while loose shale cascaded into the water. Then my companion paused: 'We seem', he announced thoughtfully, 'in an over-hang situation.' Slowly looking upwards (for fear too abrupt a movement would help my haversack to topple me backwards) I saw the red sandstone outcrop that had looked so inviting had indeed the aspect of an arch, even of a ceiling. Nothing to do but descend, and push on; there was no going back the way we had come. So, sweating, bleeding, we inched our way towards possible safety, forty-five minutes to cover as many yards, watched by a man with a short pipe in a flat-bottomed boat who can't have had such an enjoyable lunch-break in years. At last the angle began to flatten, the brambles to thin and, reaching the safety of ankle-deep ooze, pink with mud and red with bramble scratches, we marched towards Stourport for lunch. The man in the boat still watched, pretending not to.

We were walking along the Severn. We always do, at least we do every year, Laurence Whitfield and I, starting where we left off the previous year, hoping to reach Plinlimmon and the source before, like Anchises, we have to be carried. Many more cliffs like that and we'll never make it, but there aren't many, though we make the most of them when we return.

You simply follow the brown river, there is a way all along its banks and you are free to observe, and speculate, and dream. The world seems to have ignored the Severn since the war. Sometimes the motorway is only a few hundred yards away but you cannot hear the traffic and it might not exist. It is almost as though there are two Englands, one tearing up and down out of earshot and another, withdrawn, secretive, brooding. The occasional bank-side houses look like that; even if they are reached by the road, the river is their real concern. They cling to the green bank as though their owners have crawled into a good interstice and hope nobody will notice.

The bank is indeed green, mile after mile, almost endlessly green. The Severn floods every year, and so on either side are flat meadows, dotted with old oaks, and after the flats the ground rises and is wooded; one is walking inside a wide green cup. Spring had arrived, tentatively; there were primroses and wood anemones, the alder catkins were purple and red and the willows were sprouting that rather dramatic yellow colour. There were coots and water ousels and yellow wagtails; one red cliff contained a cave and in the centre of the cave, calmly watching us, was the orange and white face of a fox. It could afford to be calm because the cave was in a sheer cliff, attainable only by pitons and crampons and all the things we had wished for outside Stourport.

Not much happens on these walks, except things like foxes glimpsed in caves, but to arrive anywhere on foot is to see it as though for the first time. Worcester, for instance, wrecked in the 1960s, you come upon just below the Cathedral, it is all you can see and it is marvellous. This time we stumbled on Bewdley. Later, by chance and in the dark, old street, we fell into an equally old pub called the Packhorse that gave us fresh grilled sardines in the bar and sword-fish steaks and good wine at cost price. We still find it difficult to believe in that unadvertised, unilluminated outside, Packhorse at Bewdley.

We pride ourselves on independence so we always return home by public transport, if there is any. We leave the river, find the road, and hope for some sort of bus. This involves much desolate trudging, faces whipped by the slipstream of lorries and never a

Bankside

human soul to ask. After only two days on the river it is difficult to believe the impersonality of the road. But cold and fed-up, walking in the vague direction of distant home – 'these are *negative* miles,' said Laurie, thinking of far Plinlimmon – his face softened in wonder: 'There's a bus behind you, Patrick,' he whispered, as though afraid of startling it. 'It is going to Kidderminster, and it's *stopping*.'

1984

III

When we started we could read the map without glasses, it was so long ago. Beginning at the Severn Bridge, each year we have walked twenty miles of the river-bank and now we are on the other side of Shrewsbury. Last time we reached Ironbridge, so we parked the car there and set off again, towards the distant source. One of the pleasures so far has been that we seldom needed to look at the map at all; glasses or no, you just keep to the river.

After Ironbridge it is not so easy because sometimes the path stops, blocked by a power-station or an estate, also the river itself begins to perform such arabesques in its course that it seems slightly dotty to stick religiously to it. But every time you leave the river you are startled anew by the rush, even by the existence, of traffic. Then, when you find the river again, the sudden calm is so strong it enfolds you. The paradox is that the Industrial Revolution, therefore the modern world, could be said to have started at Ironbridge, because of the river; it is the river's gift. But, between its alders and willows and oaks, skimmed by martins, patrolled by herons and dragonflies, the river is powerful and stays secret.

The path is hardly trampled, and only by anglers from the Midlands, but you never see anyone else, and you can travel the bank for days without seeing a boat of any kind, on waters that once must have been so busy. Why so many estates in Shropshire? 'Think river', opines Laurie. The land is fertile, and money must also have flowed from the goings-on at Ironbridge: all depends on the river.

After a bad bout of traffic-walking we took shelter in the Mytton and Mermaid at Atcham. ('Mad Jack' Mytton was one of those eighteenth-century squires endearingly devoted to beggaring themselves.) 'He was laid to rest in Room Number Five', said the waiter, reverently, but it seemed unlikely. We had to eat early because tonight was 'singles' night. 'Over twenty-five. No jeans or canvas.' (Canvas trousers? Shoes?) The first 'singles' arrive, elderly bachelors in groups, one large sad girl to whom nobody talks. It all looks fairly unbearable. Then groups of youngish women arrive, defiant in finery, and groups of men, nervously noisy. Soon the large place is packed (it is miles from anywhere), they are five-deep at the bar, there is loud music and some of the women jig about, maybe hinting, looking around, but no one dances, the sexes stay separate. Laurie and I find ourselves sedulously avoiding eye-contacts. Perhaps the clue to a successful, or at least a crowded, party is to call it a 'singles'. Perhaps they became doubles later.

Next day the Severn goes wild in its contortions towards Shrewsbury and we walk every loop, discovering the town is almost encircled by river, a natural moat. The path stops, we are forced into a new housing estate; in a garden is a gnome and a miniature wishing-well. 'Back to the real world', says sculptor Laurie Whitfield, grimly. Outside the elegant gaol, visiting womenfolk queue, waiting for the gates to open; it seems an unnecessary humiliation, eyed by the passers-by. Could they not be allowed in to wait? Shrewsbury is a nooky old place, with narrow passages called things like Grope Lane. On the outside wall of St Mary's is a plaque:

> Let this small Monument record the name
> Of CADMAN, and to future times proclaim
> How by's attempt to fly from this high spire
> Across the Sabrine stream he did acquire
> His fatal end. 'Twas not for want of skill
> Or courage to perform the task he fell:
> No, no, a faulty Cord being drawn too tight
> Hurried his Soul on high to take her flight

Bankside

> Which bid the Body here beneath good Night.
> Febry 1739 aged 28

The Severn influences everyone.

One problem is how to get back. Last year from Bridgnorth we were given a lift to Hampton Loade in the guard's van of a steam train, but that was dream-like. Now we wait for a 'Hotspur Town Hopper' bus to Ironbridge, outside an office building that houses 'Rewind Video Service', 'Clowns Galore' and 'Postal Bears'. I ponder these, while Laurie, glasses on nose, has thoughts even more surreal. He measures with his thumb the distance we still have to go to reach the source. 'Welshpool, Newtown, Llanidloes. We have to think in years.' He angles his thumb up and down the future tortuous course of the river on the map: 'You'll be sixty by Welshpool.'

1986

Margiad Evans

THERE ARE some writers with whom, the moment you pick them up, you feel a snap of sympathy. Coleridge has this effect on me. But they don't have to be such big guns as that: in a sense the less well-known they are the better, because then a feeling of proprietorship enters into it – you have made a friend who is not too dauntingly the friend of everyone else as well. And if they are writers whose subject is their own personality, who, as it were, like Coleridge, invite you inside, the greater the sense of intimacy. For me such a one is Margiad Evans.

She was an essayist, novelist and poet, well enough known in the 1940s and early 1950s for profiles to be written about her in popular magazines, to be the subject of critical essays, and for her poems to appear fairly widely in anthologies. Then, as far as I can judge, she was almost wholly forgotten. Her books were out of print and unobtainable, except for one or two that still lurked in public libraries – which is how I first came across her. Of the two books I found, one was published in 1943 and is called *Autobiography* and the other, published in 1951 when she was forty-three, and her last prose book, is called *A Ray of Darkness*. These have since been reissued.

What little I have been able to learn of her life does not come from *Autobiography*, which is really a collection of nature essays. Like many writers whose work is one long self-revelation Margiad Evans is very economical with personal details. But the subject-matter of *A Ray of Darkness*, of which more later, forces her to tell us something of her practical life, and it appears she was born and brought up in the hills of Herefordshire, she was all of her life poor, she wrote when she could, which was not as often as she considered she ought to, and at the age of forty-three she had a daughter.

Margiad Evans

I'd like to quote a couple of paragraphs from *Autobiography* taken more or less at random, because everywhere the writing is as good. They are from a piece called 'The Field'.

> It is still very early but already the thresher is at work at the farm. People are fetching water, cracking faggots over their knees. They are bruising the dew, teasing and scattering the faint creations of the mist. Going to work they smear the dim grass with dark tracks. Their voices pass down the lane...
>
> The thatcher comes and heaves his ladder against the oat-rick. He tips his hat over his eyes before he goes up with a bundle of wheat-straw under his arm. Slowly he stretches his arms over the rick as though reaching into his clothes and slowly he begins his movements with his rustling hands. In response there is a harsh and restless sound: it is the last speech of the corn.

Each of these paragraphs has its memorable phrase. In the first, as people go to work they are 'bruising the dew, teasing and scattering the faint creations of the mist'. And in the second there is the thatcher reaching over the rick as though into his clothes and the noise of the straw – 'the last speech of the corn'. She is a gift to any anthologist of nature writing.

She was also a novelist, of some success. But her novels vanished even more completely than the rest of her work. In 1950 the critic D.S. Savage published an excellent collection of essays on the contemporary novel (another book, incidentally, that deserves reissue) called *The Withered Branch*. His subjects are Ernest Hemingway, E.M. Forster, Virginia Woolf, Aldous Huxley, James Joyce and – Margiad Evans. He summarises her novels, the first of which appeared in 1932, and he quotes long passages. Her last novel, *Creed*, published in 1936, he calls, firmly, 'one of the very few significant modern works of fiction'. I managed, briefly, to get hold of a copy of *Creed* – it was lent to me more or less under armed guard, so rare has it become. And it is indeed an astonishing book. It is wholly about passion, not only sexual passion but of course there is a sense in which all passion is basically sexual. The nearest parallel I can think of, in atmosphere, is *Wuthering Heights*. And certainly D.H. Lawrence comes to mind. But it has something entirely of its own. It is a description of the knots and tangles that lie at the base of our minds. Written at a consistent level of intensity, it might seem almost hysterical but for the cool accuracy, I nearly said 'wit', of the writing. The sentences are placed like pebbles. You keep having to go back to enjoy again their hard, clear quality.

Fortunately, however, D.S. Savage concentrates his attack on a book which *is* sometimes available, on *Autobiography*, her most recent publication when he was writing his essay. I say 'attack' because for the most part Savage has chosen his subjects for their distinction and for what he regards as their in some ways faulty reaction to reality. In the process he makes some palpable hits, especially against E.M. Forster and James Joyce. Margiad Evans, however, seems to inspire in him a respect akin to tenderness but he nails her in the end – and fairly, I think – by discerning that her work is death-orientated, that *Autobiography* is really an account of a death wish, as indeed, he suggests, is all intense nature writing: 'A life lived only in relation to nature,' he says, 'and not also in relation to nature's complement, history, to say nothing of personal relationships, is less than half an existence.' He questions the value of nature writing. 'If the essential meaning and value of life is to be found in this immediate communion with the natural universe, why reproduce one's observations, sensations, impressions, in the abstract mental medium of language? This is an inescapable problem for every despiser of society, of humanity, of culture, of the spirit.' Yes indeed, for anyone who does in fact despise those things. Margiad Evans gives proof throughout her work that she does no such thing. Nevertheless, these are good questions and, put in this way, I think unanswerable. But there is a kind of answer, if you change the emphasis.

When, for instance, Mr Savage asks, 'If the essential meaning and value of life is to be found in this immediate communion with the natural universe, why reproduce one's observations?' it is possible to reply: 'Because these reproduced observations put one in immediate communion with Margiad Evans.' I know of few writers I feel I could more nearly reach out and touch than I do when I read her. In this (and in other ways) she is like Coleridge in his *Notebooks*: you feel you are being let inside another person's soul. When Coleridge, for example, writes, 'Hartley fell down and hurt himself – I caught him up crying and screaming – the Moon caught his eye – he ceased crying immediately – and his eyes and the tears in them, how they glittered in the moonlight!' he is telling us in a brief space a great deal about himself. In much the same way, and also to some extent by the same means – a series of journal entries – Margiad Evans grants us a similar sense of intimacy.

Mr Savage tries to place her in a tradition: he mentions names like John Cowper Powys and D.H. Lawrence. But I don't think this is helpful. She has as many differences from them as they have from each other. A writer who cannot be 'placed' in this way sometimes irritates a critic's sense of tidiness. This may be a reason why her work has fallen into disregard. She doesn't quite fit. 'Surely,' the question may have phrased itself, 'a writer who conveys so intensely her physical experience must be some kind of mystic. If so, what kind? What God does she worship?' Margiad Evans makes it clear that if she worships anything outside herself, it is the achievements of men like Bach and Jakob Steiner, the sixteenth-century maker of musical instruments. Her devotion goes to the achievers of perfection in this world and she scarcely bothers her head about the possible occupant of any next one. What matters about this writer is not whether she was a mystic or not, but whether she expresses clearly a sense of her self, real, in a real universe.

One of the chief interests arising out of Mr Savage's remarks is that Margiad Evans read them and in her last extraordinary book *A Ray of Darkness* she tries to explain and reply. What he chiefly objected to was the absence of any God at the centre of her nature worship – which was the basis of Coleridge's difference with Wordsworth, who, thought Coleridge, could talk of stones as though they were God. Margiad Evans admits this as a fault but points out that all mystics begin as nature mystics and, if they live, go on from there. But she agrees about the over-intensity and says: 'What is wrong with *Autobiography* is the strain, the continuous effort to put into language what was in reality a deeply relaxing experience. The lapsing into quietude which I failed to convey because it was words, was what saved me for so long.'

'What saved me for so long.' I do not think she failed to convey a 'lapsing into quietude' but it is that last phrase we have to attend to now. At the time of writing *Autobiography* she had been approached by a sense of hurry. She was not, as she says herself, death-orientated so much as death-obsessed. In the years that followed, this sense of pressure fluctuated but never went entirely, until without any warning, a healthy woman of forty-two, she fell down in an epileptic fit. This, the discovery of her epilepsy, also of her pregnancy, which more or less coincided, is the subject of her most autobiographical book, *A Ray of Darkness*. Or rather, it is the theme. For although she brought to her description of her fits, especially the first, the detailed observation she had trained herself to give to the natural world, the book is in no sense merely an account of illness. It *is* that, and in detail. But it is also an examination of the creative and religious impulse, an attempt to question and disentangle the insights and the terrors deriving from her affliction. She says herself of the book: 'I can find no continuous form, in fact I can find no statement whatever except the flow of question. I am, therefore, not telling, but asking, a story.' Above all, it is a description, as accurate as only a writer of her gifts could make it, of what it was like to be Margiad Evans in a particular situation and in a particular place.

The place is of special interest to me because the cottage where it happened is only a mile or so from where I live. The smallest four-roomed cottage I ever saw, or at least it was until a few months ago: it has since been rebuilt. For some years it was deserted and I remember looking through the window and wondering how anyone could open the sitting-room door without falling into the fire, so small it was. At that time I had not read her book and did not know this was the room where she fell in her epileptic fit, the 'parlour like a nut', of her description. That she escaped burning she regarded as a kind of miracle, and so it was, especially as there was not only a fire but an oil lamp in that small space, and she was alone. Her husband worked in the valley below and could only get up the hill at weekends, they had no car.

Here is one of her brief descriptions of the cottage. I can vouch for the accuracy of this:

> It was called the Black House, for it was tarred outside. Some minute muslin curtains were made for the windows, the geraniums were set in them, the old black flagstones were polished, the coppers shone in the log-light of the open kitchen

fire. The whole of the inside was painted a clear yellow, including the charming little old staircase.

It had a parlour like a nut. There were four rooms, an outdoor lavatory, a lean-to wash-house with an earth floor, and a pigs-cot. At the gateway stood an immensely tall pine. All its branches went up in the air except one, which it held stiffly out over the roof, in a commanding gesture.

The air up there, though very, very pure, used to get involved with the clouds. At a thousand feet this will happen, particularly in winter. And it was never still. On the hottest day – we had very few, for this was the summer of 1950 – you could feel a little frill of breeze under your chin like a beard, and your hair alive.

Margiad Evans is still remembered locally as Peggy Williams, her married name, a figure in a green cloak, striding across the fields with her dog at all hours of the day and night. I've seen a photograph of her at some local fête, a genial-looking bespectacled figure, handsome in a way, a cigarette between her fingers. Apparently she smoked all the time. One person at least remembers her with great love, remembers how interested she was in everyone in the village and in everything that happened (*pace* Mr Savage), and that is the girl who sat with her each day after she discovered she was ill, a girl whom Margiad Evans describes movingly in *A Ray of Darkness*. All her descriptions of people have an epic quality, clear and strong, like a Victorian portrait photograph. (How Mr Savage came to think that she did not care for people I don't understand.) This girl lived in the Black House after Margiad Evans left it and still lives fifty yards away. Few people have been so praised, so epically commemorated, in a book they have never read.

Here now is Margiad Evans's description of how she found herself to be so frighteningly ill:

> The night was quiet and dark – I went to the door and looked out once or twice. It was about eleven o'clock when I put down my pen, feeling suddenly tired and saying to myself that I could do no more that night, so I would make a cup of tea and go to bed. I made the tea, looked up at the clock – a strange chance – and saw that it was ten minutes past 11. The

next thing I was still looking at the clock and the hands stood at five and twenty minutes past midnight. I had fallen through Time, Continuity and Being.

I discovered I was lying on the floor on my back, my head against the rungs of the rocking-chair and my body, full-length, crowded between the steel fender and the little table at which I had been writing. The lamp, a tall brass one, on a very slender base, was burning steadily on the table.

It was not until much later on, appalled and shaken, I realised how dangerously I had been placed, unconscious, certainly in convulsions, in a locked cottage alone with my dog at midnight and a quarter of a mile from the village. The space in which I was lying was perhaps a yard wide. My sleeve was charred by an ember, that was all. Had some special agent of preservation laid me down between the lamp and the fire it could not have been more dexterously done. When despairing I have often recalled this to myself.

She decides she must be ill and ought to go to bed. She continues:

But where *was* bed? The next mental process is terribly difficult to describe, for, as after all my bad fits, the brain held and let go, held and let go, a confused mass of atmosphere and memory. It worked, but like an engine misfiring and unsteered. The idea of going to bed brought an extraordinarily vivid presentment of our childhood's room where I had slept with my sister, gone these many, many years. I saw the blue distempered walls, the tallboy. This floated in my head and vanished to be followed by every room I had ever slept in, *except the present one*. Another image was bobbing up and down in me, and again it was amazingly solid, was seen and then snatched away and then seen again as though held up in the air before me, as, I have since imagined, religious maniacs behold their sins. It was a jug, a blue-banded quart milk jug.

It was the jug that aroused me, for into it we always poured our can of afternoon's milk, and I remembered that I hadn't done it. Conscience seemed to bring consciousness and strength. Conscience because the brain interrupted seems to work by precept; and it was one of my mother's housewifely rules which I had always followed to empty your milk at once so the cream didn't stick to the can.

There were still curious numb patches in my thought, and a feeling that the soul didn't know whither it had returned, to the right earth, or to an unknown one. As the air touched me I felt a cold dampness and it came on me stunningly, terrifyingly, that my clothes were wet. Horrifyingly, in one moment, I realised the incredible, impossible and ghastly truth – I had neither fainted nor been asleep: I had had an epileptic fit!

There are many gifts a really good writer can give us, and to me the feeling of actually being there in the room with them is one of the most seductive. Death-obsessed she may have been, and with reason as it turned out, but everything she writes is bursting with the sense of life.

I cannot believe she deserves to be forgotten. She was a humble, practical woman. She respected Emily Brontë because 'in her last hours she fed her dog, and in her last weeks did her housework.' But Margiad Evans herself thought she would be remembered, and says so, in one of the few flights of fancy she allows herself in *A Ray of Darkness*. Remembered, strangely enough, because of her disease: 'It seemed a Force which was determined that my soul should avoid others; that it should be sent away from earth to pray and to repair, and that, returning, it should remember nothing of its hermitage, but that nevertheless *it would be remembered* for it.' If intensity of response to living, and patient care taken to share that vividness with anyone who cared to listen, if these things have any value, I believe she will be proved right.

1971

Birdlip Mirror

―――― o ――――

AROUND HERE it is easy to think of the Cotswolds rising out of the Severn plain like a cake. A rugged and irregular-sided cake: some of the hills of the escarpment – Crickley, Cooper's, Cleeve – push into the plain like yellow peninsulas, but on the whole the jutting-up is sudden, and the top of the cake smooth, give or take a few baking-cracks and valleys here and there. This is only true of the west side, facing Wales. Approached from London, from the east, it is difficult to see how we reach such a height (where I am writing is about nine hundred feet) the ascent is so gradual. But standing on wind-buffeted Crickley Hill you are aware of it, looking down on Cheltenham and Gloucester, and across at the slow, lumping bulk of the Malverns, which dominate the scene: you are also aware of the slow drift of the Celts westward, over the fertile plains and into the far mountains, hazy, beyond.

Jan Morris in her book *The Matter of Wales* points out that the Romans penetrated Wales but the later invaders, Jutes, Saxons, Franks, did not, so that the darkness of the post-Roman centuries never fell on Wales, she alone kept intact what Morris calls her 'Celticity', as well as her Romanisation, and therefore retained, in Morris's dramatic phrase, 'the folk-memory of Europe!'

I am shy of the word 'Celts' because of the sillinesses that have attached themselves to the idea and the general vagueness (my own, certainly) which surrounds the movements and minglings of races and peoples during those distant times. But somebody certainly lived on Crickley Hill, and it must have been like living on the prow of a ship, forever ploughing into the green of the plain, for the wind tears at you, in nautical fashion. Recent excavations, however, have shown that many people lived here, for many hundreds of years, a millennium before Christ.

Birdlip Mirror

Looking down at the post-holes of their fortress, which the archaeologists have marked on the turf, and trying to imagine what their lives might have been like up here, I feel a familiar tickling at the back of my neck, bidding me look round; and I know what it is: the memory of the Birdlip Mirror.

It was found just behind me, not on Crickley but, I believe, in the bank on the other side of the road. I don't know exactly where and wish I did, because it is hauntingly beautiful. It is a bronze hand-mirror, a dressing-table mirror, exquisitely punched and scrolled and enamelled in red. It was found in a grave near the side of the road, is dated first century AD and is Celtic. Ever since I first saw it I have been wondering about the lives of people who could afford to make and possess such a beautiful and unnecessary object, and find in themselves the generosity and piety to bury it with the dead. It seems to suggest a settled and secure form of existence, difficult to imagine being lived in this nearly constant wind, perched on this crag for fear of enemies; for fear, I dare say, of everything.

Perhaps the man who made it, and its possessor, were of different races? The 'Celts', Jan Morris tells us, believe there is another world, just beyond the window. I, who assume myself to be one, have always believed that. Perhaps there is such a thing as 'Celticity' after all, and after all this time. And another recognisable trait: Posidonius, in the second century BC, said Celts 'are exceedingly fond of wine and sate themselves with unmixed wine imported by the merchants'. So Celtic artists, it appears, were paid in wine, and a modern scholar of the period has gone so far as to venture that the whole extraordinary mass of Celtic art found scattered across Europe, and the lovely thing found a few hundred yards from where I am standing, 'may largely have owed its existence to Celtic thirst'.

The lovely mirror may have been made to pay a wine bill. There is a carelessness about that, a profligacy (for all the intense care taken in its making) that consoles, that blunts the sharp tooth of the wind; which is the point of art.

1984

The Green and the Grey: Ten Miles of Wales

———o———

CHANGING A WORD in the old song, reversing the direction – 'If you ever come across the sea *From* Ireland' – you are likely to drive from Holyhead through Snowdonia. When cataracts the colour of Guinness froth, cragged heights and sheepy glens and graceful groups of mountain ash are beginning to make you sing, you come suddenly to another sight, equally awesome; you come to Betws-y-Coed, which *Nagel's Guide to Britain* innocently describes as, 'perhaps the most famous of tourist centres, and its beauty has made it famous.'

You will have plenty of time to take in the treble-parked motor-coaches, the steaming cafés, the damp queues outside the gift shops and the queues picking their way forlornly round the bonnets of frustrated cars. Somewhere under the petrol-fumes the salmon-filled River Llugwy gnashes its teeth round its boulders, each of them worn smooth by feet and occupied by at least two families.

All this happens between one moment and the next, and ceases in the same abrupt way. Within a few hundred yards, on the road to Ffestiniog, you are back in emptiness again, with only an occasional fisherman in waders, still as a heron.

You have time to ponder what is left of 'beauty' if we all rush to enjoy it, when you are hit by another sight, equally unexpected. You drop like a stone, between one green mountain-slope and the next, into a black world. You have come to the slate-quarry town of Blaenau Ffestiniog; beside you and above you, nothing but black and grey, nothing but slate.

The little town, in matching grey, has seen better days: some of the shops are for sale, the enormous chapels have an under-used look, and there are two-storeyed granite houses on offer as 'Holiday Homes'. But there is a taste of Welshness here, that tangiest of flavours.

Two names then, small as beads on the rocky bosom of Wales, clinging to the string of the A5: one appearing to contain the history of British Tourism (swollen) and the other the history of British industry (shrunk). But they are both Welsh, and Wales has its own ways of not going under.

Returning to Betws at a quieter season, it is possible to step on to the A5 and stand between the river and the hotels, looking up. You see that behind the new gimcrack frontages, plate glass, crazy-paved walls, the buildings are solid and good, of a more confident age. Betws – 'the sanctuary in the woods' – has been offering shelter for a long time.

The first hotel was built about 1790. Its present manager, an Irish-Liverpudlian, is also the cook, as his father was before him. Sitting in the bar in his chef's kit, breaking off only to tell the barman that the beans must be ready by now, he deplores the new frontages of what he calls 'Sunset Strip'. To him the point of the place is the peacefulness that his father knew, and he thinks most people come there for an hour or two only to say they have been there. For, as Nagel's said, Betws is 'famous'.

But no local will confess to minding the visitors. The secretive Welsh are accustomed to foreign occupation and, as one gently says, the season is not long, even though from June to September the population swells, by day, from five hundred to *eight thousand*... There is much talk now of trees, more interesting than foreign visitors, and one man eloquently regrets the felling of an oak, fifteen years ago.

So, after 'the Irishmen' of the Iron Age, after the Romans, after the feuding Welsh Princes, after the English, there came in the 1790s the first Romantic tourists to exclaim at the Picturesque and view it through their brown Claude Lorrain glasses.

Then in the 1840s came the railway, bringing with it botanizing vicars, hill-walkers sternly cleated and, of course, the salmon-fishermen. For all these were built the sturdy Victorian hotels. Then came the motor-car, now come the motor-coaches, and Betws has humbly laid herself out for them all.

People and Places

These three layers, Welsh, Victorian-style visitor, and tripper, can still be observed together.

In a bar, campers from Wolverhampton tell each other the story of a recent film. At the other end of the room, massively relaxed, three locals talk to each other in Welsh. And across the hall, in the Residents' Lounge, long salmon-rods stacked in a corner behind a screen, an English group in deep armchairs discuss the day's sport over whiskies and soda; a pair in a corner play chess. It is like the setting of a pre-War country-house play, and indeed, outside in the hall bookcase, the *only* books are *The Stock Exchange Investors Handbook*, forty years old, and, a year or two older, *Public Schools Yearbook (1936)*. Like something discovered at Pompeii, they give a date to the Deluge. The Old Order has yielded, but now, in the 1970s, its survivors seem to live easily enough with the New, and the aboriginal.

But changes do not end with the Wimpy Bar and the Log Cabin Crafts Shop.

Betws is surrounded by steep hills, heavily wooded, with magnificent old oaks. It is strange to hear the local people talk so much about trees, as though half-remembering ancient tree-cults. In England, practical England, most people regard trees as green things in the way of agriculture, or as dangerous things likely to fall on their houses. It is not so in Wales.

But if you climb through the oaks to gain a better view of the village you come to a standing stone brilliantly hung with lichens, proof of the pure air of the place. Then you notice that some barbarian has scraped the coloured lichen off the other side, to paint a yellow arrow, indicating a track. The Forestry Commission has struck. From that moment you pass out of the bird-haunted woodland into identical drives through conifer plantations that create a kind of night below them and an unnatural silence around. Remains of Iron Age huts, and of shepherd's cottages, are under the regiments of invading trees.

But if you keep on, armed with patience and, in those undifferentiated plantings, a good compass, you do come at last to an emptiness like a balm. We would have to be even more industrious than we are to do away with all such places.

On the other hand, it would be difficult to find any place more

The Green and the Grey

redolent of the human than Blaenau. And that is another kind of exhilaration and relief.

The approach to it is usually through drifting vertical ghosts in white shrouds, which is rain. It manages an annual ten feet of the stuff, one hundred and twenty inches, which is twice the average for Betws, ten miles down the road, and no one could call Betws arid.

Men only came to live here because of the slate. In 1765 Methusalem Jones of Caernarvon dreamed that there was slate under these hills, and there was. Now unimaginable weights of it lie on top of them, discarded. The slate boom lasted a hundred years, the town swelled to twenty thousand people, now it has settled down to about four and a half thousand, which is a comfortable number. But only a couple of hundred still work in the quarries, and you get the impression that few of these would if they could find anything else to do. The high beetling tips look as though constructed by slave-labour, or by men desperate for wages.

If you scramble among the deserted quarries you see at once how desolatingly hard the work must have been. The signs of a century's labour tower above the town. Piles of thrown-away slates like giant playing-cards, high as the natural mountains and unnatural as the Pyramids. The men must have climbed half the night to be at work by dawn. Black trackways disappear into the clouds, a pattern of zig-zag lines that turns the whole place into a sombre, abstract design. On every skyline are vast skeletal sheds, and when you reach them there are more, higher, and on and on. Sheds the size of aeroplane hangars, with one door flapping on broken hinges in the constant wind.

One still seems to have life in it, even though, in this world of slate, there are slates missing from its roof.

Inside it is like a Victorian sweat-shop. In half-light, in little booths along the whole wind-swept length of it, cut off from each other by yellowing strips of plastic, men sit in silence, alone, on wooden blocks or old car-seats with the springs spilling out of them, tapping at slabs of slate. Maybe the impression is more like a labour-camp than a sweat-shop.

Meurig Evans reckons he can just about cover the roof of a small house in a day, but then he has been at it since 1932. He says the community feeling isn't what it was in those days, and blames this on Social Security, they used to look after each other then. And looking around his hellish place of work, you think, 'And by God, they'd have to!' He agrees, cheerfully: 'We put hens in coops to lay eggs. We go into our coops and lay bloody slates!' He tells me that I should call any piece that I write, 'How Grey Was My Valley', and I remember that the book he means was originally called 'Slag'.

He says he would live nowhere else and it is still a strong place. The thirty enormous chapels are still used, even if it is only the vestry, and there is still a newspaper in Welsh – for four and a half thousand people – although there used to be three Welsh newspapers.

'Community' is difficult to define. The proof of it is perhaps in the bewilderment of the few immigrant English, all of whom claim that they came here to escape 'the rat race'. Some of it they try to bring with them. One newly-arrived hotel-owner waves his arms in exasperation, at the Welsh determination to turn any transaction into a personal matter: 'Look, I only want the bloody job *done*! Right?' Another Englishman, a sculptor, who has lived in that sculpted landscape all his life, tries patiently to explain to him that he is in a different culture, that here everything must be personal. The other stares, trying to understand, baffled, as his countrymen have always been baffled, sometimes to violence, by the Welsh and by the Irish, by their refusal, precisely, to create the impersonality of 'the rat race'.

Sheep wander the traffic-filled roadway as naturally as dogs. To keep them out of the shops cattle-grids have been dug, but these they have learned to *roll* across. What connects this place with Betws is the small space of the outrage. There, a few paces take you from 'Sunset Strip' to aloneness; here, one pace takes you from sterile slate to sheep-cropped grass. At the side of the old workings the clear waters of high Llyn Manod lap between green boulder-strewn mountains. At the end of the lake lie the approaches to Wales and Tomen y Mur, which is as far as the Romans dared. Not many invaders got as far as that Roman fort, not this way; they lost heart when they looked at the range of mountains that faced them. That is perhaps why this feels so very Welsh a place.

The Green and the Grey

Just behind Tomen y Mur, at the edge of Llyn Trawsfyndd, are the towers of the nuclear power-station, and even they look mysterious in the water-filtered light. Power stations, Wimpy Bars, industrial scars; it is hard to wreck a place if there is room enough, and that place is strong.

Or is it? Through the bottom of Blaenau runs the old Great Western Railway, its tracks bright orange with rust. But that sort of rust forms quickly in a climate like Blaenau's, and the track is used every week to carry nuclear-waste from Trawsfyndd.

Where to? Into the old quarries in the heart of the mountains, next to the innocent town? Towards the sea? No one seemed to know, or no one would say. This used to be the safest place in Britain – for all, that is, save the quarrymen. So safe that the National Gallery hid its pictures in those caverns during the war; even the Crown Jewels were here. It is remembered to this day, and with bitterness, that the Keeper of the National Gallery at that time, Sir Kenneth Clark, called Blaenau, 'that hellish place'. Easy to see what he meant. But it is not hellish – yet. It is in a way magnificent. A human thumb print on a defiant landscape. Augustus John came to live here, so did John Cowper Powys, who loved its mantle of cloud, the comedy of its people; he called it 'an Aristophanic town'. But he did not know of the load that railway would one day carry.

Blaenau, Betws, monuments to the swarming power of man and the patient resilience of nature. Each has survived, in its way. Or up till now they have.

1978

The Soft Side

―――○―――

THIS WILL BE hopelessly out of date by the time it hits the newsstands (in snow, perhaps) but all week we have been driving through bucketing rain. At night, in the headlights, it smashes up white from the tarmac and it roars under the mudguards. 'Just how much water', exclaimed an American friend, 'has come out of the sky since I've been here?' The answer, with a touch of bitterness, is 'Enough.' Not bitterness because of the rain, which was needed, but because we English know that next summer, if there should be a sequence of dry summer days, the cry 'Drought!' will ring through the land.

Jenny Pitman's Borough Hill Lad won the big race the other Saturday and she was relieved, because there had been training difficulties: 'Up to November we have had a drought,' she said. 'The going was hard. But now it is very soft.' (There is a beautiful phrase about track-conditions – 'the soft side of good'. That would make a fine title for a novel that nobody would buy; but it would be worth reading if it lived up to the title, because almost impossible to write.)

Anyway, if we have had a drought up to November, these days have more than made up for it and we should be grateful. But we are not grateful because we don't even save it up against, so to say, a non-rainy day.

But gratitude, praise, is something we seldom show much of, for some reason. We seem to prefer low spirits.

Robert Graves, in a letter, has an interesting list of writers and people whom he regards as truly great. He denies the title to Dostoevsky 'whose works have depressed more young people in England and Russia than any other novelist from the first beginnings. *Genius* does not depress.'

That sounds true. We like Dylan Thomas the better for saying

The Soft Side

his poems 'are written for the love of Man and in praise of God, and I'd be a damn fool if they weren't.' In the liturgy we are told it is 'meet and right' we give thanks – which is a form of praise. There is much before that about asking for mercy, which some might find too craven, but when it comes to the thanks and praise part that surely touches a psychic need. The trouble for most of us, I suppose, is that we don't know whom to thank.

But the need to praise exists. On some recent mornings, for instance, after a night of rain, day begins with floury clouds, grey-blue; these clear away and the sun shines on a bright wet world, crows' wings flash gold, seagulls look whiter than white and the green silage-trailer on the horizon glistens: even the cows are so content they rest their steaming chins on each other's backs and half-close their eyes: there is a need to describe such mornings, and that would be good, though it would sound a little on the soft side; they make you want to shout and thank somebody for them, and if you happen to believe there is nobody to thank there is a strong need to invent one.

Of course it goes, and clouds pile up again. Briony berries fade. The same American friend wondered why we didn't use their brilliant scarlet for Christmas decorations, but the colour has gone by then. Just as old man's beard becomes tousled, which before was so thick and downy it looked as though you could lie on it. (In America, apparently, it is called 'virgin's bower', which sounds a soft name from that hard-bitten continent. But Grigson's *An Englishman's Flora* says the name originated in Somerset.) The shine of the day goes and people in shops say 'another nasty one' and we all agree.

Though we are told it is 'meet and right' to praise we are not then told how to do this, which is a pity. Writers, in Graves's phrase, are frequently 'depressing' because it is so difficult to be otherwise without sounding like a Boy Scout. But the desire to praise the soft side of good can lie on the chest like a burden, which is why it is a relief to get rid of some of it in writing, once in a while.

1984

A Walk

——— o ———

TOO MANY PARTIES, too many funerals – the turn of the year frequently has too many of both – and I woke up in a rage. I am not sure against whom, or against what; against Time itself, probably.

The car was far distant, being serviced, and I decided to walk to it. I did not know exactly how far distant, never having walked it before; some said fifteen miles, I suspected it was more like nine, but putting one leg in front of the other would presumably get me there, and the mood, the confusion in my mind that I woke with, had to be worked off somehow. So, with a small tangerine wonderingly thrust at me as a form of sustenance, I set off.

Snow was on the ground, lumps of earth showing through it, the colour of plain chocolate. There was a northerly wind at my right ear, which hurt it, and I began to wonder about the wisdom of all this. But I arranged my scarf so that the bottom two thirds of my head sat in it, as in an egg-cup, and that gave some relief.

So little happened on the walk that it would be worth describing. I was headed for Tetbury, and there is a route to it across country through a string of tiny villages, with much vacant space between them. It is, I believe, an ancient, pre-Roman, way, very bare and handsome.

The first thing I discovered was the difficulty of embarking on such a walk at all, so near home. I had barely gone a mile before a passing car slowed and stopped; a neighbour, who offered me a lift to the next village, which I accepted, because that stretch was over-familiar. At Winstone he suggested he take me the whole way, admitting, rather charmingly, that he had nothing better to do. Sternly, I resisted temptation. In fact the white road ahead, stretching on into the green sky, looked inviting,

A Walk

and the wind had dropped. 'G'merning!' I replied to some passing horse-people, involuntarily imitating their own tones.

After that the road was empty, as were the patchy-white fields on either side. A line of bare beeches was the distant horizon, and they looked bluey-purple in the light reflected from the snow. Although the main road was far away you could hear the traffic, because the air was so still. There must have been some movement in it, however, because the occasional small beech in the hedge, its dry leaves still on it, rattled them companionably, making a noise as though it was raining. Pigeons rattled too, as crowds of them suddenly startled from the trees. I had never noticed this before, but as they fell out of the trees they made a noise like marbles shaken in a bag. Apart from them, and the beech leaves, nothing moved; except a fox, winter beech-leaf colour, that strolled casually across the road, very confident and slow, its brush at half-port.

The signposts started playing up. They said 'Sapperton 4' but after half an hour's brisk walking the next signpost said the same thing. It looked as though I would reach no pub in time for lunch. I ate my tangerine and began to sing, but stopped, because it sounded silly. After an hour another car drew up, with a friend in it. Would I like a lift? Yes, as far as the pub in Cherington. After lunch I went into the little church there and thought of the person whose funeral I had recently attended. The names on the Roll of Honour were often repeated, First World War and Second; family names, different from the repeated family names in my village. I was in different, distant lands. After that the last four miles into Tetbury passed with ease, and without incident.

Driving back (the distance turned out to be sixteen miles, of which I reckoned I had walked eleven) I hoped for a mild form of hero's welcome. When will I ever learn? Everyone was even more preoccupied than usual. An unexpected lamb had been born in the snow and was showing signs of distress. My son was trying to feed it with an ingenious arrangement made out of a tube and the inside of a fountain pen, but as what came out looked decidedly blue he desisted. They had installed mother and lamb in a room outside my study. I was slightly surprised they had not put them into the study itself. The farmer who owned it said we should have put the lamb in the Aga. '*Bottom* oven. I've lost count of the lambs that have passed through my Aga.' Mother and child are both doing well, they are outside my door now, chomping and suckling away, a peaceful sound and sight. Nor am I stiff, nor so enraged.

1985

By the Light of the Poacher's Moon

———— o ————

THERE IS NO need to feel protective about country 'characters', or fear their disappearance. The disguise they pull on with their boots every morning is self-protection enough. Give them a chance and it is like pressing a button, out roll the well-rehearsed stories – always of the past – expressed in a dialect not too difficult for the stranger to follow, and filled with the small details of period and of country craft they know to be expected of them. Even in front of each other they never let up, like an ideal theatrical company they polish their repertoire until it is oiled and smooth and impenetrable. Only a question about the present can stop them; their eyes lose their geniality and fill with intelligence instead, they take on the aspect of birds listening; then, with the briefest and politest of evasions, they step back inside their roles: 'Funny you say that, I remember the toime....'

Political questions particularly they deflect. You never hear a countryman complain, about present living conditions, or terms of employment. Or if you do you know he is on the skids, about to leave the district. In the pub an expression of bitterness causes a beat of silence, a stillness all round, and is soon drowned in conversation slightly louder than before. This is not because they are flunkeys; it is their highly developed sense of survival: they wear their hardships (always *past* hardships) like feathers in their caps; a deceptive plumage. As watchful as the creatures they know and understand without even knowing that they do, they give nothing away. They have had plenty of time to learn that in the end a man can trust nobody but himself. So they are either quiet, colourless, smiling in a corner, or they put on the slightly gaudy colourfulness of the 'countryman', content to amuse, content to be patronized, while from inside their disguise they look out, watch, and wait. The Manor is not to be confronted in broad day, but some of its riches can be filched (and some justice done) by the last light of the setting moon. Because by then it is late enough for policeman and gamekeeper to have gone, despairing, to bed, yet there is still enough light to silhouette the roosting pheasants against the sky, and soon in the full dark it will be easy to get home laden and unchallenged.

In country where there are large estates, the difference between the haves and the have-nots is very evident. The men who work the fields are forbidden the fruits thereof; not so much as a rabbit may they take, without permission. The penalties were very great. We are not so far removed from the age of man-traps. Two of those horrible engines decorate the walls of the local pub, if they have not been replaced by now by pixies.

Thus the romance of the poacher. He takes risks to redress a balance. He embodies the vague idea at the back of most people's minds, that England belongs to Englishmen, or ought to. His work is lonely, dangerous, it involves outdoor skills we all instinctively admire: stealth, cunning, knowledge of the ways of the earth. He is one, almost, with the beasts, for most of these, the predators, hunt like him by night. If he can beat them at their own game, then perhaps there is hope for mankind after all. He is our representative, out there on the fringe of survival, and his success is good news.

Ben Legge's father was a poacher, a famous one. He himself is now a gamekeeper, but is proud of his father without any sense of contradiction.

'Times were hard, sir, fifteen shillings a week he was paid.' (The old-style countryman's conversation is liberally interlarded with Sirs and Madams when addressing anyone different in education from himself; above the politeness the mild eyes watch.) 'He had a gun, sir, a Stevens, with a butterfly bolt in the middle, it unscrewed in half. Half down one side, half down the other, you could be talking to him you wouldn't know he had a gun.'

It was he who talked of the poacher's moon, standing in his neat room, small china ornaments, small ashtrays, real ducks up the bank at the back, main road outside the parlour window. 'He'd go in the pub and he'd say "I think I'll try Whistler's Wood tonight." He'd drink his fill and there'd be sure to be somebody who'd tipped off the gamekeeper. Then he'd go and get himself

By the Light of the Poacher's Moon

a bit of hay in a barn, get himself down and sleep the drink off. Then about a quarter to three, when the moon was just right and – bang, bang. The policeman and the keeper, they'd have given up, think he'd been pulling their legs.'

Ben has stood up to demonstrate the setting of the hay in the barn, the raising of the rifle to the dark silhouette in the trees. He is wearing a cream flannel shirt with a thin green horizontal stripe, so modishly backward-looking it would be no surprise to see it in Turnbull and Asser's window; it tones with his corduroy breeches in faded pink, his green stockings. He is beautifully dressed. 'I had a sort of boat pram see.' He stands to demonstrate the curved shape. 'Seat at either end and a dip for your feet in the middle. He'd put the pheasants down there, cover 'em over and I'd sit there in my sailor suit and my grandmother wheeled the pram into town. The policeman would stop the traffic – it was all horses and carts in them days – "Let the lady with the pram pass" and she'd wheel me down Miners Passage to Miners Restaurant – it's gone now, was there for donkey's years. There she'd leave the pheasants – they'd take all she could bring – and my father used to say "Now you keep the pheasant money and I'll keep my wages for beer and bacco". Big dinner parties they had there in those days. My father once said "You know, some of them gents is eating their own birds."

'Oh Lord he was caught often enough. One night in Sister's he feels a hell of a butt in the back. "Who the hell did that!"' Ben's on his feet again. 'Three o'clock in the morning, middle of the wood. Keeper. Took Dad's gun and smashed it on a stone. Just as well, so there'd be no shooting. Then by God! they had a set-to. He did three months in Gloucester for that. Oh yes.'

Now he talks of rabbits, eight hundred taken at a time. Poaching? 'No, gents' shoot. You couldn't touch 'em.' Was that not hard, in bad times not even to be allowed a rabbit? 'Ah.' A shake of the head, either in acknowledgement of the question, or of a new thought. No reply.

'But nowadays there's no poaching. They come in cars sometimes, take a pot shot. Nothing! There's nobody clever enough to do it!'

In the pub down the road after leaving Ben Legge (he could not come, he had to water the pheasants) contrasts make themselves plainer than usual. It used to be a country pub ten years ago, with farmworkers playing darts and drinking beer from wood barrels. Now it is a roadhouse. The interior has been entirely rearranged, pleasantly, if anonymously. The publican's son, a charming fellow, is a former rowing Blue. He is chatting up a row of commuting barflies, all with enormous bottoms overlapping their cocktail barstools. The talk is all of food, and cars. Everyone is on Christian-name terms, they are drinking rounds of Campari and soda, sniffing country air in the red leatherette lounge to the sound of Muzak. They give an impression, doubtless unfair, of flabbiness, and a kind of helpless greed; they compare badly with the whippet-like, guileful, wholly alive Ben Legge. Yet he would come in here in his breeches and his billycock hat and Yes, sir, No, sir, three bags full, sir. He would delight them, they had met a 'character'.

'There's nobody clever enough...'

Miss Greene-King, local magistrate, confirms this; standing with a saddle over her arm, calling her dogs about her to prevent them eating the visitor's hand. 'The occasional car from Birmingham, but they don't get much. Les Bawcombe was saying the other day when he was a boy they always got one or two for the pot, but the youngsters don't bother. Perhaps they don't know how?...

'I suppose now a tin of corned beef costs as much as a leg of lamb they may start again. You ought to go and talk to Caleb.'

All roads lead to him, Ben mentioned him, now the magistrate; the best known poacher in the neighbourhood.

His blue front door is open, behind a little gate on the village street. His wife calls him quietly: he is asleep in front of *Crossroads* in his neat sitting-room. The transition from sleep to waking is impressive, a blue eye appears in the bearded face, the look as direct as the magistrate's, but sadder.

He swings enormous shoulders forward and switches off the television set, pours two glasses of mangold wine. He has been stone-walling all day, it is his trade.

One of fourteen children, he first went poaching when he was seven. It is the same story, the 1930s, 'Times was hard, very hard.' When he says it you believe he means precisely that, just as you believe him when he says later that he didn't give a bugger for nobody. He is a man of great physical presence. If his eight poaching brothers are anything like him they must have been a formidable bunch to stumble across in the night, something out of a Western.

After the war, on paid leave, he had four months rabbiting. 'They called me the Torment. Seven hundred to a thousand rabbits they used to get, on the estate shoot. When I'd finished, last shoot they had, they got twenty-eight.

'I was caught. I've been caught three times. Never prosecuted. I'd just throw the bag down with the ferret in it and say "All right then, you bend and pick it up." No keeper ever did...'

Parsnip wine, in a fresh glass, so as not to mix the flavours. Tales of pursuits, escapes – it is fairly obvious that no one dared catch Caleb – of the policeman pulling sacks over the tell-tale traces, feathers, cartridges in the back of his van, concealing them from the irate farmer; of children put in the attic to keep them quiet when the landlord Earl is passing, lest he come into the house and see the catch strung along the beams. 'Seventy, eighty brace (of pheasants) I'd have, in three nights. Piece-work in the quarry during the day. I'd make twice out of poaching what I did in the quarry. It's not right. If a farmer or a gentleman wasn't so greedy, not letting people touch his rabbits...'

That was the staple of the poacher, the rabbit. Since myxomatosis there are not enough to be worth snaring. Its disappearance had far-reaching social consequences; it was the poor man's dinner, and many a small-holder paid his rent from his rabbits. In these parts the smallholder, like the rabbit, is no more. Now the rabbit is returning, but the big farms have too settled a grip. Perhaps with the rabbit the poacher will return, if anyone can still eat a rabbit who has ever seen one suffering from that horrible disease.

'I wouldn't eat a rabbit even before myxie. I'd find too many growths and cancers inside 'em, all of a sudden.' All the time he is giving a picture of himself, a vast slow figure bent over his snares on a dark night in a fine rain, afraid of nothing, except possibly the unnatural, or the odd. He would dig into a rabbit stop, his ferret underground, and sometimes find as many as eighteen. He would wrap the innards round a bean-pole and stuff it down the burrow to attract his ferret back. Paunching a rabbit one night in the dark he felt something hard and put it in his greatcoat pocket to show Doreen. In the light back home it was a little black foetus with hands like a baby, hard, that had been rattling about inside the rabbit. He did not like that.

Peaspod wine, twelve months old, out of a champagne bottle. He stands to talk, his eyes alight, of his old dog Whippy: could bowl a fox over, not as big as a fox. 'That dog was as crafty as I was...' One night of snow a dog-fox got Whippy by the leg. Caleb offered the fox his own hand. 'It hung on it. Bled for two hours, my hand did. Couldn't stop it bleeding, piddled on it and everything.' Doreen agrees how enormously his hand swelled. She is from Northumberland, still with the rolled Hotspur r's. They have not left the village for thirty-three years. Caleb has never left it, except for the war, when he met Doreen.

'They're murdering the countryside. Foxes, hedgehogs. Myxie is barbarous.' It is an accurate word. 'I could tell you what we'd do to him, me and my brothers, if we found somebody planting it...

'You were talking about the wild flowers they kill. I notice the birds, drystone walling. Stonechats, golden wagtails, I don't know all their names. Little birds. They aren't about like they used to be.

'No, I don't go out now. There isn't the need maybe. Police have walkie-talkies, dogs. There's not enough rabbits worth catching. Pheasants? Those fat things can't get off the ground. Have you heard the disgusting noises the beaters make, trying to get 'em to rise? And they call that a gentleman's sport?'

Reminded that there are one or two local boys who make a show of knocking off a bird occasionally. 'Poachers?' Caleb settles his feet deliberately: 'They're not bloody *poachers*!'

Another, large, glass of parsnip. We go round the back to where he manufactures the stuff, among wooden barrels and boilers and stone jars and plastic dustbins. We pass a photograph of a handsome, fair little boy with his blue eyes facing outwards on to the blind alley, so Caleb sees it each time he goes to inspect his wine.

It is easy to regret there are no more Calebs pitting their wits against the night, against their prey and against those who would

By the Light of the Poacher's Moon

send them to prison. But the economic need for skill like his has gone. Long may it remain away. Should it return Miss Greene-King may once again be kept busy – she seemed a humane woman, Caleb's equal – but would there be anyone left who could do it? As we come back to the little gate on the village street a fair boy of about ten is standing there, Caleb ruffles his hair: 'Alex, he's my grandson.' The same blue independent gaze, the same set of the thick shoulders. He strolls off planting his feet as squarely as his grandfather.

'I liked that wine.'

'Come back again and we'll make a night of it. Bring Ben.' The gamekeeper. 'He's my cousin.'

1975

Cataracts and Creeks

―――― o ――――

SOMETHING STRANGE happened to English poetry in the seventeenth century. A group of men (who weren't a group), such as John Donne, George Herbert, Henry Vaughan – and there were others – began to write a personal religious poetry in which God – or, more especially, Christ – is addressed intimately, as though He is there in the room with the poet writing; He is implored, wrestled with, defied, confided in and, above all, loved.

These poets, and others, have tended to be lumped together by literary historians under the label 'Metaphysical', which is not very helpful, in fact it is off-putting, because it tends to obscure the differences between them and also lays too much emphasis on their 'difficulty', real or presumed, of their fondness for farfetched metaphors and verbal ingenuity for its own sake. They did go too far in this direction sometimes – Henry Vaughan, however, hardly at all – but they were capable of a dramatic honesty and directness when they stared, unblinkingly, at the times they lived in and the state of their own souls.

Henry Vaughan seems to have done this with particular concentration during a period of about five years, in which he wrote most of the poems for which he is remembered. On one level, not a very high one perhaps, this is the more impressive because he, unlike George Herbert and John Donne, was never a clergyman, in whose professional interest, as it were, such fierce spiritual introspection might be. He was a doctor, a country doctor in Wales.

Vaughan was born in 1621, which means that he reached early maturity at the time when the storm broke, the reformers fought the traditionalists, and England was at civil war. A sort of Royalist, he went back to Wales from London, and took no part on either side. I say 'sort of Royalist' partly because of this nonparticipation, but also because there is little sign of anti-parliamentary zeal in his poems. What there is is an angry detestation of the social destructiveness of the Zealots and great indignation that these called themselves 'the Saints' when his idea of sanctity was different.

There is, incidentally, an argument that he did take part in the Civil War, because of the internal evidence offered by an amusing poem of his about borrowing a strange-looking cloak. But Vaughan, in 1647, was adamant, originally in Latin, about his hatred of blood-letting:

> But so my integrity and reputation may go unchallenged you should know I took no part in this great overthrow. We truly believed that innocent blood has a voice, and a power after death that teaches men to weep. Thus I have taught myself to endure, like a chaste and faithful mother, and to ease the burden of my destiny with tears. I have never desecrated what is holy with hideous violence, neither was my mind or my hand stained.

That is from the preface to his second book of poems, called *Olor Iscanus* – the Swan of the Usk. His first book, very accomplished, published in 1646 when he was twenty-five, contains love poems in the manner of his time. He could already write, certainly, but there is not much indication of what is to come.

His second book, in which he draws attention to his love of the River Usk, near his birthplace in Breconshire – indeed, to emphasize his attachment to the place where he was born, lived and died, he called himself the 'Silurist' because Tacitus said that a tribe called the Silures had lived there – contains invitations to friends to come and stay, elegies to friends killed in the Civil War, and also, evidence of how poets at any given time tend to write like one another. Here are a few lines, from a long address to the River Usk, which are reminiscent of Marvell, whom Vaughan was highly unlikely to have read, for Marvell's poems were not published until some thirty years later.

> May the evet and the toad
> Within thy banks have no abode,
> Nor the wily, winding snake
> Her voyage through thy waters make.

People and Places

> In all thy journey to the main
> No nitrous clay, nor brimstone-vein
> Mix with thy streams, but may they pass
> Fresh as the air, and clear as glass,
> And where the wandering crystal treads
> Roses shall kiss, and couple heads.

Not as good as Marvell, but like him. Then something, or more likely a series of things, happened. Whether it was the death of his loved brother in 1648, or a serious illness (which he mentions as a crucial event in his life), or disgust at the Civil War (his twin brother Thomas, a parson, was evicted from the living at Llansanffraid, near the family home), or all of these things, Vaughan changed, or, it could be said, became more defiantly himself. Certainly an important motive for change was his reading of 'the blessed man Mr George Herbert, whose holy life and verse gained many pious converts (of whom I am the least)'.

No great poet owes so great a debt to another as Vaughan to Herbert. He borrows ideas from him, phrases, images, without acknowledgement or shame, nor did he need to feel shame. They were about the same business – conversion – and Vaughan's poems, whatever their debts, are wholly his own. At any rate, after reading Herbert, from the turmoil of the Civil War Vaughan turned to himself or rather, more importantly, turned to God, in a series of intimate meditations in verse, often on biblical themes, which sometimes read like verse letters to Christ himself.

Before examining these intimacies, let us look at an example of the sort of non-intimate poem he began to write. We have just read some of his earlier lines, Marvell-like, somewhat contrived, on the River Usk. Here he is now, on a similar theme, the passage of water to the sea. There are no evets and toads and nitrous clays now. He fashions instead a metaphor. The poem is called 'The Waterfall'.

> With what deep murmurs through time's silent stealth
> Doth thy transparent, cool and watery wealth
>   Here flowing fall,
>   And chide, and call,
> As if his liquid, loose retinue stayed

Cataracts and Creeks

    Ling'ring, and were of this steep place afraid,
        The common pass
        Where, clear as glass,
        All must descend
        Not to an end:
But quickened by this deep and rocky grave,
Rise to a longer course more bright and brave.
Dear stream! dear bank, where often I
Have sat, and pleased my pensive eye,
Why, since each drop of thy quick store
Runs thither, whence it flowed before,
Should poor souls fear a shade or night,
Who came (sure) from a sea of light?
Or since those drops are all sent back
So sure to thee, that none doth lack,
Why should frail flesh doubt any more
That what God takes, he'll not restore?
O useful element and clear!
My sacred wash and cleanser here,
My first consigner unto those
Fountains of life, where the Lamb goes?
What sublime truths, and wholesome themes,
Lodge in thy mystical, deep streams!
Such as dull man can never find
Unless that Spirit lead his mind,
Which first upon thy face did move,
And hatched all with his quickening love.
As this loud brook's incessant fall
In streaming rings restagnates all,
Which reach by course the bank, and then
Are no more seen, just so pass men.
O my invisible estate,
My glorious liberty, still late!
Thou art the channel my soul seeks,
Not this with cataracts and creeks.

That is not one of his greatest poems, but it is typical. Technically, it is for the most part a poem with four beats to the line. But it begins with two slow pentameters: 'With what deep murmurs through time's silent stealth / Doth thy transparent, cool and watery wealth...' which suddenly change into two quick lines of two beats each: 'Here flowing fall, / And chide, and call...' The intention is obviously onomatopoeic, imitating the sound of water, and its slow movement to the brink, its hesitation and then its tumble. As his biographer remarks, Vaughan was the most Welsh of poets writing in English and he always had a lovely ear. But he soon abandons this alternation of pentameters and two-beat lines (as he often changes rhyme-scheme in mid-poem, without a jar, and this adds to their freshness and the sense of freedom and urgency they contain) and he writes the rest of it in four beats: 'Dear stream! dear bank, where often I / Have sat, and pleased my pensive eye.' An apostrophe and simplicity that would have pleased Wordsworth.

The tone of the poem is that of a man quietly and carefully thinking his thought through. This is one of Vaughan's greatest virtues. There is no literary lumber, or showing off, only simplicity. 'O useful element and clear! / My sacred wash and cleanser here...' In narrative intention it is a poem of hope and consolation, for himself and for us all; as most of Vaughan's poems are. There is no sense of strain. He is not trying to console, he is consoled.

'Should poor souls fear a shade or night, / Who came (sure) from a sea of light?' 'Light' is a favourite word of Vaughan's. His two most famous poems begin with it: 'They are all gone into the world of light! And I alone sit lingering here' and the other famous one that begins so startlingly 'I saw Eternity the other night / Like a great ring of pure and endless light.'

From the idea of the waterfall Vaughan has moved to the idea of the passage of the soul towards God, towards the spirit that moved upon the face of the waters: 'And hatched all with his quickening love' (the second use in the poem of the verb 'quicken', meaning to give life). Vaughan's destination, and ours, is the sea of light:

> O my invisible estate,
> My glorious liberty, still late!
> Thou art the channel my soul seeks,
> Not this with cataracts and creeks.

In other words, not this difficult, bumpy world. The poem itself

Cataracts and Creeks

comes down to earth with a bump. It is tempting to think that Vaughan is referring to his contemporary world, the Protectorate, under which he found it so uncomfortable to live. He often takes such oblique side-swipes in his poems. He is always aware of the world outside.

'The Waterfall' comes from a collection of about 130 poems, some shortish, some a couple of pages long, called *Silex Scintillans*, first published in full in 1655. There is not a failure among them and four or five are great.

I mentioned earlier that these poets seemed actually to converse with Christ, He was their intimate. Here is an example:

> Aye, do not go! thou know'st, I'll die!
> My Spring and Fall are in thy book!
> Or, if thou goest, do not deny
> To lend me, though from far, one look!
>
> My sins long since have made thee strange,
> A very stranger unto me;
> No morning-meetings since this change,
> Nor evening-walks have I with thee.
>
> Why is my God thus slow and cold,
> When I am most, most sick and sad?
> Well fare those blessed days of old
> When thou didst hear the weeping lad!
>
> O do not thou do as I did,
> Do not despise a love-sick heart!
> What though some cloud's defiance bid
> Thy Sun must shine in every part.
>
> Though I have spoiled, O spoil not thou!
> Hate not thine own dear gift and token!
> Poor birds sing best, and prettiest show,
> When their nest is fall'n and broken.
>
> Dear Lord! restore thy ancient peace,
> Thy quickening friendship, man's bright wealth!
> And if thou wilt not give me ease
> From sickness, give my spirit health!

People and Places

Could anything be more intimate and ordinary, in this extraordinary poem than: 'No morning-meetings since this change, / Nor evening-walks have I with thee'?

I have also mentioned that Vaughan often uses a biblical text as a starting-point. To a short poem called 'The Dwelling Place' Vaughan provided this head-note:

> Then Jesus turned, and saw them following, and saith unto them, What seek ye? They said unto him, Rabbi (which is to say being interpreted, Master) where dwellest thou? He saith unto them, Come and see. They came and saw where he dwelt, and abode with him that day: for it was about the tenth hour.

From that text he fashions this joyful, *homely* (the word is his) meditation.

> What happy, secret fountain,
> Fair shade, or mountain,
> Whose undiscovered virgin glory
> Boasts it this day, though not in story,
> Was then thy dwelling? did some cloud
> Fixed to a tent, descend and shroud
> My distressed Lord? or did a star
> Beckoned by thee, though high and far,
> In sparkling smiles haste gladly down
> To lodge light, and increase her own?
> My dear, dear God! I do not know
> What lodged thee then, nor where, nor how;
> But I am sure, thou dost now come
> Oft to a narrow, homely room,
> Where thou too hast but the least part,
> My God, I mean my sinful heart.

There is no shadow of insincerity, no sense that Vaughan is pumping himself up in order to feel what he thinks he ought to feel. He feels it, from the opening sentence. And how well he manages that sentence, showing a marriage of feeling and technique, the thought moving easily and logically through and past the rhymes: 'What happy, secret fountain, / Fair shade, or mountain, / Whose undiscovered virgin glory / Boasts it this day, though not in story, / Was then thy dwelling?'

Cataracts and Creeks

Vaughan asks if a star came down to shelter Christ: 'to lodge light, and increase her own?' This sense of Christ as light itself, as a being that suffuses the whole universe is, I think, peculiar to Vaughan's poetry, and has a far-reaching effect on it. In his great poem 'The Night' he talks of 'God's silent searching flight / When my Lord's head is filled with dew, and all / His locks are wet with the clear drops of night.' This is strange, as well as magnificent. But it is this sense of Christ's omnipresence – in stones, in birds, in everything – that makes Vaughan perhaps the first of our nature poets.

No man lives exactly as his poetry suggests. It would be a pity to leave a picture of Vaughan as a saintly recluse, too good for this world. That would reduce, not enhance, the triumph of his work. He not only had public troubles, harassed by the local sectaries, but private ones as well. His father had been much given to litigation and Vaughan had tangles with the law also and, most sadly, because of his children. He may have felt himself isolated, pushed into some over-quiet creek, but he was subject to family cataracts as well. His first wife died, after bearing him two children, and he married her sister, who bore him two more. The first children fell out with their stepmother and with him and, in order to make peace, he had to move from his own birthplace to a cottage, making the house over to his son. A daughter, crippled from an early injury, sued him for maintenance.

I have said that Vaughan was a poet who loved light. He is buried in the open air, outside the church his brother was expelled from, whereas people of his rank were usually buried inside the church. He lies under a yew tree, near his beloved River Usk. His stone is a horizontal slab which someone keeps clear of yew leaves. But some leaves stay, in the incisions of his name, Henricus Vaughan, 'unworthy servant, great sinner'. I hope nobody ever removes them, because they have turned yellow in the deep cuts so his name shines out, luminous, from the dark Welsh stone.

1984

Father Time

————o————

THERE WAS OCCASION blithely to mention scything the grass last week, and since none has been done, for reasons which will be given, it might be worth explaining why such an old-fashioned activity was planned at all. There are those who automatically suspect others of showing-off, of being different on purpose, who attribute just about every motive to their neighbours' activities except the obvious one that they are doing what they do because they want to and think it is a good idea.

However, for the suspicious (who are many) why, of all things, a scythe? Does the fellow, a London refugee – albeit of long-standing – see himself a son of the soil, with string round the legs of his trousers?

The answer is that the fellow doesn't see himself at all, much, but sees grass, too much of it to mow, at least for the likes of him. Of all activities mowing stands high in the tedium list. Besides, he confesses to enjoying grown grass. So, some is mown and some is left to stand. But this long grass has to be cut, about now, or it dies back and suffocates the new growth and you are left with a weedy wilderness that becomes worse every year. You can buy machines for this cutting but they are noisy and expensive, exhausting to handle and, like all machines, liable to break down in his hands. Also, there is not enough grass to justify such a machine, it would only be used once, at most twice, a year. So, about seven years ago, when the problem first presented itself, and groaning only very slightly, I went and bought a scythe.

It was a beautiful object of curved American hickory, with two simple wooden handles sticking out of it. In the shop a priest of the agricultural implement, stroking it lovingly, showed me how to tighten the handles if they came loose, and I bore off my purchase feeling (yes) a little self-conscious, never having handled such a thing before, but confident it was the obvious solution. So it proved. If your occupation is sedentary you have to take some form of exercise and useless, self-punishing forms of it have never appealed. However, it is extraordinarily pleasant to get up from your desk and, taking up this handsome useful object, go out for an hour to cut a few more swathes and so reveal the new green grass underneath.

But it has to be done within a certain time. When the grass has fallen over it becomes tangled and cutting it is a terrible labour; you long for a machine. So last week the scythe was taken out, one of those simple handles needed tightening, was tightened, and it snapped. The only thing that could go wrong did, and the scythe was useless.

This was annoying, but not the end of the world. A replacement handle could be found. Could it? No, it could not. Scythes no longer exist. In the shop where I bought it seven years ago (one of many in a rack) the priest-like figure has been replaced by girls, who are helpful, but not the sort to understand the bewilderment and despair of a suddenly scytheless man. I ransacked the town and in one place was informed, by an implement seller in his middle years, that he had never seen a wooden scythe outside a museum... I am told it took the Ancient Egyptians a thousand years to develop the scythe from the sickle, and we have been using it ever since, from the time of Moses. Therefore its disappearance *in the last five years* seems worthy of record. Not that it quite has disappeared. It is now replaced by an aluminium substitute which in desperation I bought and which I find entirely useless. However held it buries its nose in the earth, *kamikaze* fashion.

At last I found, hidden away in a back yard, the sole surviving blacksmith; a young man who saw the problem, admired the scythe, and reckoned he could fix it. I haven't yet dared to find out if he has. But now I realize, facing the possibility of his non-success, that all those who passed and saw a literary type swinging his scythe and who possibly suspected him of trying too hard to be 'Truly Rural' (as my satirical aunt used to say), that all those automatically suspicious of others' motives (and they are many), were looking, possibly for the last time, at an absurdly contented man. 1984

Green Shades

———o———

IT WAS ALWAYS a doomed endeavour in this green darkness, to try to watch county cricket on Cheltenham College ground; so we watched the hail instead, bouncing off the plastic sheets that covered the wicket. We were reduced to memories, or memories of memories: of W.G. Grace striding from that same High-Victorian pavilion; of Walter Hammond, here, taking a slip-catch so quickly he was able to put it in his pocket while the rest of the fielders ran up and down the boundary, puzzled, looking for the ball; of a young writer of stories for boys who watched a cricketer on this ground, called Jeeves, and remembered the name. We were all in the condition of Francis Thompson, with his Hornby and his Barlow long ago.

The drawn-out mopping-up operations palled as a spectacle after a while so I took a walk around the town until the next, hopeless, wicket-inspection. I called at the shop of Alan Hancox, second-hand bookseller extraordinary, and on impulse asked if he had anything on Francis Thompson. The London Library has nothing but Alan had; birdlike he flew to a shelf and plucked out, the pages yellow and brittle as winter leaves, *Francis Thompson* by K. Rooker (B.A. Oxon.) Docteur d'Université de Paris, 1913. It is surely the subtlest low-point in a reputation's decline that the only book (so far) available to someone interested in a presumably well-known English poet was published seventy years ago, in London, *in French*. It sounds rather good, what I have dared read. It falls to pieces in my hands. The poems are quoted in English, and translated into French in a footnote. I looked to see what the translator made of the famous lines – 'As the run-stealers flicker to and fro, / To and fro, / O my Hornby and my Barlow long ago.' They came out like this: 'Tandis que dans le va-et-vient de leur course fugitive les joueurs essaient de marquer des points,

Green Shades

/ O mon Hornby, O mon Barlow des jours d'antan!' In a much quoted remark Robert Frost defined poetry as what gets lost in translation, but this is ridiculous. It is enough to put one off reading translations altogether.

Apart from washing-out cricket, this present weather has made harvesting impossible and, in our small case, amid the unharvested fields, the cutting of our grass. Some of this is mown, the rest grown, and the 'mown' part is now a good, soaking six inches and the grown part, tall and yellow, tosses and tangles in the wind. Yesterday there was a phenomenon. I was told that a groundsman, attempting to remove the plastic covers on Cheltenham College ground, actually took off into the air. Up here the wind blew wildly from the east, flattening the grown grass one way, then, as we watched from the rattling window, changed direction totally in a matter of minutes, came from the west and knotted the bewildered grass into such fierce confusion that when it is possible to scythe – if that time ever comes – it will be almost impossible to know from which direction to cut.

This enforced and additional leisure has led me to another poet, Andrew Marvell, who is clearly as great an enthusiast for grass as I am. Brooding over it, outside, uncut, I was in a frame of mind to notice the extraordinary number of times he mentions grass. He even knew something about scything: 'While thus he threw his elbow round, / Depopulating all the ground.' Precisely, the stroke comes from the elbow. In 'Upon Appleton House' he has stanza after stanza about grass: standing grass, scythed grass, growing grass – even, so help us, wet grass: the meadows 'Whose grass, with moister colours dashed, / Seem as green silks but newly washed.' Then of course there is 'The Mower against Gardens' who cannot stand all these new-fangled flowers and garden statuary, grass is your only stuff: 'The Gods themselves with us do dwell.'

'Stumbling on melons, as I pass, / Ensnared with flowers, I fall on grass.' I wonder how Marvell translates into French? 'Annihilating all that's made / To a green thought in a green shade' would sound all right, even Baudelairean-sinister. It was 'run-stealers' that got them – 'les joueurs essaient de marquer des points' forsooth!

1985

Labyrinthine Ways

———o———

'DISMAYED, HE WOULD emerge from his room upon a household preparing for dinner, when he had been listening to sounds he thought betokened breakfast. He was always behindhand with punctual eve, and in trouble with strict noon.' And – 'no doves fluttered against his lodging window to wake him in summer, but he was not indolent in his struggle against indolence.'

They don't write like that any more, nor so kindly. It is Everard Meynell in his *Life of Francis Thompson* published in 1913, and, as in that example, it is a manner that lends itself to mannerism but also to good manners. When Thompson talked too much in the editorial office of Everard's father, Wilfred, 'he would be sent forth on some expedition with the children to whom he bore himself as a sweet and eager, though not from their point of view an exciting, companion.' Everard was one of those children, and it is hard to see how it could have been put more gently.

Thompson's story is all the stranger for being expressed in this way. The figure of the poet-tramp is not that unusual, perhaps, but Thompson seems to have fallen to the bottom like a stone, without even instinctively flapping his arms in an attempt to arrest his fall, just as Shelley is said to have lain on the bottom of the Arno and folded his hands across his breast.

His father, a convert to Roman Catholicism, was a doctor in Preston, and Thompson from an early age appears to have been intended for the priesthood. He was judged unsuited and for several years pretended to learn medicine. He tried his hand for two weeks with a maker of surgical instruments and then, as an encyclopaedia salesman: 'it took him two months to read the encyclopaedia, and then he discarded it, unsold.' His desperate father said in that case he had better enlist, which he meekly did, but confessed later that he never even became 'Private Thompson'

Labyrinthine Ways

because he failed the medical. (Before she died his mother had given him De Quincey's *Confessions of an Opium Eater*, and he was taking laudanum.) Finally, aged twenty-seven, he wandered from home as vaguely as he had stayed there, and for the next three years lived rough in London, not even collecting the small allowance his father directed to a well-known reading-room. This is puzzling, because usually the most dedicated poet-bum takes what is offered, if he is not embittered against the offerer, which Thompson was not; nor was he suicidal; merely indifferent.

Eventually he sent Wilfred Meynell a manuscript and, after much difficulty, that kindly editor succeeded in tracking him down and at last he appeared in his office; the biographer's description is a gift to the film-maker: 'Then the door opened and a strange hand was thrust in. The door closed, but Thompson had not entered. Again it opened, again it shut. At the third attempt a waif of a man came in. No such figure had been looked for: more ragged and unkempt than the average beggar, with no shirt beneath his coat and bare feet in broken shoes, he found my father at a loss for words.' It is the shirtlessness that sticks in the mind, because one pictures a formal black coat of the time (1888), whatever its state of dilapidation – perhaps a frock-coat – and no shirt beneath.

Thompson reveals that he over-wrote on purpose and thought himself the first to do so. He talks of his (good) essay on Shelley but doubts that it will be accepted for publication (it was not) because, 'Then I burst into prose poetry. "He dabbles his hands in the sunset. He is gold-dusty with tumbling amid the stars"' etc. 'Personally, I recollect nothing like it in English prose.' The date is about 1889 and, surely, almost everyone wrote like that then: his biographer does. The odd thing about such stuff is that though it tumbles with 'images' (as Thompson called them) no picture arrives in the mind.

Five or six of his smaller poems thrill, because of their rhythms ('To a Snow-flake', 'A Nocturn', and others). Longer, 'The Hound of Heaven' carries sensuous abstraction as far as it will go, and sustains it. But it is his life that contains the pictures that cry for a sympathetic film-maker: for example, he loved cricket, but never played it at school; instead, in a friend's garden, he bowled by himself for hours, into a net, 'which meant that he had, after each delivery, to retrieve his own ball.' In his way he continued to do this.

1985

Mr Hornby and Barlow

———o———

'IN MAKING THIS Collection I have been governed by Francis Thompson's express instructions, or guided by a knowledge of his feelings and preferences acquired during an unbroken intimacy of 19 years. His own list of new inclusions and his own suggested re-considerations of his formerly published texts have been followed in this definitive edition of his Poetical Works.' W.M. May 1913.

Hm. Let's hope Wilfred Meynell got it right. They did some odd things, those old editors. Many a Golden Lyric turns out to be snipped from a longer work, not by the poet but, later, by an editor, with no acknowledgement that this has been done and with a new title invented for the purpose.

It is to be hoped that Meynell was right because Thompson's poem 'At Lord's' is included in the *Oxford Book of Short Poems* which contains no poem longer than thirteen lines and in order to avoid the booby-traps of those unacknowledged snippetings great pains were taken by the editors, one of whom is me. (The other is James Michie.) It had to go in, if it qualified, for it is the best cricket poem – 'O my Hornby and my Barlow long ago!' – but the truth must out: it was published (though not by Meynell) in a longer version in an essay by E.V. Lucas in the *Cornhill* magazine in 1908.

The essay makes clear that the poem, with two extra descriptive stanzas, is about a match Thompson must have seen at Old Trafford in 1878, when he was eighteen. Gloucestershire, then the great county, with the three Graces, W.G., E.M. and G.F., came north to play Thompson's beloved Lancastrians.

> The long-whiskered Doctor, that laugheth rules to scorn,
> While the bowler, pitched against him, bans the day that he was born;

And G.F. with his science makes the fairest length forlorn;
They are come from the West to work thee woe!

It was Hornby and Barlow's match. In the second innings Hornby made 100 out of 156 and Barlow stayed with him while he made 80 of them. The famous line nearly became, according to Lucas, who had access to the notebooks: 'O my Monkey and Stone-Waller long age!' E.V. Lucas explains: '"Monkey" was, of course, Mr Hornby's nickname. "First he runs you out of breath," said the professional, possibly Barlow himself, "then he runs you out, and then he gives you a sovereign".'

It was surely Thompson who preferred the published version of that line, so let us believe the shortened poem was one of 'his own suggested reconsiderations'.

It was not the only thing he wrote on cricket. Lucas quotes his cricketing parody of Fitzgerald's 'Omar Khayyám':

> Wake! for the Ruddy Ball has taken flight
> That scatters the slow Wicket of the Night;
> And the swift Batsman of the Dawn has driven
> Against the Star-spiked Rails a fiery Smite.

It is a pity that Thompson called his parody (admittedly in his notebook) 'Rime o'bat of O my sky-em', but they liked such things in those days.

> A level Wicket, as the Ground allow,
> A driving Bat, a lively Ball and thou
> Before me bowling on the Cricket-pitch –
> O Cricket-pitch were paradise enow!

After a few stanzas he possibly tired of this and began to wish he was writing 'The Hound of Heaven':

> Is there a Foe that domineers the Ball?
> And one that Shapes and wields us Willows all?
> Be patient if Thy creature in Thy Hand
> Break, and the so-long-guarded Wicket fall!

He also wrote about cricket in prose. Describing a famous

fielder, Royle, he says: 'Slender and symmetrical, he moved with the lightness of a young roe, the flexuous elegance of a leopard....' Thompson went out of fashion because of his over-indulgence in lush language; in these days of plain cooks that 'flexuous' is delicious.

1985

The Mystery of Cricket

─── ○ ───

I

I NEARLY PUT 'The Mystery of My Interest in Cricket' at the head of this, because it is odd that a non-athletic person like myself should be so dotingly fascinated by a game. I mean – what is it? An absurd business that goes on far too long. Yet it has held me, as nothing except sexuality has held me, and with something of the same involuntary fascination, since I first heard the clink of pad-buckles in a cricket-bag.

Incidentally, this interest has nothing to do with imitation, is not an attempt to impress others. Those who do not see the point of cricket (perhaps there is none) often suspect that we fanatics, enquiring of each other the latest Test score, are hopelessly conventional, Basil Radfords and Naunton Waynes playing at a dream of vanished Empire. How little they know us, and what a mixed batch we are. I have spent afternoons in Lord's Tavern with a loquacious pair of Pakistani brothers who knew the second-innings scores of obscure county games that had been played before they were born. They were an extreme case but there were plenty of us to argue with them. No, our passion is self-generated, not social. I doubt, for instance, if my father even knew the rules, and at school my interest in cricket, if noticed at all, impressed nobody.

Perhaps it was indeed those pads, the kit, that first caught my imagination: the look a batsman has of being armoured for the joust; his lonely heroism walking out, his even greater loneliness walking back, peeling off his sausage gloves, or his gloves spiked in rubber, black or green, and his bat, that beautifully coloured and discoloured piece of wood, spicily redolent of putty, sticking out from under the sleeve of his billowing white shirt.

The Mystery of Cricket

I was never much good, so I did not have the incitement of talent.

I am trying to find my way back to where it all started. Cigarette cards? Those neatly open-shirted figures in braided blazers I stuck in the dun-coloured book provided? Kenneth Farnes, Hedley Verity, W. Voce: pre-war faces to be seen again (or not seen) once the war was over – that distant treat, birthday and Christmas combined, promised by grown-ups, when everything would somehow be different, and better. The name Don Bradman stuck in my eight-year-old mind, the 'Don' sounding especially romantic, like Don John of Austria in Chesterton's poem that someone had read to me.

Perhaps it was the first real cricket match I saw that made the infection bite deep into my mind. It is still the best. It was at Lord's, in 1945, I think, a gathering of servicemen, a 'Victory' Test. Learie Constantine leapt towards a ball as though his legs were a pair of compasses, infinitely extendable, and his arms stretched as though unattached to his shoulders to seize balls apparently far out of reach, to throw them at the stumps in one movement, his body almost horizontal and on-balance. Hammond scored a century, going down on one knee with the final flick of his off-drive, and Keith Miller hit a six to the top level of the stand near the pavilion. There was also a bowler with the memorable name of D.V.P. Wright, whose face, like Hammond's, had been on those cigarette cards, and he kangaroo-hopped to the wicket beating both batsman and stumps almost every other delivery... But this is not nostalgia. It is the astonished recognition that these memories are more vivid to me than almost any other memory of any kind. Why? Why do I remember those figures from such a long time ago, and so many others, their movements, mannerisms, even the way E.R.T. Holmes knotted a white handkerchief round his neck? Who on earth was E.R.T. Holmes that I should remember him when I have forgotten so much else? Or R.W.V. Robins, or Laurie Fishlock, or Long Jim Sims or, most cherished of all, the two Langridges, John and Jas.? I was besotted. I still am. A Sussex supporter, I was distraught when S.C. Griffith lost his place as England's wicket-keeper to an upstart called T.G. Evans. But when, years later, I stood next to Godfrey Evans at a bar, I stared, entranced, at his

People and Places

hammered, mis-shapen hands.

As soon as I could, at school, I set myself to learn to bowl. This is where my belief that cricket lends itself to certain kinds of obsessives, and is not a particularly 'English' game at all, receives confirmation.

My nightly companion at the corner of the playing-field, coat for a bowling-mark, oil-drum for a wicket, was a Pole, Karol Bystram. He was as fanatical as I was. We were both determined to learn the game. Every night of the summer term, *every* night, we bowled at each other till it was dark. We must have bowled tens of thousands of deliveries. In the end I think I could pitch a ball on the wicket and reasonably near the right spot with my eyes shut, and I still can. I even made the school team – just; third-change bowler never, as far as I remember, asked to bowl and always so terrified of getting out first ball that I usually did. Once, first ball, I was given the dream opportunity: a full toss on the leg. I smote it for four, the watching school broke into cheers which faded to silence as they saw me on the way back to the pavilion. In my eager swing my pad had brushed the wicket and knocked off the bail. I can hardly remember a keener disappointment. The headmaster – an ex-county player himself and much admired by me – murmured as I passed him, 'You're not a cricketer, Kavanagh, you're a comedian,' and I pretended to join in the sycophantic laughter. So it always was, a chapter of disasters, never playing the one good game I felt I had it in me to play and now I have played what I reckon is my last game and that was a disaster too. What a sad tale it is!

One odd thing is that after I left school I never played or thought of playing for another ten years. Perhaps I was ashamed of my interest. Admittedly I was abroad most of the time but I am fairly certain that I thought cricket should play no part in the life of an aspirant writer who, to save his soul, must draw a firm line between himself and the Hearties. What snobbishness! It was only when I was old enough to recognize and admit my true enthusiasms that I allowed myself to play again – in Java, of all places. In Djakarta there was, perhaps there still is, a superb cricket club called, appropriately, The Box. There, with Australians, Indians and even the occasional Dutchman, I played again, not caring about the turbanned waiters, the absurd fag-end of

The Mystery of Cricket

Imperialism it all represented, or did not represent; absolved of guilt and self-consciousness I played and gloried in it. Without success, of course. But, I fancy, with just enough stylishness sketched while the cognoscenti were looking to ensure that I was asked again.

Back in England I played once or twice in Battersea Park where as umpire I gave an l.b.w. decision against the art critic, David Sylvester. The ball was entirely white with blanco from his perfect pads but as he strode scowling past me he hissed that he had hit the ball and therefore was not out and I recognized a fellow-dreamer, and the shattered dream.

I even for a time flirted with village cricket, that fiercely competitive cauldron, but I played for a team that consisted almost entirely of relations, indeed seven of the team bore the same surname; the two fast bowlers took all the wickets, the two openers scored all the runs, and I grew tired of fielding at long leg.

Then came the great day, a game under a captain who detected my passion. I was invited to play for the magazine *Private Eye* by William Rushton, on the beautiful ground near the house of the editor. I was thrown the ball by the kindly Willie and those long summer evenings with Bystram at last bore fruit. I had not bowled for years and I took a wicket. Indeed, I took four. Incoming batsmen conferred with outgoing batsmen to discover what I was 'doing'. I was doing nothing at all except bowling with the suddenly released enthusiasm of a lifetime and enjoying myself beyond reason. This game became for me an annual event, greatly looked forward to.

Sometimes there came from the magazine less understanding captains than Willie, bearded exposers of corruption in high places, less sensitive to the subsonic bleeps of yearning, electric emanations from the figure ageing year by year in the deep field. But there were high-spots still, for me, until the year of the last game. After four years' absence I went out to face a new demon-bowler on a hat-trick. The first one hit the middle of my bat, so did the second. Was this the innings I had been waiting to play since I was nine years old? I was sure it was, confidence welled within me. Playing forward fearlessly to the third ball – had not David Steele saved England by doing just this? – I was knocked flat in a welter of blood and stars: Retd. hurt 0. Looking up through a penumbra of small boys' faces – thrilled at the sight of blood – a doctor's face loomed, his Sunday afternoon ruined. He drove to his hospital in Reading to get materials to stick my face together and, lying on a rug in the car park being attended to, hopelessly embarrassed, I acknowledged to myself that a career was over – one that had never begun. I had *watched* that ball rising towards my face, waited for my body to take avoiding action which a year or two before it would have done instinctively. Nothing had happened. I was too slow. I was too old.

It is a strange moment to arrive at: the knowledge that an ambition would never be achieved; salutary, I suppose. But the passion does not fade. I write this against the background of the Test commentary on radio. Woolmer is in trouble on his return to Test cricket. I feel for him, but I still do not know why I feel so much. The loneliness of it, of course, the uncertainty and yet the clarity of a game that makes it impossible for a man to fudge, cheat, pretend; and the smallest instinctive movement seals his fate as a hero, or as an also-ran.

Those who write about cricket are often tempted into grandiose analogies but as a game it really is rather like the writing of a poem. What you do either works or does not and no one can tell you precisely wherein you have failed, nor can you know for certain if you will ever succeed, or, if you have succeeded, that you will ever do so again. The failure is in you, it is you that is getting in your own way.

The solitariness has a tang of the heroic about it, and round the great player an aura settles. The first cricket match to which I took my son he spent the whole afternoon collecting empty Coca-Cola cans from underneath the stand while I watched the now portly Cowdrey proceed to a stately 50. When we passed the pavilion he was taking off his boots and for some reason he looked up and gave us a smile. I said, 'You'll always be lucky now, you've been smiled on by Colin Cowdrey,' and I was only three-quarters joking. Like poets, cricketers spend unimaginable numbers of hours doing something as near pointless as possible, trying to dig an elusive perfection out of themselves in the face of an infinite number of variables, and as a result a large proportion of their lives belongs to the realm of the mystical. Like poets' their faces are deeply engraved by introspection – all cricketers

The Mystery of Cricket

seem prematurely lined – because they are as deeply locked in a struggle with themselves as they are with the opposition. But they look happier than poets.

1981

II

I saw something so extraordinary the other day that I hope not too many people will switch off because it happened at a cricket match.

Middlesex were playing Somerset in a limited-overs competition at Lord's. It was the semi-final. The morning was uncharacteristically grey for this summer but in the gloom Middlesex slowly accumulated a score against good bowling and astonishingly good fielding. They were playing in front of their home crowd but there was a large and noisy contingent from Somerset in funny hats, with large plastic flagons of cider. The Lord's Tavern is now closed for a long period in the afternoon, to prevent excesses, but these day-long chanters and singers had brought their own supplies. The atmosphere was not demure.

Middlesex scored 222, which was good because they have a battery of fast bowlers capable of bowling out most sides for less.

This, in darkness that increased, the Middlesex bowlers proceeded to do. Two Somerset wickets fell for thirteen runs and this brought Vivian Richards to the wicket who is (I am trying to write this, and keep it reasonably interesting, for someone who knows nothing about cricket) generally acknowledged to be the best batsman in the world. Immediately he showed that he was, playing a different game from inhibited mortals, an indulgent father knocking about a tennis-ball on the beach. Then, unexpectedly, he was out, caught. He stood staring for a moment, in surprise at himself, before he turned and walked back to the pavilion. A couple more wickets fell and Somerset, nearly all their best batsmen out, were five wickets down for fifty and the game was as good as over. There only remained Ian Botham and a young schoolmaster called Nigel Popplewell.

People and Places

If he could stay with the great man something might yet be salvaged. He did stay, and Botham, after some initial luck, began to play circumspectly, his bat seeming to become broader and broader, and when he did hit out he hit so hugely that one six-hit went over the highest roof in the ground. Good schoolboy stuff, but I have not yet come to the great three minutes.

Popplewell, after striking some good shots himself, was at last out. All the way back to the pavilion he struck the ground with his bat, so great was his grief and his anger with himself. There were still seventy runs to get and it was now so dark and late the lights on the scoreboard looked almost as bright as floodlights. In these conditions Gatting brought back his fast bowlers (among the fastest in the world) and it was now it happened. Botham struck the first ball that hurtled at him out of the darkness so hard that not a fielder moved before it reached the boundary. It is a cliché to say such a thing but there were three of them on the boundary and I saw that none of them moved. He had barely lifted his bat, there was no flourish, no defiance; it was a perfect, no, transcendent, combination of eye, balance, wrist, temperament, instinct. What does it matter, in such a man, what his private life is like, or his intelligence, or anything else about him? The only proper reaction is grateful awe. He did the same thing, in the same way, twice more in the space of three minutes; he inspired his new companion, Marks, also to strike out, and Somerset had scored 200; victory was possible.

Almost as a tribute to those awesome three minutes he had a stroke of luck. His only false shot popped into the air, an easy catch; the bowler, Daniel, ran for it, so did Gatting. Each left it to the other and it fell harmlessly between them. They stood staring at each other with what looked like hatred; but it seemed an unconscious salute from ordinary humanity to the brief, godlike, passage that had gone before.

Somerset won, Botham 96 not out, scorning the final hit that would have brought him his century, and the crowd invaded the pitch shouting Both-*am*, Both-*am*, disconcertingly raising their right fists in unison on the second syllable. But the appearance of the great man on the balcony dispelled any niggling worry caused by such a sight. He was engagingly awkward, even bashful. He had been presented with a tie and a cheque for £250 and,

The Mystery of Cricket

uncertain what to do, he raised the tie packet and the cheque envelope to the crowd, as though they were the FA Cup or the Wimbledon Championship plate. Because half-aware of the absurdity of this he did not raise them very high, grinned, and quickly vanished. He was probably only half-aware of those three minutes, bearer of a gift which he doubtless understands as little as the rest of us, witness to what we humans are capable of, if only we can get it right, however briefly.

1983

III

Walking under the stands at Lord's before the start of the day's play in the Test match, I marvelled at the order and clarity of it all. The attendants were standing chatting at the entrances to the stands, the mowers were going precisely up and down, the cushion-sellers with their comfortless little plastic biscuits were already calling 'A day's comfort for forty pee', and the magic cry, remembered from boyhood – 'Scorecard!' – was beginning to go up. I knew I was reverting to boyhood but plenty, it seemed, were doing the same, and I acknowledged how much of the pleasure that I felt, and anticipated, was due to the formality of others. I never would have erected this vast stadium on a priceless piece of real estate, would never have formulated the intricacies of the Laws of Cricket or discussed its finer points far into the night. I would have had too much humour and not enough sense. For it is absurd, of course, but it is precisely the seriousness with which it has been treated over the years that has let the poetry in.

Those generations of pompous men in the Pavilion – a few of them doubtless were, and are – have done me and my kind a service. We may safely laugh at them but they have created a predictable frame inside which the unpredictable can safely happen. It is almost a nursery sense of order, but within it I can achieve a sense of holiday, difficult to find anywhere else.

But at the end of the day the ground, or rather the stands around the ground, are amazingly filthy. It is as though humankind can stand just so much order and then must put its dirty footprint on it, for sanity's sake. As I moved to the back gate in the evening I was ankle-deep in thousands of beer-cans, smashed plastic glasses and mounds of half-eaten junk food. Those biscuit-cushions were flying about, too, there was loud laughter, the mood was drunken, but reasonably friendly. And outside the ground, at the exit of the Members' Car Park, propped against walls or lying on the pavement, muttering, shouting, or staring blankly nowhere, the Members' cars nosing slowly between them, occupants looking neither to right nor left, were the drunkards and derelicts queueing to come in and clear up the mess.

The shock of the contrast is great. Inside there are the white seats and white flannels, the green formality of the grass, the violence of the game, contained within society, and outside, waiting, are those who for one reason or another have been incapable of playing society's game. True, there is the bridge-passage of the muck to prepare you, but they are still a shock. Nursery holidays within a sense of order are not allowed to last for long.

Their names are taken at the gate and, if sufficiently sober, they are presented with a broom or shovel. These they hold proudly, like the staffs of office, talking rather formally in small groups. We all need some formality, some society. They are unsuitably dressed for their work, clearly in their best clothes, to help them pass the interview at the gate. When one of them topples over he is cheerfully escorted back to the gate and called by his Christian name – 'Come on, Paddy, you're no good tonight.' 'I was tripped, Sorr, tripped!' Many of them are Irish. The English do not like excuses, but Ireland is an agricultural country and a big city is sometimes too much for such country people. It is sometimes too much for me. It was distressing to watch them; some had bloody scabs on their faces from falls, or fights, some had faces that seemed to have collapsed from inside. It is a kind of hell. 'I never get used to it', said Gareth Williams, who organizes them. 'Always think, "There but for the grace of God..."'.' He treats them firmly and well, knows many of their names, for some come back again and again, there is competition for the work, at two pounds an hour. The order and morning clarity of Lord's depend on these.

One addresses me, broom on shoulder: 'You meet interesting

ones here. That Brian Johnson, he's a nice man.' I say I believe he lives near the ground. 'How do you know that?' He is suspicious, perhaps wondering if I am one of the 'interesting ones'. I doubt that, I am too uneasy. I can only with difficulty bring myself to meet his eyes.

1985

A Book in My Life

―――― o ――――

IF YOU THINK of the happiness of the old Matisse, painting his lovely colours and lovely girls, and compare this with the misery and malice that disfigured (we are told) the last years of Somerset Maugham, similarly aged, only a few miles down the coast, you can't help thinking that painting, or almost any activity, is better for you than writing. There are exceptions, of course – Goethe, Blake – but on the whole writers seem to fare badly: 'We poets in our youth begin in gladness; / But thereof comes in the end despondency and madness.' Indeed, not long ago, a school of criticism was erected on this; the degree of talent gauged by the disastrousness of the life, with suicide the stamp of authenticity.

That, of course, is the worst kind of romanticism, and I have always taken comfort from the contrariness of that still insufficiently appreciated genius, John Cowper Powys. Far from deteriorating, he began his best work at sixty and after a life of struggle, penury, ill-health and very little public success, became not only happier, but in a strange way healthier. He should have been dead years before – quite early on he had so much of his insides cut away that he had what he called a 'pseudo-stomach' – but he went on till he was ninety-one, emanating more and more energy, intelligence and goodwill, genially existing on bowls of bread and milk. He would have been the first to describe himself as a crafty old saurian – above all things he admired Homeric, Odyssean guile – and he had clearly found some way of adjusting his psychic dial to wavelengths of good news. How?

In 1935, at the invitation of his American publishers, he wrote a book, *The Art of Happiness*, answering that question. (He had published another book with that title in 1923, more philosophical, but this one concentrated on the technique, the 'art'. His publishers had met him, and realized that at the age of sixty-two he had some tips to offer.)

This has been republished by the excellent Village Press which deserves an article to itself. The way John Cowper Powys writes, in his essays, *helps* people, and it helped Jeff Kwintner who had just made a million in the rag-trade, from his Village boutiques. So he founded his own imprint to reissue just about every word John Cowper Powys wrote. Kwintner deserves a statue.

Powys begins his book by disposing of the cult of *un*happiness. He identifies it for what it is, a desire to revenge ourselves on the world. 'To be unhappy in order to punish! That really does seem a human instinct. But how pathetically absurd!' Nevertheless, the problem has to be faced: 'If at any moment a sensitive person were made fully conscious of the appalling pain in the world he would go mad and die howling.' Nature herself makes sure we remain 'too sturdily selfish' for that. However, we must remain aware, and yet not 'howl' and we can do this by *controlling our own thoughts*. I italicize this because it is the core of his advice. He does not like the word 'happiness' – 'the annoying jauntiness, and even the bouncing babyishness of the word' but it differs from pleasure, or joy, in that it is subject to mental volition. He now proceeds to a series of practical tips, with examples: he calls them the 'Icthyian leap' (like a fish out of the water), 'discarnation', the 'panergic' stance. He apologizes for the names, he is the enemy of obfuscation, but is also a profound believer in the magic of naming. But it is astonishing, as he says, how we allow ourselves to be at the mercy of any thought, however banal, that pops into our heads. 'We lavish our energy on plans to improve our condition but seldom concentrate on heightening our mental reaction to the moment as it passes.' This is generally so true that anyone who can help us not to re-play an old film in our minds, or dwell repetitively on some grievance, will do us a great service. He says it is up to us: 'We can be unhappy... or we can *force ourselves to be happy*.'

In this case the italics are his, he is fond of them, but no one must have the impression that his book is a regime of mental hygiene. On purpose he avoids religious consolations (he does not want to put anyone off, and in this case he barely considers them necessary). He calls it an 'impious' book, and the recommendations towards selfishness and deception in his (excellent) chapters called 'Woman with Man' and 'Man with Woman' (his book is nothing if not to the point) might be startling to some. But as much as anything he is redefining, freshening, these words. He was the son of a vicar and he is possibly having a sly dig at the Reverend Francis Powys in his re-writing of scripture; he lays much of our misery at the door 'of those tremendous commandments, in both the Old and the New Testaments, commanding us to love instead of to be at peace in our own souls.' But what balm there may be for some self-tortured soul in his next paragraph:

'What a liberating flood of planetary happiness pours through us when we experience that great moment of Conversion, turning us from love to peace! It is then that we realise that we can be free and happy and honourable and pitiful and kind *and yet not have to love anybody.*'

That makes me smile, I'm not sure why; like a disciple at the mouth of a cave, overhearing the Master. There are many such moments: 'A woman is happier living with almost any man who does not get drunk and beat her than with the best of mothers.' 'Men, down at the bottom of their hearts, *are afraid of life itself.*' (A source of irritation to their women.) He sees life as war – not against each other, but against negation. 'There is undoubtedly something, in our abandonment to misery, of an evil and destructive satisfaction.' As so often with Powys, he prefers the attitude of women: 'To be attracted by the exquisite delight of making love to the incredible yieldingness of an enchanted body, only to discover – when he comes to live with this body – that he has landed himself with a personality ten times more belligerent than he is, is a startling shock to most young men.'

He writes, as I have said, to be understood by everybody, which is a sure way, alas, of getting yourself underestimated. But Stevie Smith has it right, as she usually has (though her drawing of a bearded, robed harp-player is, thank goodness, fanciful; the sage was clean-shaven and reassuringly jacketed.) She wrote a little poem called 'Homage to John Cowper Powys'

> This old man is sly and wise,
> He knows the truth, he tells no lies,
> He is as deep as a British pool,
> And Monsieur Poop may think him a fool.

1983

A Glastonbury Romance

———— o ————

IN DIMENSIONS, and in plan, *A Glastonbury Romance* is the kind of large episodic book stuffed with characters that was common in the 1930s, like *South Riding*, like *The Good Companions*. It is set in the Glastonbury of its time, more or less. People fall in and out of love, Town Councils are elected, factories go bust, people discuss their troubles, a plot summary could make it sound deceptively ordinary. But it is different from all other books of this kind – I nearly said from all other books – because it goes beyond social description, and psychology (though it contains plenty of both) and ventures, with splendid unembarrassment, into the indefinable area of impulses and glimpses, of joys and horrors, of miracles, of gods and devils and energies and influences, that novelists understandably shy away from and leave to poor devils of poets. And he does this without losing grip of the story or trying to carry us so far he loses his grip on us. In short, while you are reading it it makes all other novels – *all* other novels – seem thin.

So why has nobody forced such a writer on our attention? The answer is that they have. Angus Wilson said Powys would stand with Henry James, D.H. Lawrence and Joyce in the eyes of future critics. Henry Miller called *A Glastonbury Romance* unique in English literature and couldn't bear to come to the end of it. J.B. Priestley writes of Powys with the nearest approach to awe that is possible for a Yorkshireman, and Professor Wilson Knight says that we may expect his works to grow steadily in repute, until their stupendous qualities are known. Well, they haven't grown, despite the eulogies of these very different men and many others. Powys is still little read. But before we try to think of reasons why, it might be useful to say a few words about the man.

He was born in 1872 in Derbyshire, the first of eleven children, and was the son of a well-to-do clergyman. When he was eight years old his father moved to Wessex and eventually to a village not far from Glastonbury. Two of his brothers were also writers, T.F. Powys and Llewellyn. The brothers were close and this perhaps gave rise to a public impression of an enclosed Powys circle into which only the initiate could penetrate. This is untrue as well as unfair.

John Cowper Powys began as a fairly typical poet of the 1890s, which is hard to imagine when we are faced with the Olympian sweep of *A Glastonbury Romance*, published when he was sixty-one, which sounds throughout as though a loquacious and unjudging god has found himself poised only a very few feet above the ground with a pen in his hand.

He had sixty pounds a year from his father, a wife and child to support, so he gave lectures. All his life he appears to have been without ordinary vanity; this had been cauterized perhaps by his experiences at school, where his gigantic appearance, his habit of slobbering his food and his untypical enthusiasms made him the butt of his companions, until one day he verbally turned on his tormentors and found he had the gift of utterance. So he became a lecturer. For thirty years he toured the United States – one-night stands, sleeping in trains, in cheap hotel rooms, speaking to few people sometimes, sometimes to thousands, improvising without a note, mainly on books: Homer, Dante, Rabelais, Dostoevsky. What his audiences of tin miners, city clerks, and suburban housewives made of him we cannot know; perhaps a great deal, because any contemporary account of those performances describes them as electrifying. He was half-mountebank and half-sage – a Holy Fool perhaps. The young Henry Miller attended one of these lectures and Powys immediately became his god and remained so to the end. Powys was often in great pain from stomach ulcers, exacerbated, presumably, by the unusual discomforts of his life and not helped by his nervous obsessions. He had mental torments as well as physical ones: detesting cruelty he found in himself tendencies towards sadism, or so he is constantly telling us. He was also a compulsive voyeur and haunted the burlesque shows of North America in an attempt to satisfy his endearing mania for female ankles. All this he confesses, cheerful as always, in his *Autobiography*, which J.B. Priestley

A Glastonbury Romance

is not alone in thinking the best in the language. It's worth mentioning what Priestley rightly finds one of the most interesting things about Powys: the way he cuts right across our daft contemporary notion of the artist's life. We are used to the idea of the artist burning himself up, destroying his life, for the sake of his art. Powys did the opposite, he cured himself through his art, cured both his illnesses and his obsessions. As soon as he began to write constantly in his fifties, and he never stopped again, his vigour and his happiness increased. He died full of both, aged ninety-one, in 1963, and Henry Miller visited him in Wales shortly before this and says he found the same wonderful being he had idolized in youth, only he had grown younger, healthier, gayer. I look with even more respect on work that could have such an effect on its author.

In America, in April 1930 at the age of nearly sixty, after about thirty years of public performances, he settled down to write *A Glastonbury Romance*. He had written other novels before but now he had come to the end of his long apprenticeship as a lecturer on other people's fictions and was ready to commit himself full time to his own. It is a gigantic work, at least half a million words long. The effect on reviewers must have been literally stunning. Henry Miller says it took him a year to read, in joyous sips, and the average reviewer can hardly have been half-way through before he had to give an opinion. Surely this must have had something to do with the public myth of the interminable vapourings of an outmoded Sage? I wouldn't have it one page shorter, and when I tried to choose some passages to quote here I found it was like trying to tear a piece of tight knitting. Every paragraph contains a surprise: impossible to forecast what is going to happen next or even what a character is going to say next, though when it happens or when it is said it sounds inevitable. There is no skill apparent in the book, though it is skilful, by which I mean there is no sense of character-charts and plot lines pinned to the study wall. There is only a sense of a man spinning creations out of the largeness of himself as easily and unselfconsciously as God on the First Day.

What Powys did have in his American study was a large-scale map of Glastonbury and its surroundings, and his book is as localized and detailed as the Dublin of James Joyce's *Ulysses* – a book which he knew and helped to defend in court more than a decade before. Also, like Joyce, he used a peg upon which to hang his huge narrative, the story of the Grail. Unlike Joyce there is no word-play (nor for that matter any sign of old scores being settled back home) nor is the complex and ambiguous Grail legend allowed to distort or in any way change the natural flow of the story. As detailed as Joyce he is without his pedantry, as intense as D.H. Lawrence he is without his aggressiveness.

He chose Glastonbury for his Romance – and it is a Romance, with a capital 'R', there is wizardry in it – because of the extraordinarily rich history of that place. As he says himself, 'the most materialistic of human beings must allow that at certain epochs in the life of any history-charged spot there whirls up an abnormal stir and fume and frenzy among the invisible elements that emanate from the soil.'

Whether everybody would allow that is doubtful – all his life Powys had a genial faith that others thought and felt roughly as he did – but I have no difficulty; and it is into this fume and frenzy that he puts his Mayors and brothel-keepers, his several pairs of lovers young and old, heterosexual and homosexual, his sadists, maiden ladies, murderers, communists, capitalists, his revivalist preacher, his antiquarians and his aristocrats, as well as a mass of walking-on parts, and watches them submit to the forces inside and outside themselves. None of these is only a type, each of them is an individual flame, dancing with the other flames, fed by the same wantonly variable forces that are flowing through them and around them. The book is no mere pageant, though it contains a pageant, one of the great set-pieces of the story. These high spots occur regularly. There's a christening for example, where the putative father gets drunk and hurls the christening cup in the river and the sturdy old vicar suffers agonies of guilty love for his son's mistress, the mother of the child. In this scene, the cross-currents of feeling become so intricate and are navigated by the author so surely, the climax when it comes is so unexpected and right, that I wanted to take the whole thing out and put it in an anthology of great passages of the world. But I can't because it's too much a part of the book. Then there's the description of the mistress of the vicar's son preparing the nuptial couch for her lover, boiling eggs for them and making toast, which is the best account of a sacramental moment in sexual love I have read. While she does all this her unfortunate lover is condemned to stumble about outside, not sure whether what he wants to happen is going to – a naturalistic touch. But the insight into the earthy mental processes of the girl are poetry precisely *because* they are earthy. Powys's sympathy with women seems complete – elderly unmarried ones and mannish ones as well as young ones in love.

You have to be careful with Powys, not to be too overwhelmed. He should not be set up as a sage, though he entered into the business himself by publishing books of philosophizing essays. He is a magician, as he himself knew very well, not a teacher in the ordinary sense. He transmits a world that reflects in the mirror of our own world and makes ours flash.

Technically, *A Glastonbury Romance* breaks no new ground. To the possible distress of critics it shows no signs of being 'modern'; though it seems today, because of its intentional timelessness, undated, except perhaps in very minor details. What it does is to go back (consciously but not self-consciously) to the narrative speed, in which gods and men so naturally mingle, of Powys's adored Homer. And here, in these gods and energies, I think we come to the heart of the resistance to Cowper Powys, and also to his great contribution. Those readers who cannot believe in anything outside themselves must find him unendurable. Those who do so believe are likely to be some sort of Christian, and Powys's easy way with exterior forces, with energies and demiurges, from the Primal Cause to Merlin, from the Sun God to Christ to grey-eyed Athene, must often sound disturbing, not to say potty. Thus at the outset he loses two audiences at once. Perhaps more readers are ready for him now. On the other hand, writers and readers have often been impatient with the novel as a form. Analysis of human relations is not enough, nor are social observations enough; even taken together they leave out too much of the elusive richness of our experience. What Cowper Powys wanted to do, and this is why a critic has said of *A Glastonbury Romance* that it makes even some classic novels read like escapist fiction, was to put back what gets left out. He does this by endowing everything that moves, and everything that doesn't, with a life and spirit of its own, with an energy, however tiny, that affects the other energies around it. This is no more than Wordsworth did in his poems – but then the English never believe poets mean what they say. Novelists they call to account. Whether Powys believed in his Primal Cause, letting fall evil and good, arbitrarily, on poor unwitting earth, whether he believed that trees, after their own fashion, could really think, is no more worth asking than whether Homer believed in his pantheon. Powys probably did. I see no reason why he shouldn't. So possibly did Homer. He certainly didn't think them merely quaint. What is important is that this machinery of other-than-human forces gave Homer, as it gave Powys, the chance to enrich, dignify and in the widest sense *explain* his story. It gave Homer the opportunity to describe Odysseus visiting the dead. It enables Powys, within the first few pages of *A Glastonbury Romance* to describe the thoughts of a corpse in his coffin, reviewing his past life with the detached curiosity of a botanist. As soon as I read that, Cowper Powys had me at his mercy, because that's exactly how a corpse in a coffin *would* feel, if it felt anything at all. The coffin-thoughts speedily and economically help the story along.

Everything does that. Snails, lice, trees, stones, all have their part to play, their small energies mingle with the vastness by which they are surrounded – what Powys called 'The Multiverse' rather than the Universe. The wind carries the troubled dreams of sleeping Glastonbury, each of them particularized, towards Salisbury Plain.

> By burdening itself with the greedy dreams of Nell's little boy, who cried in his sleep because the nurse refused to wake his mother so that he might be suckled, and with the vegetative feelings of Tossie's little girls, who seemed perfectly prepared to let off *their* mother and enjoy alien nourishment at any moment, the wind seemed to need a greater momentum to carry it away northeast, towards its resting place on Salisbury Plain, than it possessed.
>
> It flagged a little by the time it reached West Pennard. It dropped some of its tiny moss-spores, its infinitesimal lichen-scales, its fungus odours, its oak-apple dust, its sterile bracken-pollen, its wisps of fluff from the bellies of Sedgemoor wild-

fowl, its feathery husks from the rushes of Mark Moor, its salt-weed pungencies from the Bay of Bridgewater.

That is a very particular wind, we even begin to feel sorry for it, and by the time it sinks down and falls at Stonehenge, depositing its seeds and smells and what he calls 'the more psychic part of its aerial burden', he has managed to bring in the sleeping thoughts of most of his characters, the nature and contents of the wind and, with Stonehenge, time and history itself.

This is typical of his method. In even the greatest nature-writers, at the heart of their work, there seems an inhumanity, an over-intensity; whereas in Powys, as in Hardy, nature is the backdrop. His characters are rooted in the non-human world because we all are whether we like it or not, but it is the human world which is centre-stage. Stonehenge, after all, was made by men. But he entirely lacks Hardy's pessimism, without in any sense being complacent; he seems as far above facile optimism, as a novelist, as he is above good and evil. Physical pain, hopeless poverty, he confronts head-on. So great is his mastery over the reader by that time that you wonder if at last someone is going to teach you how properly to regard such things. You are left with a feeling that he has found a way, and it is a possible one. For hovering beside his book is the captivating personality of its author, one of his own greatest inventions. There is a wonderful lack of separation between the writer and the man; you feel certain he has given himself to you fully, without evasion or embarrassment, and if you met him he would talk in the way that he writes.

He says himself of this book that it is the sort into which he flings his whole nature.

> I work almost unconsciously as far as life and reality and nature and human character are concerned... the faith I try to advocate is the acceptance of our human life in a spirit of absolutely undogmatic ignorance. Whether death is a waking from one dream to another, or a total snuffing-out and entire obliteration, we simply do not know. In either case the symbolism of the Grail represents a lapping up of one perfect drop of noon-day happiness, as Nietzsche in his poignant words would say, or as nature herself, according to the hint given us by Goethe, whispers to us in more voices than at present we are

able to hear, or to understand when we do hear.

He wrote that in 1953 during what was surely the most tentative and self-limited period in our literary, and therefore in our spiritual, history. It was an age when Philip Larkin, finding himself in an empty church, slipped off his cycle-clips 'with awkward reverence' and poets wrote poems about not being able to write poems.

Perhaps the time has come when we can find again the courage to stop limiting ourselves, to discover that our definition of what is 'real' in life is too small, that we are feeding ourselves on unnecessarily thin gruel. If the time has come Cowper Powys is our man. He doesn't shirk the pain and indignities of life – far from it – but he doesn't shirk the other aspects of it either, as many of us do. I put down his book with more life in me than when I picked it up.

1977

True Story

———o———

T.F. POWYS, author of the remarkable novel *Mr Weston's Good Wine*, whenever he felt himself particularly gloomy and rebarbative, which he often did, considered himself subject to 'the moods of God'. He regarded these changes within himself as somehow external to himself, like the weather.

There does seem to be something outside us, which affects us, and over which we have little control. A mood of depression and discouragement can arrive, exaggerated beyond reason, which seems to have no immediate cause and can even be inappropriate to the circumstances: a piece of good news, on certain days, can only depress us further.

Presumably these could be called 'negative' feelings, and are surely necessary; anyone whose feelings were permanently 'positive' we would regard with suspicion. Nevertheless, when these moods arrive, apparently untriggered, they do seem odd.

For example, here we have been ice-bound and snow-bound for weeks, a sharp wind has been permanently in the east, and I have felt reasonably cheerful; but this morning, the last of the snow melting, warmth suddenly in the air – even a lark somewhere singing – I found myself filled with the conviction that all my life I had got everything wholly and unrescuably wrong. Nor had I performed one meritorious action. It was no use my telling myself that I must have done *one* thing right, by the law of averages, and if I could not remember what that thing was perhaps there were other decencies and kindnesses which I had forgotten. No, the mood was entirely unforgiving and the verdict was Guilty.

Small birds were exploding round me with a rattle of wings. The morning was warm, sunlit, busy, and I stood inside it in a rapture of self-dislike. My treatment of my children was wrong, of my wife, of my work. There is always enough truth in such

People and Places

dark suspicions to make them truly poisonous.

Wincingly, I took a few steps from the house to see what the snow was doing. The drifts were shrinking and had gathered dirt, with black deckled edges they looked like funeral cards. I was coughing a bit, and shivery; typical, to catch cold as soon as the weather improved. But I could not convince myself that my mood had anything to do with health. No, I was wrong, always had been, and 'wrong' was the word that kept rolling around in my mind.

I remembered I had noticed something unusual at the side of our lane, near the gate, as I drove past last night. Gloomily, I went to see what it was.

Written on the grass verge, in sawdust, in letters a foot high, complete with exclamation mark, was the word 'WRONG!'

You will have to believe this. In fact, I am going out to take a photograph of it to help me believe it myself. You must also understand that our house is an isolated one, the nearest neighbours a quarter of a mile away on either side. This gave the sawdust the force of a personal message.

I stared down at the letters, greatly cheered by the mystery of it. They were well-written, neat, all the same size, almost as though laid there by a sign-writer. There was no sawdust nearby, no tree-felling. Someone had brought the sawdust there in order to write the word. Was it addressed to me? If so, why was it 40 yards from our gate? (I checked; it was the nearest point that is out of sight of the windows.) But why should it be addressed to me? I did not, in fact, believe it was. I supposed it had something to do with a 'nature trail', or rally.

That I had even considered it was aimed at me was a reminder (not needed) that all such depressions and self-blamings are inverted self-regard, a kind of sulk. I knew this of course, but such knowledge is no help. In fact the only thing that can help is to find your own verdict written on the side of the road, a foot high, in sawdust. If it had said 'CHEER UP!' then I would have been really depressed. Perhaps there is a man, a member of some new *Club of Queer Trades*, who makes it his business to cheer up people in this way. God bless him. This is a tall story, but true, and it now occurs to me for the first time that it is precisely the kind of thing that could have happened in *Mr Weston's Good Wine*.

1985

Iceland

———o———

THE FIRST SIGHT of Iceland from the air is of some islands which look like cakes which have been forgotten in the oven, cracked, burned black; a new eruption. Iceland is a palimpsest of lava-flows; the new stuff, last year's, looks like neat banks of coke in a coal-merchant's yard. There are patches of green, though, and the story is that the first Viking settlers liked the place so well they called it Iceland to discourage other immigrants. When they reached Greenland, which is indeed covered in ice, they wanted more companions so they named it more invitingly.

We spend a night in Reykjavik and in the morning are scooped into a bus by our guide Marianna, impressively booted, with the mien of a confident nun. We travel the suburbs of the town picking up the rest of the party who all say Guten Morgen, except two pairs who say Bonjour. After an hour there are twenty-two of us: four French, two Dutch girls, a Swede, a doughty elderly lady from Chicago, two English (us) and the rest a variety of Germans from the gentle to the boisterous, among them one silent, stiff-backed couple who eat constantly.

It is a new country for me and my son, and the first time we had been so long alone together, but it is this new society into which we have been suddenly compressed which most distracts us both. Marianna tells us we must become 'a group', and we have already been told in the brochure to 'bring our light mood along'.

Little Icelandic townships (which are few) look from a distance like caravan-sites; low corrugated-iron huts, brightly painted. Only about twenty per cent of Iceland is liveable on, the rest is various kinds of desert, and nearly 200,000 of the 226,000 population are clustered in the towns – 120,000 round Reykjavik alone. The rest live on isolated farms strung along the coastline. It is hard to see how these survive. Their hayfields are about the size of an average village green (though each contains a spanking new tractor) and are balanced above black lava, as though cleared for roadworks, or by the deposits of glacial floods dotted with huge boulders.

On the new lava nothing grows, on the older stuff there are the first hopeful smears of lichen and, on older lava still, this gives way to silver moss lush as a cinema foyer carpet, and to sudden surprising clumps of pink mallow flowers, white bladder-campion and inch-high heather. Along some of the small glen rivers is a moss which is a fluorescent, almost hysterical, light green; although only a few inches across at the water's edge, it is visible from an aeroplane at 20,000ft, shining, an image of the tenacity and aggression of life in the most unpromising of conditions.

Some of the crags look excitingly like old castles, but there are no such things in Iceland. There is nothing man-made, not even field walls, which is old at all. Before corrugated iron, the buildings were made of unmortared stone and turf. The absence of that kind of history weighs on one. After a wet day in a lava-desert, when mirages make distant black islands appear to hang in air, it is possible to sympathize with the old Viking's prayer: 'In that place of fish may I never come in my old age.'

But our first stop is historical: Thingvellir, where the Vikings held their open-air parliament, the Althing. The sun shines, so does the wide lake, the empty plain, the deadly-cold glacier river and the neat, iron Lutheran church. Arctic terns with long tails like swallows squabble above the sedges. I am reconciled to the thought of putting up tents wherever we go by realizing that is what the Vikings did here; Icelanders have always travelled so, on their beautiful little horses with their curiously level way of running.

Cornelius and I have our first and only continuing difference – over photography. He wants to take one thing, I another. Everyone else on the bus has provided himself with a smart black bag neatly stuffed with the impedimenta of his mystery. Their gadgets fascinate the fourteen-year-old. In a superior fashion I scorn them. Everyone jumps from the bus and claps his camera to his eye like a bandage. They leap from rock to rock, the shutter-

Iceland

fiends, with loud cries, in search of a better angle and, I tell myself, see nothing.

Back to the bus and on to the *Geysir*. These days the famous one is sulking; an old whale refusing to blow through its hole to please visitors. The aperture is crusted with white salts, maybe the remains of the Sunlight soap which was thrust down for generations to encourage it to perform. But the water in the hole, contemplatively steaming, is the perfect blue of an eye, or a forget-me-not – no, it is the dreamy, greeny blue of the Aegean, startling in the cold grey and white crust. A younger *geysir* obliges nearby with a sixty-foot spout every few minutes, irregular, teasing the crouched photographers, causing cries of irritation, as though it were indeed an animal.

Behind it are little bubblers, steaming away privately, unambitiously, and these are beautiful colours too, rust-red, green-blue and one with bright orange streaks round it like the hardened yolk of an egg. All this colour and activity takes place in a tiny area, perhaps a couple of acres; and Marianna tells us that it is, like all the astonishing earth-events of Iceland, because we are on the 'North Atlantic Drift', and Iceland is slowly breaking apart, one bit heading for Greenland and the other for the Shetland Islands.

From there to a vast waterfall, Gullfoss, a rainbow shining in its spume, and to the beginnings of undemocratic reflections on the difficulty of experiencing a natural wonder after being disembarked in a car park in order to view it.

To cover the dull bits of the coach journey the tireless Marianna tells us about Iceland. There is sixty per cent inflation; in her winter job she is given an automatic rise of thirty per cent every quarter. No one dares save any more. She also explains that you only use first names in Iceland, that is how you are listed in the telephone book. Ulaf's son is called Ulafsson and his daughter Ulafsdottir, and Ragna Ulafsdottir will be under R. 'We do not use titles like Mr or Mrs and always use the familiar form of address and that is how I will talk to you.' Her democratic and Icelandic pride is fierce. (I bought a cheap gas cigarette lighter in Reykjavik called an Elite. Cornelius notices that it is counter-stamped Equity...).

We bump up a glacial river, or rather a series of rivers in a delta, shining among black stones, between softly rounded hills like the north of Scotland. The weather holds good. We nose into the deep streams to shouts of encouragement from Erik the Swede and the man I have come to call The Merry Songster, because he sings tunelessly all day and, it sometimes seems, most of the night. A group, or a part of a group, is forming. The monolithic Germans in front of us eat and say nothing. We have opportunity to observe them because they stay in front of us; we all move back one seat each day so that nobody is permanently over the axle.

We arrive at the first campsite, which is in a green dell by the wide river, within sight of the glacier. We are issued with tents and waved in the direction of bushes. The sturdy kitchen-wagon has also forded the rivers and so, tented (in our case, after initial dismay) we sit with our trays on the grass as the sun goes down and eat lumps of meat in bowls and drink fruit soup, which seems to be made of boiled raisins (and is not bad) and wash it down with orange squash. The food throughout the trip varies from the reasonable to the pleasant, but that orange squash was a problem. There is no beer in Iceland, the place is virtually dry, and in the few hotels we came across a whisky costs £2.70.

In the morning the view is dramatic, but the two English are nearly late for nine o'clock kick-off. I am reminded of National Service. It had been depressing to peer through the tent-flap at seven a.m. and see those two silent Germans, exquisitely anorak'd, standing beside their neatly-packed tent, their neatly-packed suitcases, waiting for breakfast.

There are lavatories and wash-basins in this place and they are just about the last we shall see.

This is worth talking about. By day we would drive for hours through black lava-fields, or grey-black glacial landscapes where the terrible, flooding rivers had scraped all vegetation, or hope of it, from the earth. Then, for other parties had arrived before us, we would arrive at Tent City, in some splendid oasis whose point was its isolation, where there would be two cold taps and two earth closets for upwards of 150 people.

One of the French dared murmur at this, but was firmly put down. '*Nous ne sommes pas privilégiés,*' said Marianna stoutly, 'there is room for everybody, tourists *and* Icelanders.' Room,

Iceland

yes, but soon there will be a bit of Kleenex behind every rock... Also it is very noisy: Icelandic radio from the wagons, laughter from the cheek-by-jowl tents, as though automated, an *éclat de rire* every ten seconds. Again only the French dared complain, a snarled, *'Fermez la gueule!'* in the small hours which had no effect. Heavy-lidded in the morning they told it was the same in France – *'les Allemands'* – they had had to put up notices, 'No laughing after 10.30.'

And yet it was jolly enough, I suppose. Perhaps, after all, people come to lonely places to meet each other. Cornelius either slept through the racket or joined in. 'Look,' says the Merry Songster, pointing to a boulder poised on a glacier, 'An Icelandic meatball!' My suffering is quenched by Corn's delight; he is the perfect companion.

But we could walk alone on entirely black sands at Vik and discover that the birds on every rock were puffins, landing with a flash of scarlet which was the sun shining through their webbed feet. We saw glaciers like huge moulds, still bearing neat in their ice the shape of the huge hills they had carved. We saw desolation and devastation caused by the eruption of 1783 which made the King of Denmark declare Iceland uninhabitable. But still the survivors clung on. After an hours-long bone-jolting ride over a lava-desert, followed by a sweaty march over black featureless ash, those of us who could manage it climbed down one of the craters of another volcano, Askja, and bathed in a hot sulphur lake at the bottom, Marianna scorning a bathing-suit and the rest of us following her lead.

While swimming we brought up blue mud with our toes and smeared each other's faces with it until we looked savage, atavistic, like something out of *Apocalypse Now*. Perhaps in the end we were a sort of group. We left after nine days and knew we would miss Erik the Swede, his firm friend the Songster, even miss the silent pair who once again had piled their plates, in neat Mount Fujiamas, with everyone else's share of the smoked fish at breakfast.

But it was delight to see Lake Myvatn (like Killarney, only more so) nearly alone; to visit its smoking sulphur-painted hillsides without being told where to go; and, later, to wander concrete and corrugated-iron Reykjavik in the rain – a friendly place

– at our own sweet will. Perhaps I was wrong to think it was like Ireland without pubs or humour. The Songster was on his third trip; we met a Scotsman who was on his sixth. Maybe a Safari bus, in company, is the only way to see all the things we did. But, as Cornelius suggested, they should put their camp sites away from the beauty spots (and build lavatories), leaving visitors to find their own splendours. Though, in Iceland's fissured earth, there is always a danger of falling down the North Atlantic Drift.

1980

Is It Alas, Yorick?

———o———

RECENTLY I HAVE started doing sums in my head: how old was my father when I was my sons' age, and how did he deal with me? I am always startled. What – that fifty-year-old figure of authority that I remember? (No, not authority but confidence, completedness, a man who had solved his problems and now stood on top of the hill looking calmly back and calmly on.) Am I really his age now, who am not like that at all, neither calm nor complete, and unlikely to be so?

I try to console myself with the thought that I probably appear to my sons as he did to me (though I doubt this) and tell myself, more confidently, that he was not really like that either.

I have been reading some early letters of his, written to his distant parents, explaining why he had given up his medical studies and had decided, against their wishes, to get married. I recognized the tone at once, slightly blustering, self-exculpatory; I had used it myself, to him. One of his excuses for his lack of industry is so far-fetched as to be possibly true. Overcome by thirst in the laboratory he had swigged a beaker of clear fluid which turned out to contain some deadly acid. This affected his work and, he tells them, permanently damaged his health. As he often boasted to me that he had never had a day's illness in his life, which in my experience was true, he had either conveniently forgotten this or, to his parents, was pulling the longbow as far as his bulging cheek would allow. But there is definitely a young man's rather whingeing note in the letter; slight, but sad. So when did he become the confident figure I remember? No, that's not right, he wasn't confident, he was diffident, but I derived confidence from him . . . So do I go on puzzling, nuzzling at his shade.

If you push into a thicket you sometimes come across a greening sheep-skull. Outside the thicket, plump, living sheep tear confidently at the grass, undismayed. We are like that, and should be. We miss our dead – sometimes we even grieve. It is hard to imagine that one day we shall be among them. But meanwhile it is well to remember that through all sorts of cycles of change they nourish us, and continue to set us problems that will be with us until we die. So, having done my sums, I try to remember how he, fifty, dealt with me at fourteen – but I can't. Perhaps he didn't deal with me at all. But maybe it is not too late; he was, after all, a Roman Catholic, as in essence I am, so perhaps I should pray to him and ask his advice? But I can't do that either, can only imagine him embarrassed, evasive of my intensities, as he was in life; properly so, as I now think. Thus he eludes me still, which is perhaps why I think of him so much.

But it is also because I feel myself in a special position because of him. He was not, I feel pig-headedly certain, like any other father. He didn't even look like any other father. He wore black, broad-brimmed hats for a start. Not very broad-brimmed, not sombreros, but not neat trilbys either. He was red-faced and red-haired, balding, with a huge dome, and was stout, to the extent of appearing almost square when I knew him, balanced on tiny feet. Someone painted a portrait of him and friends complained the painting made him look like a butcher. He could have looked like a butcher but he did not. Whether he was distinguished-looking I have no idea but he was certainly distinctive. I have never seen anyone who reminded me of him, even remotely. With his neat red moustache he might have been a bank manager, I suppose, or a retired army officer – but it would have been impossible to imagine which bank, or which army. A conundrum, you just could not place him; New Zealander-Irish, he was as near as possible classless. When he briefly had a large desk in an office of his own making, even when he sat behind it, he gave the impression he was just passing through, was about to reach for his hat and go out into his beloved London – if indeed he wasn't already wearing the hat, which was usually the case.

He had no job, like other fathers, not a real one. He began adult life as a remittance man and when the remittances stopped he remained impoverished for a time, apparently not noticing.

Is It Alas, Yorick?

Then he suddenly began writing sketches for comedians and these, as the years passed, turned into radio shows which culminated in ITMA, the wartime programme that made him famous and, briefly, in funds; both of which he enjoyed. My point is this: he was, and is, my exemplar of order, an order I would like to pass on to my sons: but how can I when my own father spent his life, earned his living, presenting a sort of inspired, zany *dis*order as a source of true heart's ease? And every kind of authority as ludicrous? If he invented a mayor that mayor was amiably bent; if he wrote of a doctor that doctor was the source of every possible confusion to his patients. Each generation tries to be less pompous than its predecessor. I have watched my friends, the interesting ones, define themselves by reacting against their parents – against a too-limiting sense of class, or convention, or morality. (I have also sometimes seen them look aghast at the disordered world they have created, and attempt, too late, to swing back to the values of their parents.) But my father did not impose himself like that. Not that it was Liberty Hall. I once turned him purple with rage (an almost unique occurrence) because I used a fairly mild swear-word. But I can hardly define myself by going around cussing all the time.

His working methods were cottage-industry and bordered on the chaotic. He would leave it till the deadline and then get up in the middle of the night and sit at a tiny table in front of the electric fire, Parker pen in his stubby fingers, filling the ash-tray and sheets of lined foolscap which he dropped on the floor. By the time I surfaced he had covered the carpet with paper and was wandering in to the kitchen, reading bits out to my mother to see if she laughed, laughing himself anyway.

Of course, it (and he) was not all good. That period of unemployed impoverishment showed irresponsibility – he had a family. Later he often drank too much – in company, never at home. Indeed I suspected that, among friends, he hardly noticed that he was drinking at all, just emptied what came to hand, as he had in the laboratory. In company the puns flowed easily, without malice. They no longer work, they were born of the moment, but I remember one occasion when a friend called Watt warned him about the excessive drinking of one of my father's business associates named Blatt: 'But surely,' said my father, 'that's a case of the Watt calling the kettle Blatt?' and what could have been an embarrassing, possibly unpleasant, moment went up in a shout of laughter. I remember admiring him for that, for the quickness of it, the geniality.

The image of the sheep-skull keeps returning to me... The most famous skull is Yorick's, and he was a jester too. I have sometimes suspected that Yorick is the secret hero of *Hamlet*. Certainly he is a hero of Hamlet's: does he not, at the intensest moments of his confusion and grief, express himself in wild whirling word-plays?

My father didn't go in for giving advice (though he did once solemnly recommend that I keep a bottle of Vichy water by my bedside). He didn't himself – he drank enormous quantities of lime-juice instead and I certainly never saw him with a hangover however much he had deserved one – but he saw no self-contradiction in that. He told me that I should never go bald if I massaged my scalp in a certain way, as he always had. He placed his square finger-tips on his shining dome in order to show me how. However, when I was hit by a grief, he did venture an oblique suggestion during the course of a shy tête-à-tête lunch. 'Now that something terrible has happened to you,' he said, 'perhaps you'll write comedy.' Coming from him that is not quite the show-must-go-on, laugh, clown, laugh cliché it might otherwise sound. For what was there in my father's life? There was God, there was fellowship, and there were jokes. It is not a bad recipe. At times I have detested jokes – a son must react against his father in some fashion. I have seen jokes for the evasions they are, what Edward Thomas called the 'monkey, humour', praising Richard Jefferies for his lack of it. If you sit in a room with a television comedy going on next door and hear the automaton-like burst of hilarity it is possible to hate laughter itself.

But my pendulum swings. Sometimes I think jokes are the only truly serious response to our absurd fates. Who can match the desperate humourlessness of the adolescent who thinks he is the first to discover seriousness? (I was probably like that, which is why my father ducked.) For after all the show *must* go on. The alternative is not a joke.

Maybe what my father meant, but was too gentle to say, was

Is It Alas, Yorick?

that now something terrible had happened to me perhaps I might grow up. I would like to ask him about that now because I suspect he never quite did so himself and this has impeded my own growing-up, for which I bless him, however tiresome I may be to others. For I am never at ease with those who have come too surely to terms with life. I would also like to ask Yorick, that fellow of infinite jest, what he would have said if he had heard Hamlet say 'Alas'. Something to the point, surely, but not portentous.

So I go on puzzling, nuzzling the green grass outside the thicket.

1983

ITMA

THE ITMA YEARS, 1939-49, were the years of my childhood, so my account has to be personal, childlike, the history of my father and my family seen from the inside and, as it were, from below.

My first conscious *thought* about my father's strange work – for surely the manufacture of jokes, by the week, is an unusual occupation – was that there must be easier ways of earning a living. We were in Bristol and the house next door had been bombed and set on fire. In fact it was a smoking hole and its disappearance had exposed the side wall of the house we lived in, behind which my father sat writing, also smoking, his enormous domed forehead in his pudgy hand, his equally fat fountain pen in the other, covering sheets of blue-lined foolscap. On the other side of the wall (now, as I say, an outside wall, which it had not been when we had gone to bed last night in the cellar), firemen played their hoses to stop it cracking. It steamed gently, and perhaps to a clairvoyant eye my father's joke-brewing dome was steaming too. I don't know whether I thought then, but I certainly think now, that his job was much harder than that of the journalist who must write of what he sees and experiences. He, on the contrary, not only had to ignore what was happening but had to write as though it hadn't happened, churning out this week's laughs. I seem to remember at this time he was writing a show called 'Send for Doctor Dick', or it may have been 'Lucky Dip', for in 1940 he was a hard-ridden hack and the BBC had not yet realized that ITMA could be allowed to consume all his energies and would, in future days, be something upon which it could preen itself. At this time I think he was writing two or three shows a week and was paid ten pounds. He detested work.

How does a man start, as a comedy scriptwriter? Well, in this case, my father, of Irish stock, came from New Zealand to Edin-

ITMA

burgh to study medicine. The First World War intervened, he went into the Army, afterwards did various jobs, writing advertisements for Burroughs Wellcome, cartoon scripts, etc. He was a keen whisker-twiddler on the old crystal radio sets, one day heard a comedian he liked, sent him a sketch, the comedian (T. Handley) bought it, and so their long association began. How ITMA started is a longer and more complex story, but briefly, like so many ideas that are found to work, it grew out of a series of half-cock ideas that didn't work at all. The outbreak of war was the catalyst. It was a time of officialdom and officiousness, that curious strain of self-importance that a crisis brings out in certain of the British was ripe for deflation, and Tommy Handley, with the voice of a disaster-prone con-man, more bent than a six-pound note and cheery with it, was the ideal man to do the deflating. It was a time of pompous initials also, A.R.P., L.D.V., and so on; Tommy doodled on a piece of paper It's That Man Again, and ITMA was born.

Basically, there were three men involved and as my father points out in his book on Tommy Handley, none of them could have managed without the others; comedian, producer, writer. And the fourth participant, as important as any other, was the War. The nation blacked-out, apprehensive, with nothing whatsoever to entertain it except a comparatively new toy, the radio.

His private relations with Tommy Handley are difficult to define. Although they were friendly – very – it would be difficult to call them friends. Outside working hours they hardly met. They were both very private men, but in different ways. Whereas my father's world was one of pubs and clubs (where a man in the midst of a crowd can be as private as he pleases, all the more so if he is their accredited jokesmith), Tommy Handley liked to go home and read – at least that's what everybody presumed he did there, nobody knew for certain. Generous with his time and his extreme geniality (to the point of psychic exhaustion, which is probably what killed him), he was careful of his privacy and his money. No back-slapping, no rounds of drinks for the boys, he was either on-stage, in the public eye, or invisible, gone. On-stage, and I mean it in the general sense, in the middle of a crowd of admirers as well as actually performing, I found him, as a child, adorable. He was very funny indeed, with plenty of time, and special jokes, for mc and for all the other fringe members of any group, barmen, commissionaires, bores. It's true that sometimes, in the midst of all the laughter, my father looked a little wan. But then, it was only natural, he was bound to have heard some part of it all before. Tommy was handsome, almost in a leading-mannish sort of way, but there was a tell-tale crinkle at the corners of the eyes that mocked the effect of his electric presence even while he included you inside it. He stood outside himself, he had style, in any company or profession he would have been a star. Like all great performers he shone in the radiance of his effect on others. No one who had ever met him would call him 'only' a radio comedian, as though that is a minor form of art. Perhaps it is, but there was nothing minor about his presence.

The third member of the triumvirate was the producer, Francis Worsley, pipe-smoking, corduroy-jacketed, schoolmasterly. Any producer's role is difficult to describe but it's probably true to say that he held the three of them together. Without Tommy the words wouldn't have meant much and without Francis my father wouldn't have gone on producing the words. I remember him standing at my father's bedside taking an overdue script from him sheet by sheet as, groaning, my father scribbled it.

Some other members of the cast are still vivid from my childhood. Dino Galvani (Signor So-So) who even in real life was very much the stage-Italian, gentle, wistful. I remember him holding out his hands, gnarled with arthritis, and elegiacally remembering his matinee idol days: 'I used to pick ze ladies like ploms off ze trees – ploms off ze trees.' Horace Percival (Ali Oop, the Diver, Claude), lantern-jawed, immaculate story-teller, shakily coming down to breakfast at a provincial hotel after too long a session the previous night, and to my fascination using his tie as a sort of pulley to steady his tomato juice on its uncertain progress towards his mouth. Sydney Keith (Sam Scram), small, spectacled, and like the old musical comedy man he was, suddenly grabbing my delighted, blushing nine-year-old self and doing a soft-shoe shuffle with me across the stage of a freezing cinema in Bangor during a rehearsal. Fred Yule (Chief Bigga Banga), vast baritone, who in my father's opinion one day somewhat over-discussed his ailments. So he said 'Come on Fred, have

ITMA

a pint of pus with me'. (Invited by someone to lunch at Simpsons my father was disappointed to discover it was Simpsons the clothes shop in Piccadilly, not Simpson's in the Strand. So he ordered a boiled shirt.) Jack Train (Colonel Chinstrap), who always had a new gadget to show us, and who used to take us for drives in his car, a great treat in those days of petrol rationing. Friendly, chirpy Jean Capra (Poppy Poopah) and Clarrie Wright (*Good* morning, *nice* day!). That's what I remember about them all, extreme friendliness to each other and to a doubtless boring child. For the rest of my life I will love showbiz people, who are usually thought so steely, so self-seeking. That has not been my experience. It was all indeed a team, the secretaries Joyce Walters, Teeny Goss, the performers, Tommy, my father, Francis, there was a family feeling, because of the war, because of being twice evacuated, the shared hotels, digs, discomforts, privations. And I couldn't help noticing that as far as I could tell they all seemed to love my father.

For me the scripts contain him, as well as the particular trick of voice that made Tommy Handley so cheeky, so friendly, so unpompous. I remember my father being rather pleased when an MP, I think it was Bessie Braddock, described ITMA as 'a welter of bad puns'. He loved puns, alliterations, all forms of playing with the sound and meaning of words. So did Tommy. They must have had great fun.

One thing ITMA can take credit for, a loosening of the bonds of the possible in radio, characters entering without preamble, for no reason at all, and disappearing as fast. The speed was new, easily accepted by ear, it would have been more difficult to follow by eye. It bred a new style of comedy – perhaps a new style.

So it went on, year after year, the relations of the three central figures remaining the same and as friendly as ever; changes of cast but still the same atmosphere. You could feel it when you went to a rehearsal, and it came across in the broadcast. My father still leaving the script to the last moment, getting up at five in the morning, switching on the electric fire and working, smoking, still the brass ashtray, the fat fountain pen, so that by the time I got up the floor would be littered with foolscap and my father would keep wandering into the kitchen, chuckling, reading out bits. I'm not sure I laughed enough, or at all. My mother

People and Places

always did. But I hadn't yet realized that even grown-up Daddies need all the encouragement they can get. Then Tommy died. My father was very shaken, it had been a long partnership; in its own way, and because of the hugger-mugger conditions of the war, an intense one. But he said he felt he'd been released from a life sentence. More than three hundred scripts – it doesn't bear thinking of. He never found another tongue that could wrap itself round his words, or words he could shape around another tongue.

That unique tongue is now still, so is the fat fountain pen. Do the words on the page still have speed, flavour, reality? They certainly had plenty of those things once. Well, time only knows. Or, as the clock said, T.O.K.

1974

Fear of an Odd Sort

———— o ————

IN THE FILM of the life of Freud, Montgomery Clift offers his theories of infant sexuality to an audience of his colleagues and is hooted off the platform. Whether this really happened I don't know, but Freud's views certainly caused shock and dismay, and would not have done so if members of professional classes had looked after their children themselves; but they didn't, they left it to servants, and were therefore able to retain an abstract idea of what children were, or should be. Thereby depriving themselves in my view, of an educative experience we are now, two hundred years after Rousseau, only beginning to discover.

And are we beginning to discover it? Times have changed, domestic servants have disappeared, but this new rubbing of shoulders between children and literate parents is not often written about. In novels they are sometimes seen as victims of a marital break-up, sometimes even as malignant spies, obstacles to the course of true lust – which indeed they can be – but very seldom are children more than marginal figures, lurking, not yet old enough to be interesting.

This is especially odd because writers, male and female, are more likely than most to work at home and have the omnipresence of the characters and demands of their children brought forcibly to their notice. I am not saying that more books should be about children, only that they should contain them, as most houses do, and most lives.

After Rousseau the Romantics, above all the Lake Poets, were not least revolutionary in their attitude to childhood. 'Plain living and high thinking' brought them into daily contact with it, and they were fascinated (De Quincey, for example, writes marvellously about certain children because it never occurs to him that the fact he is older is of any significance). Coleridge even wrote

People and Places

'Frost at Midnight' with his baby in the room:

> The inmates of my cottage, all at rest,
> Have left me to that solitude which suits
> Abstruser musings; save that at my side
> My cradled infant slumbers peacefully.

A father sitting at night with his baby – a middle-class father – was surely a new picture in those times. What is more, the reader has the impression that if the baby wakes up, Coleridge would know what to do about it and would not mind, the baby being as much a part of his experience as the weather outside, and his own trains of thought. His notebooks are filled with observations of the reactions of his children: they, and natural phenomena, and himself are welded together into a whole: he holds the infant Hartley up to the moon.

But the most extraordinary description of what childhood meant to the Romantics is in Wordsworth's 'Ode; Intimations of Immortality'. I must quote it at length because it is my theme:

> Our birth is but a sleep and a forgetting:
> The Soul that rises with us, our life's Star,
>   Hath had elsewhere its setting,
>   And cometh from afar:
>   Not in entire forgetfulness,
>   And not in utter nakedness,
> But trailing clouds of glory do we come
>   From God, who is our home:
> Heaven lies about us in our infancy!

We may read that often, but how often have we reminded ourselves that Wordsworth, a great poet at the height of his powers, meant exactly what he said? Put in crude prose, he is saying that from a storehouse of souls, Heaven, a baby is sent down to earth with still some flavour, some sense, some memory of God. And that growing up is a slow process of forgetting this: 'At length the Man perceives it die away, / And fade into the light of common day.'

In plain words like that it is an idea so extraordinary as to inspire every kind of resistance, which is why Wordsworth put it into verse. But poetry, even 'old' poetry, is news about the

Fear of an Odd Sort

world we live in. Wordsworth meant it, and knew that if he said it in a newspaper column, for instance, it would look ridiculous, so he used art, which is what art is for, to carry a meaning as well as to express it. But it's not 'just' poetry, and if it's true, if Wordsworth is right, what a light it casts on childhood, and on life. Moreover, there can hardly be a parent (or an observer of children), however dismissive of the idea of Heaven and of God, and however determinedly rational, to whom the idea of a superiority in the child has not in some form occurred; to be dismissed, sometimes with shame, and even anger, because of our inability to comprehend it, and because of some deep-buried memory.

George Meredith has a genuine child in *The Egoist*. 'A real and sunny pleasure befell Laetitia in the establishment of young Crossjay Patterne under her roof... a boy of twelve with the sprights of twelve boys in him.' And he is that, a real boy observed without condescension, a sustained character who affects the heroine importantly, who is in no way diminished in significance by the fewness of the years on his head. In fact, this is the only great novel I know wherein the affective quality of childhood (not childhood 'innocence', real or imagined) is given its due weight.

Of course, children are not always a real and sunny pleasure, any more than anything else is. Unlike a child's, the grown (or older) mind needs patches of silence to graze in. Whole days spent in the company of a five-year-old leave the brain gasping, suffocated, because it has never been allowed to follow a consecutive train of thought. I didn't even know I had consecutive trains of thought until I had children to interrupt them. It is the new awareness of this pressure, surely, that makes more and more men take over from their wives when they can, in order to share, or diminish, the mental claustrophobia.

Even while the mind gasps for air, for ten minutes' 'abstruser musings', surprising things are going on underneath. Some adult preoccupations begin to look overblown, oddities are noticed by eyes two feet from the ground, strange connections and juxtapositions are made, a day-long Goon Show, by minds infinitely fresher and more joyous than one's own. I don't merely mean the funniness of children, though they can be funny of course, and that's a bonus, but it's usually unintentional humour measured against adult standards, I mean a new, or rather half-forgotten, way of looking at the world. Wordsworth again.

I believe the habit of sharing the lives of children is now more widespread than is acknowledged. I can't prove it, any more than Wordsworth could prove his more extraordinary assertions, but in some part of our society 'the nuclear family', far from breaking down, it seems to me, is being seen again as something that gives a meaning to life, even by those who twenty years ago would have been in the forefront of opposition to such an idea.

This is particularly so in the case of fathers. They take more part. Women sometimes complain, justly, of being confused by the variety of roles forced upon them. Men can be confused too. I'm not the only one who inadvertently, in some inappropriate place, produces a packet of sweets gone sticky from his overcoat pocket, or has to sweep the plastic debris off the back seat of the car when giving colleagues a lift.

Yet the colleagues are often puzzled. These signs of family life, in a working situation, strike them as odd although they are increasingly commonplace. That's because writers haven't written about it yet. Everything is odd until it has been formulated and made acceptable. The pleasant part of the history of the last twenty years is that more and more people have felt free to be themselves and have discovered they're not so unlike other people as they feared.

Long ago, tree-watchers were a lonely band until the landscape painters got going, then everybody was doing it. We should be teaching others, and ourselves, that it's all right to look at children, listen to them, and reply to them.

Deeper and more muddied centres are touched. Kingsley Amis put his finger on some of them in his address to Jesus, 'New Approach Needed';

> And what about a go
> At love, marriage, children?
> All good, but bringing some
> Risk of remorse and pain
> And fear of an odd sort.

There can be no father or mother who has not sat remorseful,

Fear of an Odd Sort

the children at last in bed, remembering a pointless irritation, lack of attention, unresponsiveness, fearing that in spite of themselves, they have helped to cast the shades of the prison house prematurely.

There is another fear too, of time, which is the most fearful of all things. Children are time made flesh. To love a child is to love a cloud; a child changes, slips through our fingers, disappears, probably physically but anyway into the adult. It is a love with no end in view save separation. It has to be unselfish enough to encourage that separation, it has no consummation, is nothing except what it is and every day is a fresh blow on the wedge.

Iris Origo says the Japanese have a word for the fear of an odd sort such knowledge causes, something like 'a death in the heart'. And it is a death, a loss, an education in time and in an impossible unselfishness. We fail, of course, but we think about it and it is worth our thought.

1975

September Song

———— o ————

NEAR THE BEGINNING of this month I was sitting in the gardens of Walmer Castle, near Deal, with my two sons. We have been doing such things together for a dozen years or more: wandering cold seasides (or warm ones), examining what there is to see and do, going in search of ice-creams – that sort of thing. I had expected to find it a bore, those years ago, and sometimes it was, but not often. On the whole I was surprised to find how much I enjoyed it, how much of a child I still was myself. Now, by the nature of things, this had to be among the last of such occasions, if not the last; I realized that to some extent I had come to depend on them.

Thinking of this, listening to the boys, you will not be surprised to hear that I also pondered the death-mask of the Duke of Wellington. The castle is the residence of the Warden of the Cinque Ports; he was a Warden, and lived there towards the end of his life. It is an unsparing likeness. His false teeth had been removed, so that his chin nearly meets his great nose. He died there, in his wing chair, by his iron campaign-bed in his small, soldierly, bed-sitting room. The wrinkled, almost sexless, image of that straightforward and useful man is moving. The austerity of his room is moving too, for it is comfortable enough, the few pieces of furniture good, but it is simple. The last palaces I looked at (and Walmer Castle is a kind of English, domestic, palace) were in Leningrad: gold piled on gold, rare marble on rare marble, gigantic salon after gigantic salon, until gawping wonder shades into distaste, even horror. Here the greatest of our Captains lived in a kind of monkish dignity (he was a widower by this time) with not a weapon or a memento in sight, if you except his campaign-bed. It seemed infinitely superior and (though the idea came too easily perhaps) 'English'. One has to remember Apsley

September Song

House. But we do seem to have a gift for the domestic.

The castle itself is English in other ways; it was a weapon of-war (and we are a warlike race) that was out of date even before it was built, by Henry VIII. It has been further 'Englished' by being turned, some time in the eighteenth century I should guess, into a comfortable *home*. The Duke's room was a gun-port, now wood-panelled and painted a soft, feminine grey. None of the rooms is large; William Pitt's is the size of a sitting-room in the average semi. The furniture is very good, but does not loudly say so.

I wondered, sitting in the garden (the mood, you will have gathered, was elegiac) how much of that sort of 'Englishness' still existed. We seem less rooted, more emptily boastful now. We would make an awful mess of Walmer Castle if we tried to turn it into a home today.

I also knew that any fun my sons may have had on these paternal jaunts (if they had any) they would only remember, inadvertently, after I was dust; certainly long after my nose had met my chin. It was windy, the season was changing, gusts tore green leaves from the trees. These lay on the grass until an odd, lower, wind suddenly caught them in a neat line and swept them, a small green wave, out of sight.

It was time to go, the summer holidays were ending; exams, jobs (or the absence of them) lay ahead. Was there anything left of England but museums, memorials; was there anything left of the inspired commonsense of the Duke? This was a legend to these two boys even when they were smaller. 'What shall I do about the sparrows in my Crystal Palace?' 'Sparrowhawks, ma'am.' They fantasized on the theme: 'What shall I now do about the sparrowhawks in my Crystal Palace?' 'Golden eagles, ma'am.' – and so on.

Then we came to the yew avenue. It is not very long or wide; a place to stroll along, not march between. But the surprise was that the yews have not been made rectangular, not cut into box-shapes. They have been allowed to grow, but trimmed. The result is a double line of joined yew trees in irregular scallops and scoops and plateaux of different greens, from almost black to almost lemon, as if floodlights played on them, causing highlights and shadows. It is man and nature working together, the

People and Places

trees allowed to grow and helped not to straggle; and this had been understood now, was being continued now, inspired commonsense in fact, and the sight, even in my farewell mood, was strangely cheering.

1983

Other Men's Trousers

———○———

I

IT MUST HAVE begun a couple of years ago when I sat sucking my pen and staring out at the rain and decided I needed a change. Not a complete change of life – pen-sucking and pen-using was right for me – but an occasional, brief, relief. Holidays are no use, I find them exhausting. Besides, I needed colleagues, I hadn't worked in the company of anyone else for years.

The only other thing I had ever done, reasonably successfully, at a time when even the sight of a pen was abhorrent, was to earn my living as an actor. So, when I was next in London, I found myself outside the office of the excellent woman who had been my agent twenty years before, Jean Diamond. Still not quite admitting to myself what I was doing (an excellent device in such circumstances, indeed in most: give the subconscious a chance) I allowed myself to drift into her presence. She was even grander now than she had been then and to my surprise she thought it an excellent idea, even an excellent joke, to take me once more on to her books.

It was a relief that nothing much then happened. What did turn up I was easily able to wriggle out of, the whole thing remained a pleasant possibility that I need not take too seriously. Then, recently, there came the chance of a part in a new Michael Caine film, which chance I turned down. To my astonishment the casting director persisted, implored me to come and meet the director. One is seldom implored by casting directors – unless, I suppose, one is Michael Caine – and it occurred to me that it was only fair to her, and to Jean, that I put in at least a token appearance. We had lunch and the casting director told me I was exactly right for the part, in a film to be called *Half Moon*

Street. When I read the script and discovered it was that of an arid journalistic ex-general who could not stand Americans (and who, incidentally, in a script put together long before my advent, wrote occasional pieces for the *Spectator*) I was unflattered or, perhaps, de-flattered. But there began a series of chauffeur-driven dashes here and there – a change as great as the one I had desired and which I now realized I did not want – and I was given the part.

I feel both pleased and idiotic, as well as nervous. At first I determined to keep it secret but then I noticed that the few intimates I told became strangely excited. If they had heard that I had written the best book of poems since Henry Vaughan's *Silex Scintillans* they would have been interested, fairly. But at the mention of a part in a film their eyes flashed, the air crackled with their eager questions. Ah, the silver screen....

There are some, I suppose, who will never take me seriously again. But I have always felt that life was too serious not to be taken lightly, when that is possible. (A sentence that needs expansion, but some will understand what I mean and in my experience others, who do not, can understand no explanation.)

Anyway, that is how I came to find myself in Moss Bros, being fitted for my general's pin-stripes. It was a lordly experience, the designer buying me shirts, shoes, cufflinks, ties. I had never been to Moss Bros and I was impressed by the assistants and by how well the suit fitted. Eventually I returned to my cubicle and put on my own trousers. They seemed rather tight but the general's had been rather loose-fitting. It was on the train home that I began to wonder. I found a strange handkerchief in my pocket. As soon as I crossed my domestic threshold the cry went up – 'Where did you get those *trousers*!'

At first I was appalled, at the thought of their unfortunate owner capering about Moss Bros in his underpants. But it has turned out well. He has them again, and I have mine. He had to buy a suit in order to get back to the office. He has courteously said he found it 'an amusing incident'.

But I can't help seeing it symbolically. I was, after all, trying on another man's trousers, the journalistic general's, and was being told, emblematically, that was the mistake. (Give the subconscious a chance.) But the process had to be gone through again and I emerged this time with my own clothes. The image

Other Men's Trousers

had been changed from pin-stripe to tweedy: ah, the silver screen.

II

As it is unlikely that I shall ever again spend a day in a caravan in Bedford Square, it might be worth trying to describe it. The caravan itself is comfortable, furnished in tasteful shades of oatmeal and brown. It is not easy to see what is going on outside the caravan, because the curtains have to be kept drawn otherwise parties of people peer in. London is full of peering parties at this season.

Through a crack in the windows I see, as I write this, that a man with two bottles in brown paper bags has set up camp on the pavement opposite. Now he is standing up and relieving himself thorough the iron gates of Bedford Square gardens. Now he has begun to sing, in good voice, but the contents of the bottles in the brown paper bags seem to have affected his sense of melody, and pace. I think I can distinguish the tune, very slow indeed, of 'O come all ye faithful'. It seems mean not to share my large caravan with him, but I do not do so.

I see the plane tree leaves reflected in the windows of Sigourney Weaver's Winnebago, see the top of her tracksuited knee as she reposes herself inside it. A Winnebago is an even larger caravan with 'restroom, toilet, dining-area' a member of the crew informs me. She certainly needs it, poor girl, for she finished filming at 11 last night, after an 8 a.m. start and after spending six hours driving round Soho in a taxi with me.

When I say 'with me' I mean with the director also, and the camera operator and the lighting camera-man and the sound-recordist and their vast lamps and equipment, all in the back of the taxi.

Sigourney is a tall, intelligent young woman, fit-looking, like the nicer kind of lacrosse captain. She is the female star of the film we are making – *Half Moon Street* – and the male star is Michael Caine, who has not yet started filming. I have an opportunity in the taxi to ask Sigourney about her first name and she confesses that she was christened Susan and at fourteen could no longer stand being called Susie. She found Sigourney in *The Great Gatsby*.

We are very hostile to each other in the taxi – I mean our film characters are – or, as Sigourney would say, 'hostel', which does not sound so bad. Nevertheless I am disconcerted by the loathing in her brown eyes whenever we play, and re-play, our scene in the jam-packed stifling taxi, more lamps wobbling outside it, attached to it like wings, as it slowly makes its way up Dean Street, down Frith Street, over and over again. It is difficult to know where we are because white reflecting-card is taped to the windows.

It is very intimate in the back of the taxi, five of us, with cables and equipment. At one stop at a Soho kerbside the make-up girl, obviously unable to get in, asks Sigourney to rearrange my hair behind my ears. She does so, murmuring with teasing surprise, 'Oh such soft hair! Such soft little ears!' That is altogether more like it, and I tell the director, squatting agonisingly among the legs and equipment, who also wrote the film, that that is the scene he should have written, instead of this hostel one. He tries to laugh but he is engaged in what appears to be a passionate embrace with the lighting camera-man who is trying to reach past him, round him, through him, to adjust some paper masking on the lamp. 'God! I could lick the hair on your arms!'

That was yesterday: the master-shot and Sigourney's close-ups. Today I am sitting waiting for the whole process to be repeated, for my close-ups. We are quite a village in Bedford Square: two canteen wagons with good food ('Shooting Break' and 'Set Meals'), a posh lavatory (considering) and teams of friendly, helpful people whose jobs I have not yet identified. I shall miss Sue, and Terry, and the rest.

Now I am called to enter the dreaded taxi again to be photographed in a way that will make my soft little ears four feet high. I note in the caravan mirror that I seem overnight to have grown a promising carbuncle on my nose, just in time for the magnification of that organ, and acknowledge with grim pleasure that at least my *id* is in good order. Then it will be back to the soaking hedges for a while, that care nothing for noses.

Other Men's Trousers
III

'Turn over' *one-two* 'Running' *one-two* 'Mark it' *one-two* 'Shot 85 Take 3' *one-two* 'Action!' It is metronomic; the lead-up to the photographing of a scene in a film could be written down in rhythmical lines of varied length, like an eighteenth-century Ode. It is a ritual as formal as High Mass at the Brompton Oratory and is an incantation that can never be heard by an actor, however miniature his part, without an involuntary tightening of the stomach. We all sweat a lot, and it is not just because of the lights. Lovely ladies dab our faces with powder-puffs, murmuring 'Are you all right, my *love*? *That's* better, my pet,' as though they really mean it. Perhaps they do; the Action gets to us all. There are other, preliminary, reasons for tension: the cry 'Save the rehearsal light!' (which has been winking on and off, warning everyone inside and outside the studio). Now it turns to constant red and a bell goes off like a fire-alarm, all falls still and the Ode stanza begins – 'Turn over'...

We are on Stage 5 at Elstree, a bleak hangar large enough for Concorde and called by the crew, derisively, 'the Shed'. It has grass growing out of its roof and looks as though nothing has been done to it since Alfred Hitchcock's English days. It even has a resident pigeon, gargling among the roof-girders. No matter, in this case, because a large part of *Half Moon Street* is to be filmed on location, but today, in the centre of the dark shed, there is a brightly lit cubicle, 'my' dining-room.

Before anyone imagines that the writer of this is playing a significant part in the enterprise it must be explained that although it is 'my' dining-room and 'my' dinner-party the point of the scene is Sigourney Weaver's encounter with a dicey banker and I spend most of my time busily rhubarbing behind the multiple candlesticks. For quite a long while *silently* rhubarbing, an activity new to me. When, later, I was asked to vocalize this mime in order to create a dinner-party hubbub, I found I had been telling my astonished neighbour, in dumb-show, that the pictures on my wall had been smuggled out of Manchuria by Bobo Prendergast labelled 'High Explosive' and I didn't mind telling her this had caused an amusing fuss at Southampton, a chappie rang me and – 'Cut!' Thank God for that.

But this was late in the evening, about half-past nine. We had been picked up at 6.45 a.m., on the set dressed at 8.30 – there had been time to observe the pattern of life in the shed.

It took place almost wholly in the dark. There was some light reflected from the open top of the cubicle of the tiny set, and from one lamp pointed up at a reflector just outside it. This cast enormous shadows on the far end of the building if anyone moved about it, collecting a plant, or a girder, or a plastic beaker of coffee. There was much ingestion, all day, among the riggers and lighters and carpenters, but they had been on the set even longer than we had. They still leaped to their tasks, with pliers or plugs or some other tool of their mystery, with as much alacrity at the end of the day as at the beginning. It was extraordinarily reminiscent of the army: the same stunning idleness punctuated by brief flurries of activity at the word of command, the same suppressed guffaws at involuntary breaking of wind, the same teasing garrison-complaints to the Asian who, through the for-once-blessedly-opened doors, motored in the chow-wagon, backwards. The doors were at once shut again, and to universal grumbles he besought us to take more sausages, more chicken. In the dark it was impossible to see which was which.

So the long day passed: 'Settle down studio. Save the rehearsal light.' Clang. Against the back wall the tiptoeing shadows flicker to and fro, to and fro, O my Formby and my Harlow long ago. Nothing is quite what it seems, or as expected. For instance, in our dressing-rooms we have luxurious showers and lavatories of our own. But they are miles away and all of us have to use a Hitchcockian-epoch Toilet by the back door. If we do so we are surrounded by midgets in mediaeval costume, dozens of them, swaggering up and down in pointed shoes as long as themselves, actors in another film.

The director, Bob Swaim, confides to me that nobody knows just how tedious film-making is, how long it takes to get it right. Just like square-bashing; but I am on furlough till September. I hope the pigeon escapes.

1985

A Way of Escape

———o———

AT BASTIA in the evening, newly disembarked from the ferry, we sat at a café table and looked about us in a certain wonder – it was so long since either of us had had no one to worry about but himself. The island, and the time that stretched ahead, was ours. We carried haversacks; escaping from wives, children, hand-luggage.

There was a place to the north, Cap Corse, sticking up like a finger towards mainland France; we had been told it was desolate; perversely, it drew us.

How to get there. We could not walk, it was already evening and the distance was too great. There were no bus timetables, no discernible bus stops, it was Saturday and every source of information was shut. Luxuriously unworried, we asked the waiter. He scowled. He had been scowling before we asked him. He listened to my question, paused, flicked his napkin over his shoulder, said, 'Je n'ai pas du temps,' and walked to the dark interior of the bar where he stood, still scowling, and polished a glass.

Patrick Creagh, his ear attuned to Italian, unaccustomed to the sound of Corsican French, asked what had been said. He looked blank for a moment, and then, laughing, decided that he liked it. It was at least direct.

I mention this because of what follows, and because both are typical of the Corsican manner, which is at first startling. For the waiter returned and asked me to repeat the question. Presumably he had now finished polishing the glass. Re-launched on my careful French he cut me short and flicked the eloquent napkin towards the road – Ask him over there. Across the street an elderly man in a white open-necked shirt sat in a saloon car apparently doing some sort of calculations, his car door open. Frowning, he jerked his chin interrogatively so I spread the map over the pavement at his feet and on my knees began again, supplicating. He was the bus driver. Not only that, he was the driver of the bus we wanted. And not only that: after long exchange of courtesies, smiling on my part, level-gazing on his, he, personally, captain of his ship, would see that we arrived within a couple of miles of our destination and would find us beds there. 'You,' he said, tapping his chest firmly, 'come with *me*.'

This is how it always was in Corsica, for us. Like Ireland, personal, but without the Irish extravagance of charm.

He dropped us in green twilight at Morsiglia where the incredible Boswell stayed on his way to meet Paoli, the great Corsican liberator. He was pleased with his reception there, being well-feasted, but he would not be feasted now. It hangs, with houses like smooth cliffs, on the mountains above the sea, picturesque, handsome, and nearly deserted. There is a little bar, where the bus stops, with a few male locals inside, but for the most part the tall houses are empty, their painted stucco faded, their blind eyes looking downward to the sea. So it is all over the whole of Cap Corse. Ladies with shopping-baskets got off at various stops and bustled off into high, well-built villages, set in the hills out of the reach of pirates, but they looked, as they disappeared, like the last survivors. They walked past carved doors long unpainted, and windows with weather-beaten shutters long unopened; and below and above the villages are overgrown vineyards, tangled orchards, and on hillsides once painstakingly terraced all that grows now is the sharp invading *maquis*. Cap Corse is depopulated and so for the most part is the rest of the island.

This leads to some curious effects. At Centuri-Port, where we were headed, where Paoli, unbelievably, built the Corsican navy, in a harbour the size of an average suburban garden, it is difficult to discern a local inhabitant. There are such; occasionally a fisherman floats slowly in with one fish, which he delivers to the restaurant. But the fifteen or twenty people who are there mid-September are slightly wan visitors, Swiss, Lyonnais, Marseillais. There is nothing therefore, in the human line, to look at except each other. Sharing a foreign isolation with only other visitors for company is claustrophobic. You cannot even walk, because there are only mountains, the sea, and the one main road. In the

A Way of Escape

restaurant we all whisper, as though dining on top of a corpse.

There is a track between the steeply rising mountains and the green sea. I bathe from a rock naked. This in itself is escape, from clothes. I had forgotten what a musty envelope I kept my body in. Patrick does not bathe; he sits in the shade of a rock translating Leopardi, drinking wine; he farms a vineyard in Tuscany and long days in the sun have made him seek shade as eagerly as an Italian.

Talking of bodies, the Corsicans are well connected with theirs. They walk erect, loose-limbed; are of several physical types, all good-looking. They are always touching each other. But not like Italians, softly, as though seeking to confirm a physical existence outside their own, but with a curiously transmuted aggression. A man will creep up behind another, tip his cap over his eyes and then hide, grinning. Each time the victim reacts angrily, shouting. They will kick the foot of a friend as they pass him sitting at a table and dodge away, laughing, from the return kick. Even the women are not exempt. In Bastia a smiling man sketched a blow at the smooth morning coif of a marketing woman. He aimed it carefully, so as to miss, but she ducked and passed on muttering, carefully feeling her hair as though he had indeed hit it. It may only be ritual horseplay, but it is received with odd seriousness, as though it could be more than that. There is some social kissing between men, between women, but it is stiff-necked, like storks mating.

Hidden by tamarisks among the rocks we come upon a typical Corsican sight: step after step of abandoned terracing, rising right up the mountain to the car-less invisible road that hangs like a chimney-piece over the sea. Little wheat fields the size of a cramped bathroom, fruit orchards, olive groves, vines, each on its tiny step in a staircase scraped laboriously out of the rock. Now deserted, an Inca-like persistence, abandoned. We sit on one of the still stout terrace walls, grateful for the shade. Only the sound of a distant goatbell, the transparent sea very quiet under the relentless sun. Losing the track we make our first acquaintance with the *maquis*, from which the French Resistance took its name. Here it is waist-high. It looks like sweet tangled bushes, myrtles and other herbs, but there is not a leaf without a sturdy spike; it can skin your legs in a minute.

People and Places

At evening the port is thin green, green roofs, green sky, green sea, the sea and the sky indivisible, then pink, then a soft darkness with one bright star.

We sought people, at St Florent, a recognized resort. But that was not the place either. Part of the old port filled in to make a pedestrian precinct, old houses restuccoed beyond recognition and round the harbour an unbroken series of restaurants, boutiques and shops for amateur yachtsmen. We sat and watched the bra-less beauties until even that palled. We took refuge in a dark bar in the back streets and talked to an old Corsican. It was not that we were hard to please. We sought some new experience to lighten the weight of our packs on our backs. Here we could have been anywhere, pleasant enough, the South of France, although that would have been cheaper. The Corsicans, though honest, are bland bandits.

We headed for the mountains.

There may be greater pleasures than setting out on a crisp Mediterranean morning, with the promise of heat to come, with a not-too-heavy pack on your back, but not many – and few so cheap. Within a day my companion was wholly converted.

The rhythm of the physical action sets your mind free. Patrick said at the outset, speculating on the escape-nature of our trip, that the important thing was not to think too much. And when you walk your mind is slowed to walking pace, which is a speed with holes in it, there is room for the outside world to enter. You notice everything. Even the dull bits play their part, you can't skip them, and the same thing, seen again and again, begins to yield up its specialness. You live in a world of details, and the world is made up of details. We walked along roads because tracks were few and doubtful, the *maquis* impossible. We never saw another walker. Sometimes, for hours at a stretch, we never saw a car.

At first, small, kept vineyards, and large unkept ones. We ponder the impossibility of escape. All summer Patrick has been planting vines, harrowing vines, now he is breaking his neck to look at them. We carry our preoccupations with us, as well as our haversacks. At the roadside is a new, rough building: a wine factory, its huge doors open. Patrick peers in, pokes about, ex-

A Way of Escape

claiming. A long figure uncurls itself like a snake from behind a barrel. He shows us round, offers us wine ladled from an enormous vat. He fought in the war and stares at us sternly with his light blue eyes. 'Vos compatriotes....' he says, and finishes the sentence by slowly raising his thumb to waist-level and pushing its broad blade towards us.

We begin to climb, past cork oaks, their trunks where the bark has been cut a rich umber, the colour of Hereford cattle. Stone huts with earth roofs are the same colour where the red earth has run down the walls, bright rust. Figs hang over the track we climb to Olmetta, black, refreshing. We look down at the Gulf of St Florent through sharp yellow crags we have circled on our ascent; sit on the terrace of a little bar below the road, shaded by creeper. The *curé* slowly passes on the road above us, revealing below his soutane that his socks are green. In his church the clock ticks, very slow and very loud, a feature of Corsican churches, the noise of a gigantic death-watch beetle.

On the shadowy terrace we eat cheese and feed the ingratiating parrot. It takes a piece of cheese delicately between its second and third claws like an over-refined person smoking a Russian cigarette, and eats it carefully with its hooked beak ill-designed for cheese. The proprietor talks politics, about ARC – *Autonomie Regionale Corse*; the letters are painted everywhere, on rocks, on the roadway itself. Signposts are defaced as they are in Wales, French being changed to Corse, the jealously guarded local language universally spoken in the north, which is neither French nor Italian. St Florent is changed with paint to San Firenzu, and so on.

The weather is breaking: thunder, occasional drops of rain. Clouds now obscure the view across the craggy plain to the sea. We are after all in the Nebbio, which derives its name from the word for fog.

We climb on, briefly in the company of the tobacconist. Hanging over the village, way up, is another long cliff of a building, grey, blank. 'A score of families lived there once,' he mutters. Only thirty years ago.

Horse chestnuts now, prickly pear, and at the roadside where the tarmac ends a continuous line of sweet-smelling herbs and shrubs, rosemary, spearmint, myrtle; and there is another, very common, which has a smell half-enticing, half-not, fleshy, and it leaves the fingers sticky with honey. The first bird for a long time overhead, large, with ragged wing-tips and a sad lonely cry like a buzzard; but it has a forked tail. A kite. There are few birds at this time of the year in Corsica and those few are shy, because of *la chasse*. Always just out of eyeshot, or on the weather side of a bush, so small and fast they are like motes across the eye, or quick shadows.

At the top of the pass, 1,500 feet, crags rise above our left shoulders, tall ferns fall away to our right. Far below, neck-high in ferns, a solitary cow watches, puzzled; its presence puzzling, the only living thing.

A moorland, with broken walls rising up; boring. Suddenly, round a corner, we are in a pastoral landscape, neat and fertile as the Dordogne. Muratu; a little church on an eminence built in green and white stone patterned asymetrically, standing on its own cropped sward with a single well-placed tree. The first man-made elegance we have seen in Corsica; below is a rushing stream, bordered by tall poplars and little plateaux grazed by goats like silky greyhounds, brown, black, cream.

The school bus passes us, exploding with laughing children. In the main street of the village is a deafening jukebox, hollow-sounding among the hills; in a dark room open to the street bony nine-year-old girls dance solemnly with each other.

We go to the bar, hoping for beds, tired. The barman is friendly but doubtful, the card-players look up guardedly and return to their game. It is cold at this height now the sun is down. We have no sleeping bags. We postpone our worry, and drink. The barman comes to our table with two *pastis*, unordered, 'Paid for by that gentleman there.' At the bar stands a stocky handsome man like Jean Gabin. We thank him. Return the compliment. Men silently leave and come back with bottles of wine they politely exhort us to try, wine from their own vineyard gardens. One is dry and naturally fizzy, delicious. Our appreciation is received with great pleasure. More is produced, and others, of different kinds. We had already been told that the best wine in Corsica is kept by private growers for themselves. It is true. We are allowed to pay for nothing. Jean Gabin is a retired soldier.

A Way of Escape

('We treated them badly in the colonies – les Jaunes, les Noirs. They are men like us. We could still be there.') He is vehement, almost crying, afloat on a sea of *pastis*. '*Je suis un pauvre type....*' He is not, he is intelligent, probably lonely. The others crowd around, nodding, smiling, happily liberal in their solutions to the world's problems, as people usually are in places that for centuries have had the dirtier end of the stick.

Next morning early they are all outside the shut pub sitting on a wall. In surprisingly good condition, considering. Gabin stands over us as we rearrange our packs, inspecting our buckling and strapping with a soldierly eye. He watches us out of sight, raising his arm in farewell.

Briefly we descend, to the glassy river, 'like diamonds in solution'. I shave in a pool, without soap so as not to spoil it. Stubbled Patrick admires the pure water – not only a shaving basin, a shaving mirror.

We climb slowly for the rest of the day, through oaks, Spanish chestnuts with fruits like unripe lemons, furry, past pigs eating chestnuts in little enclosures under trees, laden mules tethered in shade with grey luminous muzzles, among butterflies the colour of egg-yolk; at the side of the road are the usual sweet herbs, and autumn crocus very proud and upright, so confidently scalloped they might be made of plastic.

The Corsicans are very fond of plastic flowers, using them in enormous quantities to celebrate their dead. Round every village, like miniature suburbs, are the family vaults; anywhere, among trees, in little meadows, on crags, are these toy chapels, white and grey. Each surrounded by plastic flowers. But not a few, whole gardensfull, in sprays, swags, huge complicated 'arrangements', chrysanthemums, roses, crocus, dahlias in every possible, Mediterranean, tone and colour. The result is extremely pretty.

We come fully into the region of the hill fires. The last, dry, summer a million acres of Corsica were burnt. The porcelain pots of the telegraph poles hang shoulder-high on blackened stumps, or trail among the charred remains of the *maquis*. Licking round the chapel tombs the fires char the young cypress and wilt the plastic flowers so they hang, dulled, like real flowers ready for renewal.

People and Places

At 3,000 feet, ears popping, we are on a mountain moor again, shadeless on the burning, burnt hillside. At the side of the broken road is a yellow generator, of the kind used to drive pneumatic drills. Across the front of it is pasted an oleograph of St Joseph and the child Jesus, who has long yellow curls that fall to his shoulders. Patrick contemplates it, muses on the oddness, if St Joseph were to be the patron saint of generators...

Suffering now, towards evening we sit at the side of the track and look pensively at the towns, shuttered, half-deserted, that hang on the side of every mountain before us. Corsica, in the middle of Europe, is an underdeveloped country.

A shepherd greets us softly, with his long, soft sheep. A snake rears up, at bay, harmless. The sky darkens, thunders start bouncing round the crags above our heads. Below us is a village, Volpajola. Everything around it, below it and above it, is burned: careful little gardens, bean-plots, vines, all black. It smells like a room after a soot-fall.

Rain. Mountain rain, an awesome unburdening. The only inn shuttered and barred. Benighted again, soaked. A Corsican youth offers us his house, with a simple gesture, opening his cupboards for us, opening his wine. He works in mainland France, so do his parents. But he loves his village, returns when he can. There is no work there. He is a Communist, he believes we should all live in communities, share all we have. He shares all he has with us.

Next morning in the valley at the decrepit wayside station, blackened all round, the young stationmistress in black, even her stockings black, bids us adieu as she waves her green flag tied to a hazel twig.

We are bound, via Corte, for the Niolo. The central plateau of fabled Stone Age shepherds, a law to themselves throughout Corsican history. We climb on foot to their fastness up the Scala de Santa Regina, a suffocating corridor between yellow pointed mountains, below the road the green River Golo between smooth white boulders. Cut off until the end of last century by this dreadful pass, the shepherds had every chance to stay shut inside time and inside their own manners. Apparently, despite surface appearances, they still are.

A Way of Escape

The village at the top is deserted after nine o'clock, dead. In the only bar still open after dark some oddly elegant young men gather and drink, standing, a bottle of Johnnie Walker. A late arrival enters, long and thin, perhaps nineteen years old, beautiful, with an extraordinarily decadent grace. He kisses one man with great care, goes to shake hands with another and with a swift tug unseats him, kicking his chair away. Smiling, he reaches a chair for himself, twists it one-handed, throws himself into it and sprawls. The whole performance is filled with grace, arrogance and a kind of smiling cruelty. They all look formidable, with close-together gangster eyes. Yet they are shepherds, they can be nothing else. About eleven o'clock, the village asleep for a couple of hours, a little hush falls followed by a sudden commotion. The bar door is shut, a table is spread quickly with a green cloth, chairs are scraped noisily into position and the card-school begins. Poker, played very fast, no one drinking, and for enormous stakes. Ten pounds each in the kitty, which is frequently topped up. Then there is another commotion, chairs scrape again, they all kneel on the floor, intent, laughing. On four lighted matches placed in the form of a cross they are roasting a spider. When it is shrivelled and still they relax, a tension spent, and return to their game...

In the morning it rains, with fog and thunder. We try to walk, and find ourselves in Arcadia. There are mountains but they are wide apart, there is a sense of height but none of confinement. Between the mountains are pastures dotted with thick-trunked chestnuts with little black pigs rootling underneath them. There is an impression of leisure, sweet herbage, of more than enough to go round. Shepherds on a doorstep call to us not to go on, that there will be a storm, we shall be lost. Timidly we try anyway, it is a landscape that draws us like an old memory, and the air is high-octane. Around are the pigs, the park-like trees and the brown autumn grass, ahead is another mountain pass and below it the promise of the green sea. It pulls us but we walk into rain like a wall, are jostled by pigs scampering for cover. We shelter forlornly in a bar and watch the rain, drinking. We had glimpsed a tough paradise before the curtain came down. It had to be enough.

People and Places

In great winds at the coast we waited for the ferry back to Italy. When it arrived late its bow doors opened to emit, not cars, but a disconcerting amount of sea-water. Hardened by our footloose adventure, many days at the mercy of Corsica and we had survived, this made us laugh. We were not laughing twelve hours later. The crossing was meant to take not more than six, and after twelve hours we knew that we were still barely out of sight of the island. Not that we could see it, for it was now midnight, the night was black and tremendous, waves were crashing over the boat which seemed barely under control, and most of us were being sick. Then an alarm-bell went and Patrick and I walked, as steadily and unconcernedly as we could, to the card of instructions in the passage. The bell-sound, we read, was the order to climb to the boat-decks and prepare to abandon ship. There was no point in going to our boat-deck, the waves would have washed us overboard, so we stood where we were, knowing, for a long enough moment, that we were going to die. The rest of the passengers seemed resigned, some were praying. 'Why don't we just *sink*?' groaned one Italian, particularly badly struck by *mal de mer*. The only life-jackets were on the stewards who scurried, whey-faced, up and down the companion-ways.

Then it turned out that the alarm had been set off by a sliding car. The captain was going to circle in the lee of a small island and wait for dawn. Next morning, shaken, we were back in Corsica, the crossing had proved impossible and, we were told, it was the last time that particular ferry-boat would attempt it. We had been sent to Corsica to write about 'escape', but escape is not so easy.

1976

Liquid Light

———o———

I PROPOSE to write in praise of the month we have just enjoyed, the wettest, darkest May (1983) anybody can remember – which is to say since last year. I praise it sincerely, not perversely, or smugly (well, perhaps a little smugly), because I have genuinely enjoyed it and, besides, it is time someone spoke up for misunderstood majorities, like wet springs.

In the first place, the weather has made it much easier to get out of bed in the morning. Instead of blinking in the brash, imperious light of day you are able to gentle into a dawn-like gloom not at all hard on the nerves but, in its clear intention of remaining that way, rather soothing. Indeed, to be up and about in such days has not been all that different from remaining in bed, though not quite so warm. The sky has been so low it has been like bedclothes, 'the air a blanket, weighing on like wool', as the poet Ivor Gurney described such weather in these parts.

In the second place, I praise the weather because it has made gardening impossible. This is a very considerable boon, conducive to calm reflection, and contemplation. It is possible to dread the arrival of 'busy old fool', the sun, heartily stripping back the bedclothes.

Gardening has been impossible, of course, because of the wet, which has been vocal. If you take a step it is answered by tickings and clicking from yards away, as if you have disturbed a set of indignant creatures, underground. It was interesting to see the players in the Cup Final at Wembley creating bow-waves as they went into sliding tackles. I have never seen this before, when it was not raining at the time, and the commentator began to mutter darkly about a patch of clay near the centre-circle that had newly appeared, as though clay patches travelled. Perhaps they do, but I wonder how.

People and Places

The rain and the lack of gardening has had a spectacular effect on weeds. Nettle clumps look, for once, edible. Tall and rounded and neat, like plumped-up cushions. Every year is a good year for one weed or another (or wild flowers, if you prefer): there is a year when meadow-cranesbill does very well, another when it barely appears but willow-herb clearly enjoys itself, and so on. One of the advantages of staying in the same spot is that you slowly realize how little repetition there is, everything is slightly different every year. This year it is the turn of a very tall, green, straight plant with tiny white flowers at the very top. It is everywhere, very soldierly and forthright. Reference to a gardening book shows that it is called Jack-in-the-hedge, which is the perfect name: strong and sturdy and pleasant, with not much in the upper storey.

Because of the weeds there seem to be many more birds; more to eat and more places to hop hidden, I suppose. Plenty of linnets, which are common enough but not round here. Delicately coloured, with an introspective, private song like little needles.

All very pleasant and nobody struggling with it very much. All the seed is in, and sprouting, and the farmworkers are about peaceful indoor tasks, and contemplating also, no doubt. All the trees are not so much coming, as bursting, out. If the oak leaves appear before the ash it is supposed to suggest a reasonably dry summer, but they are running neck and neck at the moment. This is unusual; in these parts summer is nearly over before the ash trees decide the atmosphere is conducive to their refinement.... This may all sound like the Nature Notes found in small print in some newspapers, but it is the extravagant theatre into which we were all born, all of us, wherever we live. We do our best to wreck it. Sometimes we have to, but somewhere it still goes on behind our backs, ignoring us. It has been interesting to notice how comparatively unimportant what we would call sunshine really is. England looks lush and green and more like Ireland than it has any right to. Interesting that, as in Ireland, liquid is more important than light.

1983

Ruined Irish Houses

―――― o ――――

THERE IS NOTHING sad about ruins. On the contrary, there is something cheerfully uncorseted, a sense of release. Now there is no more strain of underpinning, shoring up, keeping in shape. The building is no longer imposed on the landscape, an effort of alien will (which so often proved too much for the heirs). These houses have become what they always wanted to be, a part of the landscape itself.

Of course, we can make ourselves feel a sadness if we want to. We can try to people the deserted ballroom with ghostly dancers, the arrow-slits with bowmen, the drive with dog-carts. But we never really see them, the ruin itself is too strong in its new-found contentedness. It is not the swish of crinolines that we hear, nor the singing of arrows released from crossbows, it is the sighing of ivy that nearly fills the windows, the groan of wind in the ruined chimney, the barking of a distant dog. We remain in a present enhanced, made more sharp, by the past that surrounds us.

This is the real pleasure of ruins: a delight that nature, of which we are a part, has had her way at last and nobody could do anything about it. Also that nature, and this is even more important, has made the building more beautiful, because more appropriate, than it can ever have been when wealth, greed, war-prowess or dogged determination kept the show going the way poor deluded mortals thought it ought to go. Children sense this at once, whooping up the ruined steps, straddling battlements, rolling in the now dry and harmless moat. Children and mice and owls and every kind of herbage come into their kingdom, and (above all in Ireland) so does every trick and change of the light. The sun dramatizes these ruins, its sudden withdrawal even more so.

People and Places

The truth is that most of these places should not have been there anyway. They are a fluke of history, of the eighteenth-century wealth of England and the artificially imposed poverty of Ireland. Non-Roman, non-Saxon Ireland where 'the air alone makes one do unexpected things' absorbed the 'new Irish' from the mainland of Britain and changed them. They came for cheap land, cheap labour, cheap status, and found all these things. It must have seemed a paradise, and for some it was. But the Irish temperament with its wholly different order of priorities, its subtle potency (not nearly as 'comic' as English caricature at once began, rather fearfully, to pretend) entwined itself around the new landowners' minds and hearts as the creepers entwine themselves around what remains of their houses, castles and follies. Thus was born that special case we call today 'the Anglo-Irish'. They were dependent on the English connection to protect their lands and wealth. But as the years passed the influence of their surroundings soaked into them; surroundings which, to this day, are unlike anywhere else in Europe, and are almost Oriental in the strangeness that lies below their apparent similarity. It is no accident that the leaders of Irish revolts from the eighteenth century up to the twentieth were for the most part drawn from this class, the Anglo-Irish Protestant Ascendancy.

The new landowners, embedded in their apparently perfect life, seemed to lose heart early. It is as though they sensed the paradise was too artificial to last. Terence De Vere White, who wrote a book about them, says that after 1800 their diaries bear a resemblance to General Gordon's when he was waiting for the Mahdi at Khartoum. They sought their pleasures in England, regarding their vast Irish properties as if they were estates in Basutoland. They still collected their rents of course, or had them collected by agents, almost universally detested. The surprise is not that most of these houses were burnt down in the 1920s, but that they were allowed to stand for so long. It is not Irish hatred the student of Irish history notices first, it is the lack of it.

Today, parts of these lands are bought up by new 'lovers' of all things Irish, who become equally disheartened. Kate O'Brien tells of watching one of these grow increasingly exasperated as he had his car loaded with groceries in some quiet village street. 'No!' he shouted. 'Not there, man! *There!* Do I have to say everything twice?' and so on. She became angry at his hectoring until she caught the eye of the shopwoman, who was smiling. 'He seems annoyed,' the woman said. 'You know, when I hear them kicking up against us like that, I say to myself that so far as I ever heard no one ever sent for them.' Indeed. No one ever sent for those earlier settlers (although many were sent, with grants of land), and they too must have been maddened by that easy tolerance, a superiority deriving from roots they did not have, could not understand, and therefore despised, which watched its new masters as though they were descended, briefly, from the Moon.

'A little bit of Heaven dropped out the sky one day,' says Tin Pan Alley, and there is something celestial about part of Ireland in certain lights. You cannot blame the eighteenth-century grandees for wanting to make it their own. Perhaps they were baffled in this, as much as by anything, by Irish contradictions. Kate O'Brien tells another story, of the Italian novelist Ignazio Silone who had been staying with her in Connemara; enchanted, bewitched, as I never heard of a visitor who was not. She saw him off at Galway railway station, which was being refurbished. 'You've given us fourteen days in a Japanese paradise,' he said. 'We say goodbye at a junction in West Poland.'

It was inevitable, for these big-house dwellers, that the dream of a good place should die; it was based on nothing more substantial than power. But, although it was the cause of many cruelties, there was nothing cruel, initially, in the dream. It had to die, or become a part of Ireland, which is precisely what is happening to these ruined houses. They record an inevitable, one might say triumphant, process. Most of the houses were blown up, true. But late, and with an odd courtesy. Once again one wonders why it took so long, when they were the symbol of so much.

It was going to happen anyway: Ireland was bound to absorb these anomalies into her air, into her earth. Of course, some flickers of the old life remain, here and there. It is a process, not a catastrophe. By an Irish irony, it seems that many of the old houses that still remain are inhabited by writers chronicling their demise: some wildly, like J.P. Donleavy, or quietly, like David Thomson in *Woodbrook*, or best of all, because he deals with the waning life and cracks in the walls before the IRA explosion,

People and Places

by J.G. Farrell in *Troubles*. Echoes of the old life still linger round the eyeless windows, the jackdaw-haunted chimneys; echoes which a future generation may no longer be able to hear. Like the poet in the Anglo-Saxon *Wanderer*, who stood uncomprehending among Roman ruins, they may stand among these and ask what race of men could have built them, and for what?

1980

Sheep's Lib

WHEN WE CAMPED outside the walls of Coole Park, the thought of Yeats inside, being fed tit-bits by Lady Gregory, made me muse (in the field in my sleeping-bag) on the nature of walls.

They only retain their power as long as those outside believe in it, and those inside believe in it too. Lady Gregory ceased to believe in her wall because she fell in love with Ireland, invited Ireland inside it, and therefore connived at its inevitable destruction. Admittedly, her wall still stands, enclosing a forestry plantation, but her house is gone.

The notional nature of walls was illustrated next morning when our little encampment was investigated by a herd of heavy cows. They meant no harm but there was danger of our shelters being destroyed. My wife, brilliantly resourceful (was it not I, pondering the mystico-political nature of Limits, who should have thought of it?), hastily rigged-up our washing-line on sticks and this emblem of a fence kept out the cows till we had packed up our things.

It was a confidence trick but to play such a thing you have to have confidence, and this is not always easy to maintain. If you go into a field, for instance, on a misty morning, the sheep gather together on the high ground like a cavalry squadron, watching you, and if they charged, you would certainly be overwhelmed. They do not do so, and go on being pushed around and fleeced and eaten, but they only need a leader.

Perhaps they have found one: if not a Lenin, certainly a freedom-fighter. I have been doing battle with him over the last days. He is black, or at least tawny, and horned, and has discovered he can jump over our wall.

This is no flimsy emblem, but a drystone wall built by a shepherd decades ago, still in good repair, which has kept out

People and Places

sheep ever since. Until, that is, this one discovered he could jump it. It was only half a day before a select company of his ewes discovered they could jump it too.

So I began to surround us with barbed-wire. He sat and watched me, his yellow eyes with their strange horizontal pupils particularly hard on the nerves. He revolved grass in his jaws, as Clint Eastwood chews on his cheroot. When I stood back to admire my work he slowly got to his feet, cheroot, as it were, still in his mouth, and *charged* the fence I had just built. It held. So he moved to another point close by me – there was no mistaking his defiance – and charged again. Then, with an unmistakable gunslinger's saunter, a slow roll of the hips, he went to the gate itself, which is as old as the wall, and shoulder-charged that, side-on, staring me out. Reader, this is no ordinary sheep.

I addressed a few words to him at this point and went in to announce my fortifications to my soppy household, all of whom wanted him to stay inside because he was obviously hungry. But I am made, albeit post-Imperialist, of sterner stuff.

An hour later I was told, with irritating satisfaction, that he was back in the garden, this time with two white companions. He raised his head briefly when I approached him, then went on eating.

Next day I was out again, with posts and wire, feeling a fool. For perhaps the day of the sheep has come and I am opposing the tide of history? But a man has to do what he has to do, and there are signs that the victory for the moment is mine; there are lumps of black wool on the wire; but he watches me from the field, baleful.

No, he is back, enough of his wool on the wire to make a liberty-bodice. He is a worthy opponent and begins to inhabit my dreams. An even more shaming admission is that his fleece is so long it is uncertain whether it is a 'he' at all. In a sexist fashion it seems that any creature so rebellious and bloody-minded must be male. Should Clint Eastwood (it is the only possible name for him) turn out to be a ewe it will be even more disquieting. There are so many more of them.

1985

Finding a Voice

———o———

POETS ARE USUALLY delighted to talk about poetry: not necessarily about their own work, nor as critics – they are not always equipped to be critics – but because of all artists they are the ones most likely to feel they have some explaining to do. They work, bring back their discoveries and nobody, or hardly anybody, listens. And listen is the word, because a poet hopes not only to be read, he hopes, above all, to be heard: the noise he makes is an essential part of his meaning and why he used verse in the first place. If he is met with puzzlement, or indifference, he cannot go back to his poem and make the sense of it clearer, or more punchy, as he might in an article written for a newspaper. Because if he did so he would change the sound of his poem and the sound is as much a part of the web of his meaning as the dictionary meaning of the words in the poem themselves. Touch the web and it collapses, it can't catch flies anymore, or readers.

This importance of sound in poetry, and in all writing, is what I want to talk about and immediately I am in deep water, with a sinking feeling. Much has been written about metre, about its psychological and physiological basis, which is outside my competence, or, as an early instructor of mine used to say when baffled by a question, 'beyond the scope of this lecture'. Side-stepping all that, I'd like to talk personally as a reader of verse and as a practitioner.

Some lines from the Irish poet James Stephens have stuck in my mind for years, so I'll use them for a starting point:

> Nothing is easy
> Pity then
> The poet more than other men
> And since his aim is ecstasy

> And since none work so hard as he
> Forgive the poet poesy.

I'm quoting these lines from memory and I suppose when I was younger this whimsy, with its underlying note of toughness, spoke to my condition. It stayed in my head of course because of the rhymes, 'ecstasy' with 'as he' and 'poesy' and because of the pleasant, rather predictable rhythm. It is also, if you happen to have read anything else by James Stephens, unmistakably in his own voice, which is that of an intractable pixie. In other words it was the *how* that stayed with me rather than the *what*, the way it sounded regardless of the truth or otherwise of what it said. This is maybe a fairly obvious point to make about poetry but I believe it is equally true of prose. The sound of the words chosen is a part of the sense conveyed, entangled with their dictionary meaning. Faults of 'style' – that dangerous and unhelpful word that muddled me so much at school: for a long time I thought style was trying to write like Robert Louis Stevenson at his most ornate – faults of style are faults of feeling. In fact, if we've given a writer a chance and we still feel in reading him, or her, as though we're being dragged on a hurdle over a bumpy road, we are entitled to suspect the truth, for the writer, of what they are saying. As Coleridge said, 'Heart speaks to heart untrammeled'; he also said 'What comes from the heart, that alone goes to the heart' and we are justified in thinking that when expression comes out in an ugly fashion mud has got into the works somewhere. Of course – and this is a warning note – Coleridge's use of the word 'heart' was an austere one. It's no use at all having an emotion and then to think you've done your job by telling everybody about it; you don't have to tell them, you have to show them, you need art as well as heart, you need sound.

When I was fourteen I was leafing through an anthology during a lesson and I came across the following:

> The hunchèd camels of the night
> Trouble the bright
> And silver waters of the moon.
> The Maiden of the Morn will soon
> Through Heaven stray and sing
> Star gathering.

Finding a Voice

It was somehow that hold-up, the slight hesitation of the extra syllable before that last rhyme: 'sing' and then 'star gathering'. The lines took me and swung me out of the classroom into a world of imagination and possibility: into a world I knew to be more real, not less, than the reality towards which the rest of my education seemed to be pointed. I also knew that this was the world I wanted to inhabit. To be able to express such feelings in such sounds seemed to me the highest of human activities. It would be possible to say that those lines changed my life.

But not what they said. In so far as they said anything to me, I now see that I misunderstood. Let's have the whole poem, which is by Francis Thompson:

> The hunchèd camels of the night
> Trouble the bright
> And silver waters of the moon.
> The Maiden of the Morn will soon
> Through Heaven stray and sing
> Star gathering.
>
> Now, while the dark about our love is strewn,
> Light of my dark, blood of my heart, O come!
> And night will catch her breath up, and be dumb.
>
> Leave thy father, leave thy mother
> And thy brother;
> Leave the black tents of thy tribe apart!
> Am I not thy father and thy brother,
> And thy mother?
> And thou – what needest thou with thy tribe's black tents
> Who hast the red pavilion of my heart?

I see now that it is a request to a lady to elope – or is it? Probably, on another level, Francis Thompson being a poet who was apt to write about mystical matters in fleshly terms, it is about the longing of Christ for a human soul; but that and the love-stuff apparently, only apparently, passed me by at the time, even the sound of it, even 'the red pavilion of my heart' which I expect I found then, as I do now, a bit overblown, even butcher's shop. And the first lines gave me hardly any picture at all, or certainly not the intended one. I liked the hunchèd camels and I saw them swaying over the desert casting their reflections into puddles. What puddles would be doing in the desert didn't seem to bother me, and the Maiden of the morn gave me no picture, or an unsatisfactory one of a lady in sandals, dressed in a Pre-Raphaelite fashion, wandering in mid-air with a basket under one arm. But it didn't matter. I now see that Francis Thompson meant the hunchèd camels as clouds passing across the face of the moon, which is better, which is very good, but in terms of the experience I underwent it didn't and doesn't matter; the feeling he had given me, or at least *a* feeling, had come from the sound alone, or very nearly alone. And strangest of all, despite the misunderstandings and adolescent wooziness I have described, what Francis Thompson was saying did in fact reach me. Whatever his precise meaning, the poem is an impassioned call for escape to another higher reality and that is the call I heard.

At all events, when I came to try to write poems, which was about that time, I found it was a tune, a cadence of words that set me off. Nearly always a conversational cadence; I have never written as grandiloquently as Francis Thompson, but a poet cannot choose how, or even what, he writes. When he follows the tune of his own discovery, the trick of speech that set him off, he quickly finds that the sounds in his head begin to obey their own laws. You have to follow the sound of the poem you are writing as well as try to keep, as nearly as you can, to the sense you intend. It really is as though you are straining to hear the poem you have not yet written. Perhaps this is where the idea of inspiration comes from. It seems that as you write you are a beat behind the sound commanded and it often takes you in a direction you did not intend and did not want. Poems creep up on a poet sideways, to the corner of his eye – if he turns too quickly they disappear – and if he's careful and not too impatient he feels a movement inside him, a shape of words – and of course a shape of words is always a series of sounds – and there in that rhythm and tune he briefly finds the importances and connections that before eluded him. Although thinking of death he may find himself writing of a bee, or a bus, or, in my opinion with less likelihood of success, of the Eumenides or King Arthur, if it is a good poem, if the feeling was true and he caught it in the right

Finding a Voice

melodic shape, it will contain, whatever its subject, much of what he originally felt and something more. It will surprise him. It has to surprise him in order to surprise the reader. If you write a poem knowing too clearly how it's going to finish you have to distort it, contort it, to make it reach its Q.E.D. And it will read like that.

Am I saying, therefore, that poems come from the unconscious? This is a word I'm wary of in this connection. It suggests too easily that poems are a matter of dark and dreams, whereas the best poems are filled with daylight, sometimes harshly so, having been dragged into the daylight. I prefer to think of poetry, perhaps of all art, as an act of remembering a forgotten harmony.

Having heard something so portentous and vague the reader, kind enough to turn to my own work, would be entitled to ask 'Where is such a remembering in your own work, in poems about small events, a walk with a child, rain in October?' I can only bow my head and ask myself the same question, looking up to say that poems that stick to large abstractions are usually sorry stuff and bounce harmlessly off the mind, leaving no impression. And if poetry relies on sound, it also heavily relies on the carefully delineated particular.

As for the act of remembering, let me put it this way. All of us are, I think, conscious that we live most of our lives at half-throttle, there are parts of ourselves that we seldom use. Love wakes us up, or luck, sometimes even extreme fear or pain wakes us up, and we look out on a world that is clear and significant. This fades and we go on as before, but what is odd about this awakening experience, at any rate as far as I am concerned, is that it always contains the quality of memory. It contains no surprise at all, it is as though I am looking at something I have always known but somehow temporarily forgotten. Yet when I search my past I can find no clear reason why I should think this, or whence came this apparently inborn assurance of the importance and connectedness of life. There is a part of ourselves therefore that we do not normally use, cannot use, and from this I believe derives the psychologically satisfying idea of the Fall. We are *aware* there is something of which we are *un*aware. Between art and that sense of the extra-human which is usually channelled into some form of religion, I can find no essential difference. There may be a distinction, but when we insist they are quite different we go wrong and art ceases to be a vehicle for the significant movements of our spirits. It becomes dry, an ornament merely. The poet's job is to catch these moments of awareness, stay in training for them, and over and over again he has said there is a listening quality, a straining to hear. Stevie Smith puts it with her usual deceptive simplicity and directness:

> Dear Muse, the happy hours we have spent together.
> I love you so much in wet or fine weather,
> I only wish sometimes you would speak louder
> But perhaps you will do so when you are prouder.
> I often think that this will be the next instant.
> Meanwhile I am your most obliging confidant.

Straining to hear, he makes demands on himself and on others. So a culture as practical as ours asks, resentfully, about people as socially unimportant as poets, 'Who does he think he is?' That's precisely it. He's trying to discover who he is, who we are. It is not for nothing that great poets are regarded as the most significant figures of their periods because they embody them, give them a shape and voice unrecognized by their contemporaries and perhaps by themselves.

It is always a mistake to complain about the present, it always sounds peevish and anyway we can't see it clearly enough. But it is possible that the musical power of poetry is being neglected because there is emphasis on content, on whether the poet is explicitly concerned with newspaper matters or his own private desperation. A relatively recent example of this is the work of Edward Thomas who has been blamed, and was for some time overlooked, for not being a War Poet, for not being Wilfred Owen. His work is imbued with the pathos of a vanishing England, vanishing because of the war, though he hardly ever mentions either, just describes a bed of nettles, a ploughman ploughing. To concentrate too much on what a poem merely says, on its prose contents, is fatal to the seeking, allusive quality that is poetry's great gift to us. If you listen to Edward Thomas there is, in his very lack of easy music, a noble sound that includes and transcends the trenches.

The poet William Empson told a story: 'I was hearing', he says,

Finding a Voice

'a young poet give a reading of his work and he was explaining afterwards how much he hated all the other ones of his age. He was talking about one of these and I said "He has a singing line doesn't he?" Meaning, as I thought, that he had the root of the matter in him. This chap pounced and said "That's it, you've got it! Just a writer of lyrics!" He thought that if it sounds pretty that means you're bad. Well, I thought *he* hadn't got the root of the matter in *him*.'

The root of the matter. The singing line.

Poetry is there to stretch our experience beyond the merely verbal, which tends to limit it – we stick to words and the words stick. It is there to push tentatively, fearfully, into the significance that surrounds our lives. Or insignificance, if that is what it finds.

Coleridge wrote better about the writing and reading of poetry than anyone else – incidentally, a charge of obscurity is often brought against what is always called 'modern' poetry by those who surely do not try to read it, or any poetry, very often; it was Coleridge who said that poetry gives most pleasure when only generally and not perfectly understood, that is, when the mind of the reader gives itself wholly up to it. If poets nowadays are sometimes obscure, and they are so not nearly as often as is sometimes imagined by those who haven't dared to look, it may be because they are only too glumly aware how few readers will give their minds wholly up to them. It's a circular process. One always talks badly to someone who isn't listening. That is unless one is a very special kind of bore.

But to get back to Coleridge. In his Ode called Dejection he describes the inspiration of his poetry quite specifically as a voice, a sound:

> And from the soul itself must there be sent
> A sweet and potent voice, of its own birth,
> Of all sweet sounds, the life and element!
> O pure of heart! thou needs't not ask of me
> What this strong music in the soul may be!
> What, and wherein it doth exist,
> This light, this glory, this fair luminous mist,
> This beautiful and beauty-making power.

Earlier in the poem he explains dolefully how he believes his own gift is going. He no longer receives the same excitement from the weather and the landscape of the Lake District. The sights no longer cause emotion in him and he complains 'I see, not feel, how beautiful they are'. He could as easily have said, from what he had said before, 'I see, not *hear*, how beautiful they are', hearing and feeling being for him and for most poets, in the special sense I have been trying to suggest, almost the same thing.

The problem for a poet is to find the true voice of his own heart. Then the job, apparently so simple, is done. The heart, on the rare occasions when we are privileged to hear it, and not just think we hear it, always speaks simply and surprisingly. To quote Coleridge again 'What comes from the heart, that alone goes to the heart; what proceeds from a divine impulse, that the God-like alone can waken.'

Coleridge uses words in a special sense but always carefully. He was a great psychologist of the creative process. Wakening the God-like in himself and others, a task indeed! A poet gets in his own light and falls deaf as often as everybody else. Still, forgive the poet poesy.

1975

Trifles

———o———

IN A RECENT article in *The Times* about the marketing jamboree for the Twenty Best Young British Novelists, the Literary Editor, decently wanting to do the sale of books and 'culture' a bit of good, began thus: 'In the line of business one continually meets pessimists who say that the English language is dying. (They usually also assert that civilization as we kno it is coming to an end...)' It was the 'kno' that did it. Here he was, poor chap, just setting out to convince us that things are not so bad as all that, are looking up in fact, when along comes the typesetter, before he's even really got going, and hits him in the back of the neck with a loaded cosh.

I became interested. On the back page of the same issue, in less than half a column, were 'atmoshere' (shome mishtake shurely), 'per cnet', 'intrammelled', 'vate' (Vating for Godot), 'vitue' (ladies of easy), and 'bogy-man' (isn't it usually 'bogey'? Well, let that pass). The jumbled ones are all right, though they hardly make for comfortable reading, but 'intrammelled' – is there such a word? What concerns me is the effect reading *The Times* may have on my spelling.

Does it matter? Is this the end of civilization as we kno it? It depends where you put your disaster threshold. Put it too low and you're a pedant, too high and by the time you notice things have gone too far it is too late. Doubtless the Literary Editor's pessimist would say that the generation now growing up can't spell anyway, but what chance has it of ever learning to do so when, from an early age, memories photograph words which are printed wrongly? My own view is that it matters more than the people at the *Stime* seem to think it does. We have to communicate with each other and, apart from a limited set of grunts, gestures and grimaces, language is all that we have for that purpose and we had better keep it as precise, in every way, as we can.

A curious example of the importance of this has come to light in *PN Review* (No. 30). It has been discovered by one American poet, Donald Hall, that a scholar has been meddling, since his death, with the punctuation of another American poet, Robert Frost.

This is particularly interesting because Frost was greatly concerned with the *sound* of what he said, relying on sound, more than most poets, because of the simplicity of his language, to give point to his meaning. He talked of 'the sound of sense' by which he meant that pitch, tone, cadence, pauses, hesitations, hurries, were all a part of the total meaning, in ordinary speech as well as in a poem, and he orchestrated his poems accordingly, by means of punctuation. He was in fact a punctuation buff, though his rules may have been his own.

Take, for instance, a poem of his that just about everybody knows, 'Stopping by Woods on a Snowy Evening' – the one that ends: 'And miles to go before I sleep, / And miles to go before I sleep.' It contains the line, read out loud by Frost himself in the fashion indicated, thousands of times: 'The woods are lovely, dark and deep.' His posthumous editor won't have that. The line is now: 'The woods are lovely, dark, and deep.' which is not the same thing at all. Frost says the darkness and depth of the woods is lovely; not, i) lovely, ii) dark, iii) deep. In another line from the same poem, Frost has: 'His house is in the village though.' His editor now has: 'His house is in the village, though.' This, as Hall points out, makes Frost sound altogether more calculating: 'Okay to stop by these woods, their owner won't see me', which is indeed his meaning but is now overemphasized.

Punctuation. Spelling. Small matters. But a poem, spelled and punctuated as the author intended can slightly change our view of the world; and we ought to be able to read half a column of a newspaper without having to look up 'bogy'. Details add up. Was it Michelangelo who said, to someone who told him he was worrying too much about detail in one of his paintings: 'Trifles make up masterpieces. But a masterpiece is not a trifle.'? He ought to kno.

1983

The Real Thing

———— o ————

WHY DO PEOPLE go to poetry readings? Perhaps not many do, but if you count up the readings that go on all over the country, all the year round, these people must amount to many thousands. The official stars of the reading circuit can draw hundreds to a single performance. I took part in one that contained Heaney and Hughes, as well as others, and because of those two names we had an audience of over two thousand people. That, I admit, was exciting. But none of us knew for certain why the audience was there, or for that matter why we were. Of course, people come to see what the writers look like, which is natural, and to hear what they sound like, which is useful, but the odd fact remains, easily proved by the sales of the poets' books afterwards, that many more people will come to hear a poet read his work than will read it themselves later.

I ask the question with the half-hope of being able to answer it. I recently went to a poetry reading, because I knew and liked the work of the two poets involved and, to be truthful, out of politeness.

I enjoyed it. They made an effective contrast: Norman MacCaig, very Scottish and gaunt, lovingly fashioning with his Edinburgh tongue each syllable of his wry, surprising, observations, so that you could hear the careful rhythms; Tony Connor, despite years of teaching in America, still baritone Mancunian, reading his intricately constructed syllabic poems, and even his rhymed ones, almost as though they were prose, almost making it difficult for the audience to distinguish the end of the poem from his introductory remarks to the next one. Poets often do this, scorning to pretend to be performers, trusting to their work on the poem. 'I want people to go away and read them, *then* they can see how they are made', said Connor, in some exasperation because, as is usual, although the sale of books at the end was good (there were about fifty of us there) it bore small relation to the size of the

People and Places

audience. Yet we had all enjoyed ourselves, if the intent faces, laughter, volume of applause, were anything to go by. Something had happened in the room, experience was shared, communication, however fragmentary, had taken place. We had come in search of the Real Thing, and whether we found it or not is for each individual to judge. It takes time, but our presence there was an acknowledgement of its existence, and our need.

I talked to Norman MacCaig beforehand about the Irish poet, the late Patrick Kavanagh, in some of whose poems I discover the Real Thing. MacCaig agreed, although it had taken him time to discover this, as it took time for me too. It always does. 'Difficult to trace *influences* there,' he said, meaning that too much talk about poetry inevitably limits itself to such academic detective-work, which can be of service, but brings us no nearer to defining the elusive Thing we are looking for, and which is perhaps also a reason for Kavanagh's academic neglect. I remembered a story in Anthony Cronin's little masterpiece *Dead as Doornails*, an hilarious/tragic book about his self-destructive friends, Brendan Behan, Kavanagh, Flann O'Brien, and others. Cronin reports Kavanagh as saying:

> That fellow Auden has a well-stocked mind. He has a lot of furniture, a lot of philosophy and psychology and that sort of thing. Of course it's junk, but it does to make a blaze, it creates energy and a sort of warmth, and when you get the blaze going you might succeed in saying something. But I've read nothing and have no rubbish to burn. None at all, no philosophy, no nothing. And you can't go on writing lyrics.

Apart from the astonishing honesty of that (honesty is a feature of his poems) the remark contains a great truth – 'of course it's junk'. We don't go to poetry, or not primarily, for cleverness or knowledge or even wisdom. These can 'go to make a blaze' but it is the blaze we are after, the unpredictable conflagration of the Real Thing that illuminates what is real in ourselves, and which we share with others. Which is why people go to poetry readings, in hope of it. Though why more don't take the seldom expensive brazier home with them, to peer more closely into it (when they are interested enough to turn out *at lunchtime* and to pay to hear the reading), remains as mysterious as the Thing itself. 1986

An Appetitive Decorum

―――― o ――――

GOOD POETS WRITE about poetry better than anyone else. There is no exception to this rule, from Johnson to Coleridge to Randall Jarrell. Confronted by a poem and a poet they are neither impudent nor awed. The recently published *Selected Literary Criticism* of Louis MacNeice is more proof of this; but first comes the poetry, which is the reason why good poets – practitioners – write well about it:

> The dazzle on the sea, my darling,
> Leads from the Western Channel,
> A carpet of brilliance taking
> My leave forever of the island.
>
> I shall never visit that island
> Again with its easy tempo –
> The seal sunbathing, the circuit
> Of gulls on the wing for garbage.
>
> I go to a different garbage
> And scuffle for scraps of notice,
> Pretend to ignore the stigma
> That stains my life and my leisure.
>
> For fretful even in leisure
> I fidget for different values,
> Restless as a gull and haunted
> By a hankering after Atlantis.

'Leaving Barra' (1937) continues for nine more clear and controlled verses, and is a test-piece for anyone who wants to discover if he is willing to succumb to the glamour of MacNeice. It con-

People and Places

tains his dazzle and his jazzy quality; his romanticism; his command of technique and his scholarly eclecticism (the haunting amphibrachs at the line-ends, the structure from Sir Philip Sidney); his sense of the 'stigma' of being middle-class and expensively educated in the politically-conscious 1930s; his 'fidget' for different values – he could never bring himself to accept any of the available panaceas; and his metaphysical 'hankering'.

It is in a sense a poem, as MacNeice considered himself the poet, of the Ordinary Man of no particular class. Admittedly, a self-conscious and conspicuously literate Ordinary Man, but there can be few who could not recognize the internal weather, and external dilemma, the poem expresses. In writing it MacNeice casts a cloak of elegance round the experience and round himself, but it does not muffle, or deceive. His prose works the same way.

When MacNeice died, in 1963, W.H. Auden said that of all the poets of his generation, MacNeice had the least reason to be ashamed. His characteristic note from the beginning is an untimorous, indeed in some circumstances positively courageous, hanging-back from easy solutions and public allegiances, while examining them all, holding them up to the light, in his verse. He was bombarded with questionnaires, all writers were at that time, the pressure was to toe the line: 'Do you take your stand with any political or politico-economic party or creed?' he was asked in 1934. MacNeice was not a ruralist, musing up a country lane, he was near the centre of the debates of his generation, but his reply is firm: 'No. In weaker moments I wish I could.' He never yielded to such moments.

No system satisfied him, political, religious, aesthetic; nor was there consolation and encouragement to be derived from the past. He returns throughout his career to all these matters, not sceptically, but probing, testing. He particularly returns to Christianity, but his hesitations there can perhaps be traced to his childhood (he appears to have traced them there himself). His father, a Protestant clergyman in Ireland, used to seat the young Louis on his knee and imitate trains. 'That was pleasant but what my father did by himself was frightening. When I was in bed I could hear his voice below in the study – and I knew he was alone – intoning away, communing with God. And because of his conspiracy with

An Appetitive Decorum

God I was afraid of him.'

> My father made the walls resound.
> He wore his collar the wrong way round.
> *Come back early or never come.*

(In his unfinished autobiography, *The Strings Are False*, MacNeice shows himself almost obsessed with his childhood, and it furnishes much of the imagery of his adult poetry.)

As a classicist, MacNeice turned to ancient history for some model of a political and cultural solution, interrogating the shade of Thucydides, addressing him as 'Master'. But that master/father fails him also, tells him that Periclean Athens had greed and cruelty in its public affairs, as did every other place and time.

His consequent inability to latch on to anything but the shifting surface became his theme. It could be called his fruitful pain: all his poems are a form of search, because he believed that no poet could be great who did not have a coherent system of belief. But in this, too, he most nearly approaches everyman, with everyman's distrust of dogmas, and his reliance on the everyday to provide at least some discernible good, even if it is only a cigarette or a glass of beer – or sex. (If MacNeice is ever tiresome it is in his over-facile discovery of a possible solution in some 'not impossible she'. It is a faith that remained with him to the end of his life, is endearing rather than otherwise, and he seldom lets it intrude. When it does it is oddly unconvincing. But perhaps in this too MacNeice saw his identity with other men.) In 1938 he was asked again (in an edition of *New Verse* called 'Commitments') where he stood. He answers almost impatiently: 'I have been asked to commit myself about poetry. I have committed myself so much *in* poetry that this seems almost superfluous. I think that the poet is only an extension – or, if you prefer it, a concentration – of the ordinary man. The content of poetry comes out of life. Half the battle is the selection of material. The poet is both critic and entertainer.' It is this definition of the poet that makes him such good company, in his poetry and in his prose.

In a small sense the title of these prose pieces, *Selected Literary Criticism*, is a misnomer. MacNeice could write extended criticism: his book, *Modern Poetry* (1938), has forthright chapter-titles like, 'Imagery', 'Diction', 'Rhythm and Rhyme', and proceeds with unusual helpfulness and clarity to address precisely those things. In these ways he was a systematic critic, and this selection contains lengthy forerunners and afterthoughts to that book, which are useful, as *Modern Poetry* is out of print. However, for the most part, the criticism here consists of reviews – of Malory, Sophocles, Vergil, Auden, George Herbert, Apuleius, T.S. Eliot, among others, to give some idea of the variety – and these rely on the cast of his mind and his tone to hold them together. But this works; it is not unlike reading a book of prose versions of his poems.

There is an additional ingredient in his tone which ought to be mentioned and explained, especially to non-English readers. Time has perhaps diluted the significance, but MacNeice was 'a Double First'. Which is to say he gained, at Oxford, a First Class degree in the first, Languages, part of the Classics course, and a First in the second, Literature, part. This was probably more important in his day than it is in ours (in which it may already have become eccentric), but for a hundred years it had been the passport to the higher reaches of the governing Establishment of Britain, the undisputed signal of 'a first-class mind'. Whether MacNeice regarded it as such can be doubted, but the academically-derived confidence is there, his ease with distinctions and definitions in argument, his cool regard bent on temporary fashion. There is a sense of a head cocked and of eyes narrowed (a favourite mannerism of his) and, if such can be imagined, a benign looking down the nose. Although he is the poet of doubts and hesitations (as well as celebrations) these are never, on the surface, self-doubts, or if they are he has them under intellectual control; they are not messy or over-confiding. He contrives to make this confidence one of the most attractive things about his writing; the reader feels safe with the author's knowledge and intelligence, and is in no anxiety that his lapels are about to be grabbed.

This selection begins with an early, wristy review of Auden's *Poems* (1931): 'God (or Nature) has a diffuse style which poets have often been busied correcting. Especially modern poets. Mr Auden's attempt is to put the soul across in telegrams.' Early Auden does sound like that, and MacNeice is equivalently confident and terse in his review. He writes often of his contemporaries: Spender, Auden, Day Lewis. He could be said to have

An Appetitive Decorum

had a hand in the creation of what Roy Campbell christened 'the MacSpaunday', a composite left-wing 1930s poet. But the four had little in common except, in the case of the last three, their political views, and then only for a time. When we consider how those views changed, we recognize the force of Auden's remark that MacNeice had least to be ashamed of. William Empson was surely fanciful about the public recantations of the others, but he was right about MacNeice, when he said in a radio portrait: 'After the end of the war, the poets nearly all said how bitterly ashamed they felt for having turned out so dreadfully wrong, and said now they weren't left-wing any more... But Louis at any rate never appeared in a white gown as a penitent; he went on being sardonic and responsible, hardly surprised even when appalled.'

MacNeice continued to be appalled, increasingly so, but evidence of the width of his sympathy is in his praise of the awkward honesties of Stephen Spender, for the two men were so unlike. MacNeice was deft and agile, valued those qualities in himself and others, but he could see the point of Spender. Later, equally unexpectedly, he came under the spell of Dylan Thomas, whom he loved as a man as well as a poet, and some of the most surprising pages he wrote are about Thomas. Thomas spoke no Welsh, but he could not have written as he did had he not been Welsh. MacNeice, living in England, never forgot he was an Irishman, and detected a non-English affinity between them.

An early essay (1935), 'Poetry Today', continues to be more helpful than most that have been written on the subject since. He manages a swift and convincing over-view of the twentieth century poetic scene, American as well as English, from Yeats and Housman and the Georgians to his own day. He shows how one fashion and tone succeeded another with apparent inevitability, and we feel that we grasp the process. He is always fair.

To those who disliked the innovations of e.e. cummings, for example, he makes a classically cool response: 'This has irritated many people but I cannot remember meeting, in *is 5*, any typographical oddity which I could not see a reason for.' This is not only all that needs to be said on the subject, it is the application of the *reasonable* to verse, which is a healthy process. (Incidentally, it may not only be pedantic to notice that he ends that sentence with a preposition, which it would have been easy to avoid. He stays, on purpose, with the living speech.) 'A good poet is no more a conglomeration of the typical and the derivative (and the peculiar) than of the grammatical. As for bad poets – there are also people who write solely to write grammar.' (The more one thinks about that last remark the more true one realizes it is.) In 'the Oxonian scholar', as his present editor Alan Heuser introduces him, such an anti-pedantic and anti-academic stance is cheering, as though the ordinary man has found a champion who has the equipment of the other, dominating side.

He was by nature however a dandy, in dress as well as in verse, with a taste for exotic dogs, such as borzois. In later years Geoffrey Grigson, an early publisher of MacNeice in his *New Verse*, who had endured the dogs and admired the man, whenever the subject of MacNeice's elegance came up, used to growl, '*Dirty fingernails!*' (A remark which always caused the company to look covertly down at their own hands.) There was certainly a streak of bohemianism in the dandy MacNeice, an interesting tension, a near-contradiction, but a poet is in a difficult position who has a bishop for a father. At all events, he came early to his credo of the common man or, at least, to his 'anti-literary' bias:

> The literary critics fail through being literary...Homer, Aeschylus, Bunyan, Dante, did not live in literary self-containedness. Not only the muck and wind of existence should be faced, but also the prose of existence, the utilities, the *sine qua nons*, which are never admitted to the world, or rather the salon, of the Pure Artist...'We live in our own corner' the poets had been saying, 'apart from the rest of the room'. It did not occur to them that there is no such thing as a corner in abstraction from a room.

The poet, then, should live in the world and write about the world and MacNeice is as good as his word. But metaphysical 'hankerings' can persist, and twenty-five years after that last quotation MacNeice comes near to a simple explanation of what these were in his case. In a review of the poems of George Seferis, in 1960, he uses the image of a 'corner' again, as though he felt he had been forced into one – by the prose of existence. He begins by quoting some lines by Seferis:

An Appetitive Decorum

> We knew it that the islands were beautiful
> Somewhere round about here where we are groping,
> Maybe a little lower or a little higher
> No distance away at all.

He adds: 'Which perhaps *is* an answer; on a plane just above or below our own or just round the corner which after all is our own corner so near and yet so far in fact, which might make sense of both our past and future and so redeem our present.'

His firmness and attractiveness is displayed in his defence of W.B. Yeats. Yeats, with his doctrine of the Mask, and his esoteric theorizings, has often been suspected in England, even by good critics, of being a phoney, and what is worse, an *Irish* phoney. MacNeice cheerfully admits the charge, adding that he is also 'a miracle of artistic integrity... even though as a man he may sometimes have been a fraud.' This would be a little hard for some English critics to take, approaching as it does the contradiction of an Irish bull. MacNeice cunningly, Irishly, defends his position by summoning to his aid the archetype of English commonsense, Dr Johnson. It is an example of the fun and practicality of MacNeice's criticism, his tendency to personification, and his sense of the arbitrariness and usefulness of *form*.

> We must not be discouraged in Yeats by his self-stylisation. Dr Johnson, who had a hard head, yet suffered from neuroses, one of which (I have forgotten the exact details) was something like this: whenever he had to pass through a door he would start counting in the attempt to cross the threshold on, say, the thirteenth step and on the right foot. To have such rules in life is awkward, but I can imagine that someone thus afflicted, who had a flair for elegant deportment, might conceivably turn such a tic to artistic account, always entering doors with a noticeably graceful rhythm so that people might even come to speak of him as The Man who goes through Doors So Beautifully. Such a one is Mr Yeats; such perhaps are all poets to some extent.

Academically garlanded as he was, MacNeice started out as a teacher of Classics, first in Birmingham, then in London. But soon he drifted into writing and producing features for the BBC. Not quite, perhaps, 'the muck and wind of existence', but not an Ivory Tower either. In one of those exquisitely oblique blurbs that Faber and Faber affected in the 1940s (impossible not to believe that T.S. Eliot wrote them himself) it is hinted that MacNeice is slumming:

> Those admirers of Mr MacNeice's peculiar lyric genius who may have feared that he had given up to the B.B.C. what was meant for mankind – in other words, that he had reserved for radio drama those gifts which should be more variously displayed – will be reassured, first, by this announcement of a new volume of poems, and, second, by the volume itself when it comes into their hands.

That was for *Holes in the Sky* – and they don't write 'em that way any more.

In the course of making one of those 'radio dramas' (*Person from Porlock*), MacNeice unnecessarily went down into an underground cave to be with the recording engineers, ('the muck and wind'), caught a cold which turned out to be a rare kind of pneumonia, and died. He was fifty-six.

Very shortly before that, and it ends this book of his criticism, he wrote a little piece about his latest volume, *The Burning Perch*. Of recent years he had been accused of having become garrulous but, although he had tended to write at greater length, there is more to be found in those poems than has yet been admitted. However, it was generally thought that in *The Burning Perch* he was back in something like his old form, although he confesses himself dismayed at the gloom of some of the poems. He also explains his partial return to the classical world in his verse:

> I notice that many of the poems have been trying to get out of the 'iambic groove' which we are all born into. In "Memoranda to Horace" there is a conscious attempt to suggest Horatian rhythms (in English of course one cannot do more than suggest them) combined with the merest reminiscence of Horatian syntax. This technical Horatianising appears in some other poems too where, I suppose, it goes with something of an Horatian resignation. But my resignation, as I was not brought up a pagan, is more of a fraud than Horace's. "Memoranda to Horace" itself, I hope shows this.

An Appetitive Decorum

Why did he hope so, and in what way does he show it?

These essays send the reader back to the poems. There is in the 'Memoranda' a deepening dismay at the contemporary world; MacNeice certainly went on being 'appalled', but for a middle-aged poet that is nothing new. There is also the affirmation of a belief in grace, and style, as of the Man who goes through Doors So Beautifully:

> Though elderly poets profess to be inveterate
> Dionysians, despising Apollonians,
>   I find it, Flaccus, more modest
> To attempt, like you, an appetitive decorum.

It is an attractive position and a classical one, hardly un-pagan. There is however a circling here, an identification, a kind of return across swathes of time, which goes with a recognition that he, MacNeice, belongs to a different dispensation, even though that too may have become tired and in some ways discredited.

MacNeice was never afraid of the predictable and obvious – it was part of the useful legacy of the common man. He had written in homage to clichés and later he wrote a poem in homage to 'The Truisms', in which he remembered the father whose booming prayers he had heard from his boyhood bedroom. It would be grotesque to try to entrap MacNeice within any of the systems he had so warily circuited all his life, but there is something seemly, an exact decorum, in such circlings and dreamed-of returns: he is the poet of a masculine yearning; his system was non-belief, hope-filled.

> His father gave him a box of truisms
> Shaped like a coffin, then his father died;
> The truisms remained on the mantelpiece
> As wooden as the playbox they had been packed in
> Or that other his father skulked inside.
>
> Then he left home, left the truisms behind him
> Still on the mantelpiece, met love, met war,
> Sordor, disappointment, defeat, betrayal,
> Till through disbeliefs he arrived at a house
> He could not remember seeing before,

People and Places

And he walked straight in; it was where he had come from
And something told him the way to behave.
He raised his hand and blessed his home;
The truisms flew and perched on his shoulders
And a tall tree sprouted from his father's grave.

1987

Orthodoxies

———— o ————

I

ENGLISH POETRY 1900-1950. An Assessment (how like C.H. Sisson to choose so dry and forthright a title) is precisely what it says it is, and that is like him too. It should be thrust into the hand of every schoolteacher and university teacher and every reader and would-be reader of poetry. It can do nothing but good, the cackle is cut and, what is rare, it is a pleasure to read; there is no jargon, no vapour, no genuflection before reputations and no silly desire to cut them down to size either.

'The object of this book is to show where the best English verse of the first half of this century is to be found, to indicate what its qualities are and – since these things are not separable – what sort of men wrote it.' That is his useful intention and he carries it out, with rigour: '... more than thirty poets find a place in the history. A moment's reflection on any other fifty years of English literature will suggest that the number is too large rather than too small.'

He has a theme and a measuring-rod: the nearness of poetry to the ordinary speech of its period. 'This is because there is a general, completely inartificial conversation among contemporaries of which what remains as the literature is, in some sense, the finest expression.' He is careful, with that 'in some sense', but the general proposition can hardly be argued with, it removes so much obscuring dead wood. He quotes Ezra Pound with approval, 'Make it new' – poetry's job is to refresh and cleanse the language – but also a way must be found 'to re-establish the link between verse and the language that is spoken. And this, as much as anything, is what the history of 1900-1950 is about.'

So the measuring-rod is set up but it is usefully extensible. It can include Lionel Johnson's 'By the Statue of King Charles at Charing Cross' on the grounds of 'purged rhetoric'. Though we may be sure that it is the purgation, rather than the rhetoric, of which Mr Sisson approves. He is predictably good on Thomas Hardy, rightly resurrects John Davidson and, unexpectedly, finds a place for Walter de la Mare. 'Grave and a little precious, the lines none the less have the rhythm of speech.' It is a very sensitive measuring-rod that he uses. Of T.E. Hulme he says: 'he does not turn aside for beauty. No good writer does.' In that bald statement is he not, for the first time, constructing a rod for his own back? Or a boomerang? *No* good writer, ever? No 'magic casements'?

Edward Thomas, of course, passes all the tests with flying colours. (And this book, first published in 1971, did not have the benefit of the general acceptance of Edward Thomas that has taken place, to a large extent, since.) But his close inspection of Wilfred Owen – of the whole idea of 'war poets' and 'war poetry' is invigorating. One of the hardest things for a critic, or a poet, to get across is the idea that poetry is not journalism. That a poem is not necessarily good because one approves of its sentiments, or important because its subject is important. This is crucial, and Mr Sisson is worth watching as he goes to work on Owen's much-quoted statement that ends, 'The Poetry is in the pity'. Making due allowances for Owen's youth, and the experiences he had undergone, Mr Sisson concludes: 'It comes near to being absolute rubbish', and explains why. This is splendid to hear because he is talking about one of the accepted, unexamined, texts of the age. His intention is not to destroy Owen but to rescue him from nonsense and the wrong sort of admirers.

He tries to do the same for T.S. Eliot, preferring the early work (in which he is surely right) and in the process defines the serious intention of this book. 'But the identification of the point of his failure, and its nature, are of public importance because it is not for the health of the literature of the English-speaking countries that attention should be deflected away from *The Waste Land*, "Sweeney Agonistes" and "Prufrock".

This concern with the health of literature (i.e. language) is indeed of public importance, and anyone who regards as irrelevant these discussions of the relative merits of seldom-read poets is mistaken. Nevertheless, it is in his no-nonsense, healthful approach to the poetry of W.B. Yeats that Mr Sisson begins to run the risk of sounding bossy in a particularly English way. It is the Irishness of Yeats that he seems to object to. He can't even stand his famous epitaph:

> Cast a cold eye
> On life, on death.
> Horseman, pass by.

'Yeats was a great egotist, and frivolous enough to think it worthwhile cutting a figure even after his death.' But, say we *like* the figure Yeats cuts for us and, even if sometimes affectionately amused, are grateful to him for it? After all as W.H. Auden said, not all poetry has to be, 'Plain cooking, made still plainer by plain cooks.' Oddly enough, the sentiment of the epitaph is the sentiment of many of Mr Sisson's own poems and he should perhaps have remembered that he has written a (good) poem about his own epitaph, or rather, about his regret that he has not composed one.

On Yeats the rod raps often, and hard: '... when it comes, as he said in an earlier poem, to dining with Landor or John Donne, one can only conclude that though he may dine with Landor – no mean company – he will never dine with Donne, whose poetry is immeasurably nearer the bone.' There is a touch of England v. Ireland here. The thespian Irish like to act out their idea of themselves. The English – who produce the best actors in the world – regard this as play-acting and tell the Irish to come off it. It is a misunderstanding that has caused many tragedies.

Perhaps the root of Mr Sisson's objection is here: 'Yeats always seemed to demand to be listened to on his own terms. The test of a poet, in the end, is, however, the extent to which he can be taken on other people's terms.' True, or at least true enough. But Yeats can create the terms on which we listen to him, draw us in and on, and when he 'turns aside for beauty' we go with him. Are we to feel duped?

But the book is full of things well said. Of a poem by Robert Graves: 'That is poetry which cannot be made up by any skill or ingenuity. It is a reluctant deposit on the floor of the mind.' He can be directly funny: 'From the first (George) Barker exhibited a slightly excessive facility with evocative words. It was as if he could sit burping gently, whatever his thoughts, and enjoy the aroma of past feasts.' Perhaps best of all is the giant periphrasis in favour of Hugh MacDiarmid: 'A certain arrogance is not out of place in one who has done so much, in the face of so many difficulties, but it cannot be said that his boring Scottish insistence on whatever he happens to be saying has done his work no harm.' England 4, Scotland 1½. But the point is that he *likes* both Barker and MacDiarmid, and tries to help us to read them. These thrusts are part of his method and his mind, the mind that begins the Conclusion to this historical survey: 'History does not end; at least it has not done so yet.' Accurate to the last.

It is to be expected that his *Selected Poems* should show the spareness he looks for in other poets but its slimness is startling when one thinks of the amount of poetry he has published. Also, his selection gives no suggestion of the variety of his work. The poems are in chronological order and it causes dismay to find one called 'On my fifty-first birthday' far too near the beginning of the book.

Mr Sisson spent most of his life in the Civil Service and was surely a splendid composer of Memoranda: the facts laid out, not a word wasted, the truth told, or as much truth as was practicable in those circumstances. So it is with these poems he has selected (where are 'Trafalgar Square'? 'The Discarnation'? 'The Reckoning'? Good poems, different kinds of poem, from earlier collections. Perhaps they did not pass the memoranda test.) Here we have the facts, not a word wasted, and the truth, all of it. He makes few gestures towards the reader. He, more than Yeats, requires to be read on his own terms. There is a sense of 'the reluctant deposit on the floor of the mind'. He appears to embody a kind of Christianity without hope. That is probably rather far up the ladder that mystics climb. But the view is bleak.

1981

II

I have found myself speculating how an old, intimate friend would take the subject-matter of C.H. Sisson's poetry. It is, to an extraordinary degree, about glimpses of Nothingness, outside or beyond, and as for inside, well, if we only knew what a worthless fellow he was, malicious, deceitful, etc... Would the old friend find himself wondering whether Charles really was like that, more so than most of us and so depressed? Or would he, observing him at work in his garden, or among his books, suspect him of laying it on a bit thick?

In some form these thoughts may occur to the reader and it is good to approach all verse with a certain scepticism, so long as we are prepared to relinquish it. Of course, a poet only partially represents himself, the poem itself has to come as a surprise, a kind of mystery tour. 'There is no question, as it has come to me, of filling notebooks with what one knows already,' says Sisson, and Larkin has remarked 'the poems one wants to write are not always the ones that get written'. Sisson has arrived at the same conclusion: 'The writing of poetry is, in a sense, the opposite of writing what one wants to write...'. Thus, a good poet can fail throughout his writing life to express satisfactorily some of the things that have moved him most deeply. (Otherwise, perhaps, the canon would be overburdened with poems about the deaths of children.)

What it is overburdened with is poems that can be loosely said to be about 'love' and from this we readers have always concluded that subject is not especially important to the poet, at least as he writes, because he is cool enough and clear-headed enough to employ his art to assist his expression and our pleasure in it. We make an exception for good religious poets; we reckon they mean what they say, and their versifications and verbal flights are a dressing-up to impress not us, but God. Sisson is a religious poet who refuses to dress up. His subject is a sort of spiritual rock-bottom, or maybe bottomless swamp – even in the womb 'hope lies / Crouched for its disappointment' – and his aim is to express this starkness without apparent artifice, to the point of almost abandoning art, or seeming to, because such spareness is appropriate to the bleakness he faces. 'Are there any more words to say? I do not think so.' It is a measure of his authority that we do not feel inclined to laugh at him for then going on to say a great many.

Sisson does not reach the point of giving up art, or even approach that, but his work does raise a question about whether poetry can go further in his direction, which is towards silence; whether the spareness of his effect does not derive too much of its force from the previous loquacities of others. (There is a story of one film star asking another what he intended to do in the next scene. 'Nothing,' was the reply. 'Listen, bud,' said the senior actor icily, '*I* do nothing.') Sisson called his collection of essays *The Avoidance of Literature*, and we cheer him for his dislike of literary showing-off, but it is possible to doubt that he grants enough power to the mysteriously spell-binding properties of literary artifice. This is probably what leads him so curiously to undervalue Yeats. (Though we do find an unexpected enthusiasm for the poetry of George Barker.)

In what follows I may appear to be making a moral judgement on a man rather than appraising a poet, but it is the kind of judgement Sisson solicits because he is constantly making it on himself; it is part of his method, and also his subject. His poetry presents us with a form of despair for which he considers little reason need be given. It is hard to say he is wrong in this, but, if he was truly in such despair, it is a reasonable philistine thing to say that he would not be writing a poem but staring in apathy at a wall. To take a different case: G.K. Chesterton's deliberate decision to be 'jolly' is at least as serious as a decision to be the opposite. It is not always easy to see the justification given, in his poems, for the permanent bind this poet is in. He seems to dislike himself: 'my heart is a sink / Where ambition swills round with lost lust / And even the last words are spoken with envy.' That is enjoyable, it sounds accurate and is good, confessional stuff. But a wise priest in the confessional would detect a whiff of overscrupulousness, which denotes Pride. There is Pride in Sisson's work, certainly, as well as pride of the admirable, lower-case kind; as though he is the last man in the world, determined to go down unassisted by illusion.

Sisson's Anglicanism is as important to him as Catholicism became to Chesterton. That it led the one to a determined gaiety and the other to an equally determined dismay is a possibly interesting, possibly historical, difference. Certainly Chesterton could have made something genial and intelligent out of it. Perhaps, with his acute sense of Englishness and of English history, Sisson regards himself as *fin de ligne*, the Last Anglican. In

Orthodoxies

his excellent essay 'Reflections on Marvell's Ode' he marks the point where the tide turned in the wrong direction: the execution of Charles I.

But mention of Englishness, which Sisson pre-eminently represents in all his writings, leads to another man, of the other party, a Regicide probably, described by his biographer as one of 'God's great awkward squad of unorthodox, dissident Englishmen' – George Orwell. If you open Sisson's *The Avoidance of Literature* at any point you could be in the literary and moral presence of Orwell. They both detest fuss, cant and any form of sloppy thinking. I do not mean that either imitated the other, I mean that both are of the English 'awkward squad' and show it in the same way.

'If you compare commercial advertising with political propaganda, one thing that strikes you is its relative honesty.'

'It is an odd thing, but the English are the last people to be allowed a nationalism of their own.'

'Whether or not new wine is being poured into the Civil Service these days – and it has been habitual ever since the Fulton Report to assert there is some heavy liquor about – it is certain that the old bottles are there to receive it.'

I quote at random, only taking care not to have them saying much the same thing (although that would be possible) because it is the similarity of *tone* that is striking. It would be a good game to quote more sentences and see how many the reader attributed rightly. I should guess he would have to end up tossing a coin. In this case only the first quotation is from Orwell, who was also a keen definer of 'Englishness', and raised the same doubts concerning the permanence of the Civil Service after the Labour victory in 1945.

But the point is that Orwell went with the post-Regicide tide, albeit awkwardly, scourge of both far-Left and Right; he was recognizably a man of his time. To be the Royalist Sisson, concerned with the protection of older orthodoxies, because he considers them preferable to the new ones, is much more difficult and lonely. You feel that Orwell is sustained by his sense of belonging to a movement and Sisson has the movement all against him; that he feels, as I have said, the last man in the world, or at least in Europe. (Orwell's first title for *1984* was *The Last*

Man in Europe.) Orwell could write happily about comic postcards and boys' comics, composing an anthropology of English mass culture. Sisson is in a different position, the vulgarization of intellectual and moral life has accelerated wildly since then. It is not certain that Orwell would be so blithe about popular culture today (though retaining, certainly, his faith in the Common Man, who may yet save us from our worst excesses by simply taking no notice of us). I believe Orwell and Sisson have more in common than a good prose style. They can be seen as unblinking representatives of the English official class, a type that has always seemed to be defeated by smarter-alecks, by careerists, but which has in fact made England. Possibly they represent the best of the two sides in the Civil War, a conflict which is still at the heart of what is important in English life, though the politicians (with the exception of Mr Benn) seem to have forgotten. A number of good minds changed sides in that war, some of them more than once, so finely balanced was the matter. Orwell surprised his friends by directing that he be buried according to the rites of the Church of England. (He also contributed early on to *G.K.'s Weekly*.)

However, there *was* a Restoration of the Monarchy – and it was henceforth different. There is a sense in which historical change belongs to the category of fact. It must be defined, and criticized, but too fierce an opposition can lead to a stranding, an isolation that is to be found in Sisson's poetry and is also a source of its power; for we are all so stranded, one way or another, though we pretend otherwise in order to appear to keep going. But like every strength, it can also be a source of weakness, can lead to a suggestion of crustiness. We should like to think that the Sage of Langport has not washed his hands of the world, and of us, as he appears to contemplate doing in some of his recent poems. They speak from a secret never-to-be-divulged wound and move towards the same point in us – which is perhaps the religious instinct itself. His is not that of Crashaw, to be sure; it is without sensuous ornateness; of George Herbert perhaps, but a Herbert without solace; whose only comfort is that there is none:

O light, I do not want you
The years have taken away
Whatever there was lovely
In the day

The land stretches to doomsday
The rivers to the sea
And nothing done and nothing said
Matters to me.

1984

Dun Roamin'

———o———

'ACCENTORS ARE SMALL grey and brown thin-billed birds of retiring habits.' Not a very exciting description of a bird that fascinates me, and for some reason moves me: the hedge-accentor, dunnock or hedge-sparrow. It is in appearance indeed undistinguished and creeps about the bottoms of hedges, mouse-like, the colour of earth and dead leaves. One often mistakes it for a mouse. But it can perch and it can sing, for it isn't a sparrow at all.

It is the song that is surprising. Sometimes here it is the only song there is, at morning and evening, and it is very thin, but melodious and varied. Listening to it, I have had a sense of a thin needle-like beak emitting these thin thread-like notes and it seems to be stitching, or embroidering, the beginnings and ends of the day, sewing dawn on to morning, evening on to night. This is fanciful, but I cannot get the idea out of my mind. It is a celebratory, tidy bird.

Why anything quite so subfusc, secretive and dun-coloured should hold my attention so completely I do not know. ('Dunnock' is apparently a country name for any small brown bird.) Grey and brown, it is like the paintings of Gwen John, which also move me. I suppose, to discover why, I should have to psychoanalyse myself, and this is not the place. Even Mr Geoffrey Grigson, a generous observer, characterizes its song as 'without strength or urgency or courage' whereas I find it stuffed (discreetly) with quantities of all three. Maybe I am lucky with my hedge-sparrows – an old book says it has been known to imitate the nightingale (another undistinguished-looker) and that is what, recently, they have been reminding me of.

I was sitting outside just now, watching a pair of them courting (or two cocks mock-fighting, I am no ornithologist). They flew at each other, or flew side by side, altering course simultaneously, fast as fly-catchers, with an intention-transference as quick as an

Dun Roamin'

electric current. Then they perched and gave vent to this extraordinary, and at this season powerful and varied, song. I pointed this out to my companion, a visitor from London, and he was less interested than I, preoccupied with his own affairs. This did not make me superior to him (except in my pleasure of the moment), there would be other occasions when he was interested and I was not, but it would not be in hedge-sparrows. I asked myself why did I derive such particular, serious and to me significant pleasure? At that moment I remembered, with sinking heart, that a man from the BBC was coming that evening, Mr Gerald Priestland, to record my impromptu contribution to a programme called something like 'Why I believe in God'.

I have been avoiding such occasions and questions all my life, preferring to roam the bottom of hedges, dun-coloured (sometimes singing, but not so as anyone would notice). Besides, the question, and any answer that could be summoned, is an invitation to impertinence. I have a picture of puffing out my chest and congratulating God on my belief in him, while the Almighty, viewing me with a glazed and indifferent eye, says briefly 'Ta' and turns to something, someone, more interesting. Up to now, faced with such questions, I have always pleaded the fifth amendment, unwilling to incriminate myself. For how can I explain it is a feeling, not a thought; and that the feeling is precise, though it cannot be precisely expressed? That it has something to do with the pleasure I am getting from the hedge-sparrows – that it *is* the pleasure?

For I know that our reason is as important as our emotion. I admire the people who have classified the dunnock as an accentor, rescued it from being just a small brown bird. I am told that in Arabic there are only two names for a flower – 'rose' and 'onion'. Distinctions, categories, *thought*, add to our capacity for praise. But what definitions am I to offer Mr Priestland and his microphone, trapped into it by a silly civic sense that it was time I dun roamin' the hedge and at last perched to acknowledge the great luck of belief? It will probably sound 'sweet' and 'charming', as this may do, whereas it is fierce and sometimes difficult, and the expression of it certainly dangerous, because it can be taken away. I shall have to try and remember the defiant-sounding hedge-sparrow and remember, also, that it lays particularly beautiful eggs most attractive to the cuckoo, who turfs them on to the ground.   1984

Images of Heaven and Hell

——— o ———

AT ONE PERIOD of my life it seemed to me that I was being given images of what heaven is like. Or, to be more precise, was being given a sense of 'heavenliness' – the condition, rather than the location. I was young, I had experienced a grief, and the sequence of visitations lasted, off and on, for about six months, maybe a little longer.

It is by far the most extraordinary thing of that kind that has ever happened to me, yet there was an air of ordinariness about it, of inevitability. What I saw and understood was oddly familiar, as though I was remembering something I already knew.

The experience, which seemed to be fuelled by something inside me, seemed to come from outside as well, as though it rapped on my windows and drew my attention. It did not arise from any virtue of mine, nor from any attempt at concentration or meditation. It came, when it did come, unsolicited, involuntarily, and went away when it wanted to, leaving behind a residue in which it was impossible not to believe.

It is best described, I think, in terms of colours. I was living in London at the time and had lived in towns most of my life. I was invited to the country for a few days, and stood on a little bridge in Gloucestershire, over the Windrush river, suddenly astounded by the variety of greens that unfolded themselves in front of me, layer upon layer, tone upon tone. It is necessary here to say that I was not long returned from Java, where the greens are darker and more uniform (and more threatening) and therefore was in a mood particularly receptive to 'the sweet, especial rural scene' of England. But the experience contained more than that obvious sense of contrast. On top of the extraordinary springing vitality of the sight before me, and contained in it, was a certainty of benevolence, which was there to be co-

Images of Heaven and Hell

operated with, or not, as I chose. There was no cause, no just cause, for anxiety, now or ever. Not even anxiety – that least of all – about death.

The word 'religious' ought to be defined before one uses it, but that sudden removal of anxiety is of course a religious feeling and is at the heart of all religions. It felt entirely and peculiarly sane. It *was* sane, no 'felt' about it. There is a sense in which all such clarities are delusions, as 'romantic love' can be called a delusion. But anyone who has experienced that emotion knows it is nothing of the kind; what are false are our expectations of it, for which the reality cannot be blamed. I knew if I fell in that water I might drown, no heavenly choir would hold me above water; I knew that if I stayed too long among those greens I would become cold and ill; that in the grasses and among the trees all sorts of assassinations were being committed, appetites appeased at the expense of other smaller appetites. But what I was being told I was being told. It was all wholly innocent, and good.

Nor was it only when confronted by a fortunate landscape that this sense of an innate and mysterious tenderness arrived. The 'country' aspect of it was fortuitous. I remember being halted by the sight of an advertisement-hoarding. Successive posters had partly peeled off, they were faded, rain-stained, wind-tattered. It was entirely beautiful, and gave the impression of patiently waiting for this to be noticed.

It also happened among people. I was taken to a party where I knew hardly anybody, after a period of being protected, and when it was still too soon for me to take part in such things. As I stood by myself and watched the faces (it was a late, dark, wild sort of party) I possibly expected to feel, with a part of my conscious mind, a disgust at the contrast they made with the beauty of the experiences I had recently been undergoing. Perhaps at first I did feel that, but then, unexpectedly, involuntarily, I found myself filling with small bubbles of Mozartian laughter. It was quite unsatirical; it was not laughter *at* anyone, not even at myself. Indeed, there seemed no self in it. It was pure laughter. I was its spectator, its container, it filled me of its own accord. I do not believe that I physically laughed. When it stopped, as though I were a jug and was now full, I felt refreshed, internally cleansed,

People and Places

as after a fit of weeping. Nor had I any idea of the extraordinary nature and quality of this experience, because it seemed so natural. Such a thing had never happened to me before, nor has it since. It was wholly and undeniably good.

It is important to emphasize the lack of self there was in these visitations, or revelations. They were, in a sense, nothing to do with me. Even trying to describe them in terms of my own experience makes me uneasy, as though by bringing in myself I may traduce them. Yet they were not secret, to be hugged and hidden. They were reality, everyone's possible reality, briefly revealed.

I kept a journal at this time (filled with references to colours) in which I wrote down something from Coleridge's Notebooks which seemed nearly to correspond with what I was seeing and feeling: 'In looking at objects of Nature while I am thinking, as at yonder moon dim-glimmering thro' the dewy window-pane, I seem rather to be seeking, as it were *asking*, a symbolical language for something within me that already and forever exists, than observing anything new.'

That is almost it, for he says that this happened to him when he was thinking, presumably about something else. This is analogous to perceiving a dim star by looking to the side of it; stare straight at it and it disappears. It is nevertheless still there. Also, he talks of becoming unexpectedly aware of 'something within me that already and forever exists', and that is a precise formulation of the strange familiarity I have been trying to describe.

This, then, is my idea of heaven: an unanxious perception of the innate goodness of physical reality which is like a symbolical language for something within us 'which already and forever exists'. I have difficulty in imagining a *place* called heaven – I should think we all do – and yet, although there is something passive in the experience in that it cannot be sought (it is true, however, that the chances for it can be destroyed) it causes such a gratitude of relief that praise is an instinctive reaction, and is like a kind of internal singing. One knows what he meant, who first talked of the music of the spheres.

I also copied out something from the letters of W.B. Yeats. He says to one of his correspondents: 'Yet why not take Sweden-

Images of Heaven and Hell

borg literally and think we attain, in partial contact, what the spirits know throughout their being? He describes somewhere two spirits meeting, and as they touch they become a single conflagration.' I like that Yeats/Swedenborg idea, which would certainly solve the prosaic idea that afflicts most of us, of a heaven hopelessly overcrowded; but these are images, pictures, and they become absurd if we cling to them.

Nevertheless, physical reality is what we know, and no other, and heaven must lie within it. As Blake says: 'He who sees the Infinite in all things, sees God. Therefore God becomes as we are, that we may be as he is.'

It will be said that what I experienced was the result of shock, was some kind of hyper-aesthesia. Also, being alone and afraid, unable to bear the full burden of the fix I was in, I was compensating with spectra of happiness and relief. Naturally, I would believe in what was so pleasant to believe. This may be true, but does not explain (at least to me) the power of these things I am talking about; they were neither for me nor from me. Blake has a look at this power of belief. He puts it in the form of question and answer, with Ezekiel: 'Then I asked, "Does a firm persuasion that a thing is so, make it so?" He replied: "All poets believe that it does, and in ages of imagination this firm persuasion removed mountains; but many are not capable of a firm persuasion of anything".' Blake quoted out of context can be used to support most ideas, and we don't like 'firm persuasion' nowadays. Few people could have been more firmly persuaded than Adolf Hitler.

The mention of his name brings us naturally to the idea of hell. Hell, I take it, is the permanent deprivation of what I have suggested is heaven, or the direction in which heaven lies. That heaven which, as I have suggested, can come briefly visiting. 'If the doors of perception were cleansed, everything would appear to men as it is, infinite' – Blake again. But what if we know this, need this, but have lost all faith in our capacity to attain it, and therefore any real belief in its existence? Blake has the answer to that: 'If any could desire what he is incapable of possessing, despair must be his eternal lot.' In other words, hell.

His use of the word 'could' is significant – 'if any *could* desire' – as though Blake is saying that a man *cannot* desire a good he is incapable of possessing, and that his desire for it is proof of its existence.

177

People and Places

We live in times that are particularly conscious of the hellish nature of the world. We *should* be aware of suffering, torture, injustice. There are, however, times when our preoccupation with these things, and scepticism about the idea of 'beauty', would seem to imply that our forefathers lived in kindergartens and sucked their thumbs, whereas we alone have found the courage to open our eyes and look at the world. It seems unlikely that all our forefathers were deluded and all their conclusions, wherein they differ from ours, were wrong. To take only a single instance, they were intimately acquainted with death, of their own children, to a degree that most of us are not.

Pain is true, and is a truth easier to observe and examine than any other kind. We can come to believe, therefore, that it is the only truth. We run the risk of evading truths that are more difficult and elusive and perhaps, dangerously and fashionably, we flirt with hell, which exists.

Saul Bellow puts this well in *Herzog*. Herzog inveighs against the detested Himmelstein:

> Everybody was in on the act. "History" gave everyone a free ride. The very Himmelsteins who had never even read a book of metaphysics, were touching the Void, as if it were so much saleable real estate. This little demon was impregnated with modern ideas, and one in particular excited his terrible little heart: You must sacrifice your poor, squawking, niggardly individuality – which may be nothing anyway (from an analytic point of view) but a persistent infantile megalomania, or (from a Marxian point of view) a stinking little bourgeois property – to historical necessity. And to truth. And truth is true only as it brings down more disgrace and dreariness upon human beings, so that if it shows anything but evil it is an illusion, and not truth.

The reality I have been trying to describe is under attack from me, as well as from the sceptical world. I contain within myself all the negative force necessary to put heaven beyond my reach. I also know that I may be wrong, and that the world may be only the lightless abattoir that some say it is. But say I stood up and joined such realists, denied all I have been trying to describe, for which I have no proof? No cock would crow. What I saw (or

Images of Heaven and Hell

thought I saw) does not need me in order for it to continue to exist. Besides, I could never believe my own denial.

But 'the rainbow comes and goes', of course it does, as Wordsworth admits in his Immortality Ode, which is one of the great affirmations thrown in the teeth of disillusioning experience. 'Those shadowy recollections', he calls them:

> Which be they what they may,
> Are yet the fountain light of all our day,
> Are yet a master light of all our seeing.

1981

Soame Jenyns

———o———

IN A REVIEW of a book about Purgatory, James Fenton asked the question: 'But the starving man has often wondered: if God is all-powerful, and he does this to me, can he also be said to be good?'

This immediately reminded me of what I had barely forgotten; an exchange between a Russian poet and an English novelist, in the 1960s. 'D'you believe in God?' asked the poet, Russian fashion. 'If I did I should hate him,' replied the novelist, and they embraced as brothers.

The point of view suggested by this is attractive. It is proud, clear-headed, defiant. I would greatly like to be able to share it and become indeed a member of a brave, rational brotherhood, with common sense on our side. The trouble is, twist and turn as I may, I have long been convinced that most of our human ills are not to be blamed on any external agency (should one be hoped or feared to exist) but on ourselves; to a distressing degree our wounds are self-inflicted, or are given us, however indirectly, by other humans.

This has been much in my mind of late because I was unwise enough to blurt something along these lines (that we 'complain too much') into the tape-recorder of Mr Gerald Priestland, who was compiling a radio programme about such matters, and what I said impromptu he has bruited abroad more emphatically than I expected. This has given rise to one or two gently remonstrative letters, pointing out to me that some of us have more to complain about than others, which of course is true. If we are in any state of reasonable health and prosperity we should check our complacence level daily. And however carefully we check there will always remain some of the stuff, undetected, at the bottom of the tank. It is not possible for a man to imagine himself *in extremis* the whole time. Which makes me wonder how Mr Fenton is so

Soame Jenyns

sure he knows what a starving man has 'often wondered'.

Nevertheless, the problem is real and important and I owe the reader an apology for introducing a name much mentioned of late, because of his anniversary. Over Christmas I was unwell, in a foreign hotel, and was reduced to lying in my room clutching for companionship the vast Oxford Authors paperback *Samuel Johnson*. It was thus I came across 'Sermon 5'.

It is interesting that Johnson wrote this pseudonymously, or at least in the name of a school friend, the clergyman John Taylor, who published it as his own. Perhaps the disguise gave Johnson freedom, for it is a most dangerous topic; in the Sermon he magisterially discusses, point by point, what Mr Priestland oddly (and in my view deceptively) called 'The Case Against God'. And, point by point, this least complacent of men demolishes it. I might have guessed, but I did not know, that I had so magnificent an ally. To anyone who wishes to clarify his mind, or marshal his arguments, on one side or the other, it is impossible to recommend this piece of writing too highly. Johnson, who lived his life in a state of holy terror, is nowhere more careful and profound and clear.

But he was not content. He knew too well this danger of obfuscating complacence. So – it is like a companion-piece – he wrote an enormous review of Soame Jenyns's *A Free Inquiry into the Nature and Origin of Evil*, which had to be spread over three numbers of the *Literary Magazine*. For he did suspect, in Soame Jenyns, this very complacence, as he suspected it in Alexander Pope. He also detected a lack of logic. So, almost but not quite in contradiction of 'Sermon 5', he points out in one of his most eloquent passages the varied and insupportable ghastlinesses that attend so much of human life. The passage begins on page 535 of the paperback. He makes such an ass of the unfortunate Jenyns that he renders his name, otherwise surely forgotten, possibly immortal, which is why it is at the head of this piece. Let it stand as a warning to anyone, to me most of all, of the dangers inherent in this topic. It is a theme too vast for this column to support.

But if in the course of referring to it I cause anyone to get hold of that paperback and to read what Johnson has to say on the matter, the risk will have been worthwhile and much silliness, on both sides of the question, may be prevented. 1985

Dis-conglobated

———o———

THE INFLUENCE of a great man can take us by surprise.

In Capua Vetere, in August, they had lined the streets with wooden arches, set with lights, for Ferragosto. When these were lit they appeared to cover the street entirely, a canopy of light, a brilliant, coloured arcade. The solid effect was puzzling, a trick of perspective, for the arches were set fifty metres apart, I paced the distance out. As I counted the paces, in the hot south Italian night, I realized I was doing this because Dr Johnson had done so at Inch Kenneth, in the Hebrides.

I had been reading the fine new Penguin edition of *A Journey to the Western Islands of Scotland*, which I recommend. Johnson, impatient with the extravagant unreliability of travellers' tales, set himself to be as accurate as possible, pacing out distances, measuring heights with a carefully notched staff. He believed that without accuracy of observation 'particular features and discriminations will be compressed and conglobated into one gross and general idea.'

He was equally suspicious of MacPherson's claims to have discovered a body of Gaelic verse, by 'Ossian'. He measured all he was told in the islands against his own observation and experience. Seldom does a reader feel so sure that he is in the presence of a writer he can entirely trust.

I had thought of Johnson as a master of the massive, usually incontrovertible, generalisation. His curiosity, and humility before the facts, came as a surprise. So now I am reading *Rasselas* for the first time, and Walter Jackson Bate's biography, which has further opened my eyes. For although I knew that Johnson was physically afflicted I had not known the extent of the psychological impediments he had to surmount. He is a hero of self-creation, and his methods – his 'measures' – must be of great interest.

Dis-conglobated

Once back in London I hastened to the Johnson exhibition at the Arts Council. (The taxi driver was playing Haydn from a cassette, which seemed a good omen.)

The second most striking thing about the exhibition is the number of *prayers* Johnson invented and wrote out. It may have been a common activity of the period, for laymen to compose and write down prayers, I don't know. But surely Johnson is unusual in the amount, and the care he took. It must have to do with his love of accuracy, he wished to make the formulation exactly measure up to the emotion, and the need. He prayed before writing the essays that make up *The Rambler*, because he wanted them to be useful.

But Mr John Wain, in his introduction to the catalogue of the exhibition, suggests that in Johnson this emotion was mostly fear – of damnation: 'the impression one gets is that he is pleading with a tyrant little inclined to make allowance for human weakness.' This is a commonplace attitude to supplicatory prayer but it is not the impression these prayers give me. 'O Lord, forgive me the time lost in idleness, pardon the sins I have committed... look down with pity upon the diseases of my body, and the perturbations of my mind.' The impression is of a great soul baring itself, in 'Hope and Fear'.

Put it another way: we all have an idea of possible perfection, of behaviour as well as of performance, which we fail to reach. Johnson is asking that idea of perfection in himself (call it 'super-ego' if you will, but that is not of much assistance in this case) to forgive him for not reaching it, and to strengthen him in his further attempt. He is performing a psychological salve upon himself, a complex man returning, by an effort of will, to a simplicity that acknowledges its need for help.

> Still Raise for God the supplicating voice,
> But leave to Heav'n the Measure and the Choice.

It is a sane activity and nothing, or very little, to do with grovelling at the feet of a cruel master. He is putting into it the utmost honesty of which this entirely honest man is capable. Of course for him it was more than a psychological trick. He was addressing a God in whom he believed. Doubtless he had an exaggerated idea of his own imperfections, which can be dangerous, as he knew, but is better than no sense of them at all. So these were the measures he took. Were they accurate enough? In his portraits he looks formidable, dyspeptic, dangerous, the great Cham. But the most striking thing in the exhibition is his death-mask. Some will say it is a deceptive grimace, they may be right, but some people will say anything. He looks as though his measurements were not 'gross and general', but were correct; the expression is smiling, relieved, assured.

1984

Aesthete

────── o ──────

GREY AND YELLOW syenite, green and black diorite, baleful basalt, piebald breccia, alabaster, nummulitic limestone and striped aragonite – the ancient Egyptians made small and pleasant vessels out of all these, and it is pleasant to reel off their names. The natural stones had to be noticed, appreciated, then hollowed out and shaped and smoothed – and are now in a glass case in the Burrell Collection outside Glasgow.

Not too many of them, about fifteen, with breathing-space around them and, through the glass wall, trees behind. This part of the fine new building which now houses the Collection, opened last year, was called by the architect, a 'walk through the woods' and it is like that; a ceramic Buddha-worshipper peacefully squats, apparently surrounded by full-grown chestnuts and sycamores that also frame a porphyry head of Zeus.

What must it be like to be a 'collector'? Ceramics, tapestries, armour, stained glass, paintings, sculpture, clothes.... They are all selected and put into order here but what can it have been like for Sir William Burrell? He must have sometimes been overwhelmed by the mounting, toppling pile of his possessions.

Born into a Glasgow shipping family in 1861, he made money by selling his fleet when times were booming, rebuilding it cheaply during a slump; and when times looked up he could undercut everybody else. In 1916 he sold it finally for four times what it had cost him and after it had already nearly paid for itself. With a nearly bottomless purse he now devoted himself to buying objects and continued doing this until he died, in 1958.

The Collection (or selection from it) is wonderful, so is the building that now houses it. Kenneth Clark called Burrell 'more than a collector, an aesthete' and the quality of the things he accumulated is undoubted but, like so many things, raises some uneasy questions.

The paintings and drawings are all right in this respect, they were made to be bought and sold (though one is less easy about altar-pieces). The Egyptian collection is all right (I suppose) because it was for so long open season for tomb and temple robbers. But what about the superb vestments from a Yorkshire abbey? (All right, Reformation loot that has now found a good and public home.) But the entrances to some rooms are doorways from mediaeval churches; one is from the parish church at Montron; what happened to the church? (All right, it was being demolished and a dealer happened to be passing.) And what is the crusader tomb effigy of Don Ramon Peralta de Espés doing there? It should still be in the monastery near Huesca. He was a doughty fighter, Don Ramon, and his tomb has nothing to do with Glasgow except for its 'beauty' and the fine detail of his accoutrements pointed out in the catalogue, poor man. There is stained glass from Rouen ('provenance unknown') and even from Canterbury Cathedral. If the Elgin Marbles ever go back there will be some angry people besieging the Burrell Collection.

Parts of the Collection are like an expensive junk shop of Christendom, which many would regard as fair enough. But beauty related to nothing else has shallow roots, that dry out. The only relation between these objects is that one man with a good eye bought them.

I enjoyed the Collection and am now being puritanical, but it is indicative of unrootedness and some mental muddle when secular objects (mirror backs) are put in the same case as sacred ones (pyx, which belong on the altar) because of similarity of materials and workmanship. And what of the workmen, the artisans and artists who made these objects? They did it for pay, but whatever extra they put into it came from somewhere else.

Whatever I say, the Collection is worth an enormous train fare to go and see. But if you should happen to be haunted by the hands that actually made the things here, brought – you could say wrenched – together from the sale-rooms of the world, go and look at a presumed self-portrait by Hokusai. He is intact from sale rooms, and from collectors, however good their eye. He is bald and blissfully smiling by a river, fishing-rod over his shoulder, a pipe in his mouth. There is probably something

Aesthete

stronger than tobacco in his pipe but he is in a world where beauty makes him happy and has no need of inverted commas because it is rooted and connected with, arises from, things other than itself.

1984

Edward Thomas and Richard Jefferies

―――― o ――――

FOR THE MAJORITY of readers, living in towns, the phrase 'country writer' suggests a writer who brings them news of a distant, holiday world, which they can sigh over for a minute or two, if they want to, before they turn back to the real business of urban living. It is a tag that can put a barrier between a writer and his audience.

There was a rough similarity between the subject-matter of Edward Thomas and of Richard Jefferies – that is to say, hedgerows, old barns, country characters, which superficially makes it seem natural that the younger man should have responded to the work of the older one, and, twenty years after Jefferies's death, which was in 1887, should have written an appreciative book about him. Here are another two 'country writers', it might be thought.

But their temperaments, I should guess, were nowhere near akin. The ecstasy and self-surrender portrayed by Richard Jefferies in *The Story of My Heart* would have been quite impossible for the sceptical and self-conscious Edward Thomas. Jefferies's views, especially the over-hearty, over-simple ones of his early writing, clearly irritated Thomas.

In fact, what fascinates about the two men is not the apparent enthusiasm they shared for rural matters, but the odd parallels of their artistic developments. For when Thomas describes Jefferies's journey towards clarity, simplicity and mastery, part of the excitement, for us who love Thomas, comes from our knowledge that Thomas was to take the same path himself and to arrive as an artist, as Jefferies did, only a few years before his own death.

Edward Thomas and Richard Jefferies

From the age of twenty-one, Thomas was tied to the treadmill of writing, and writing fast, in order to feed his family. This induced such fatigue and frustration in him that sometimes he feared insanity. He worked so incredibly, almost insanely, hard, that Norman Douglas, a contemporary, said of Thomas's life as a literary journalist that, for himself, he would sooner have been blacking boots. Then, suddenly, encouraged by Robert Frost, in December 1914 – helped, perhaps, by the fact that literary commissions were harder to come by, and his world appeared to be breaking up, anyway – he wrote his first poem. It seemed to come out whole, in a style not quite like anyone else's, and for the next two years he continued at a great rate, sometimes writing two poems a day, until the end of December 1916. The following February, he was in France, and two months later he was dead, on Easter Monday. All his poems were crammed between his thirty-sixth and his thirty-eighth year.

It is a wonderful story, a miraculous one, and the similarities with the story of Jefferies are clear to see. Jefferies, too, wrote to order, to please editors, and clearly wrote under pressure, at pace. Where Thomas was tortured by his melancholy and frustration, Jefferies was latterly tortured by his terrible illness, some kind of tuberculosis of the spine that sometimes made it impossible for him to walk, or even stand. But gradually the great last work of Jefferies began to come: two novels, *The Dewy Morn* and *Amaryllis at the Fair*, and the essays of the last few years.

Thomas wrote of the clarification and refinement of Jefferies's genius in 1907, when he himself was thirty years old. Was it possible he hoped the same might happen to him? I would like to think so, but I doubt it. Thomas's despair was almost wilful in its consistency, though I am sure he could not help it, and am sure he saw no light at the end of his tunnel. It is our pleasure to know that there was such a light. However, Thomas's sense of defeat in no way diminished his joy in the victory of Jefferies.

In fact, this biography was written, of all his books, in the most favourable circumstances. The subject was one he would have chosen himself and he was allowed a whole year in which to write it. The result, in Q.D. Leavis's words, is 'a classic in critical biography, to stand with Lockhart's *Scott* and Mrs Gaskell's *Brontë*'.

People and Places

Jefferies was born at Coate, then a small village near Swindon, in Wiltshire, the son of a small and failing farmer, in 1848. His disinclination for farm work, his habit of wandering the lanes and fields alone, apparently abstracted, earned him the local nickname of 'Loony Dick'. Nevertheless, no one was working harder, at observation, at the reception of clear impressions of his native place, and so Thomas begins his book, very properly, with a chapter called 'The Country of Richard Jefferies'. This will serve as an example of all Thomas's country descriptions, excellent at times and at others, to my taste, too flowery – sometimes literally too flowery, as in this sentence about Liddington Hill:

> As he [Jefferies] took deep breaths of the air about its harebell, eyebright, clover, bedstraw, scabious and fine grass, his brain was burrowed and sown with the thoughts that ripened in *The Story of my Heart*.

A little of that goes a long way. Apart from such botanical litanies, Thomas's prose, still, in 1907, contained some of the 'dead rhythms', the literary language unrooted in common speech, which he so detested and struggled so hard to get away from. (In the end, he *did* get away from them.)

However, even in his description of Jefferies's countryside, he soon strikes the note that concerns us. Here he is talking of literary matters, even when describing the Wiltshire Downs:

> Taken separately, the Downs have lines as fair as those of animals: the light wavers on their smooth and, as it were, muscular sides as it does on the rippling haunches of a horse. Yet they have a hugeness of undivided surface... They bring into the mind the thought that beauty – whether of a poet's lines, or of a melody, or of a cloud, or of shining water – is the natural and inseparable companion to passionate, bold, true-hearted acts and thoughts and emotions.

'Passionate, bold, true-hearted acts and thoughts and emotions': he is claiming for art the highest moral significance. For Thomas is a moralist, as was Jefferies and, as I believe, is every great artist.

Thomas then goes on, in two separate chapters, to deal with

Jefferies's ancestors and his boyhood, a careful and detailed job. He always gave his publishers full value for their money. Again, it is the critical asides that stand out. He describes how Jefferies saw the disinterment of a skeleton, and how the sight haunted him. He adds: 'One sorrowful impression of this kind can furnish an acid by means of which even the joyous things bite deeper into the brain.'

How relevant that is to Thomas's own poetry, not yet written and not yet hoped for. He knows too well the gap between insight and expression, however. He says: 'Jefferies early possessed such an eye, such an imagination, though not for many years could he reveal some of its images by means of words.'

From now on, he gets down to the work of beginning at the beginning, the stories published in the *North Wilts Herald*. He is no idolator. He describes them as having 'much facility and exuberance of trashiness'. He is short about Jefferies's early political views as expressed in a pamphlet called *Jack Brass, Emperor of England*. 'It is a jaunty, humorously intended by-product of his conservatism, which served its purpose, if it gave him as much satisfaction immediately as disgust later on.' Of the first novels he writes pages, with pages of quotations. But he sums up his view of these in two cool sentences: 'His characters are persons with much leisure for passions... He is trying to imagine the motives of people who give sovereigns to footmen.'

Oddly – or not so oddly, if we abandon the misleading term 'country writer' – it is the move to the suburbs of London that Thomas believes marks the beginning of Jefferies's maturity. Thomas calls him 'one of the great Londoners... It is not the least of that city's praises that it was part of the culture that made Jefferies's mature work memorable.' He notes, above all, an increase of naturalness. This, he regards as the core of Jefferies's excellence.

But even about the mature Jefferies, Thomas is cautious:

> His judgment... was uncertain. He had, however, by the constant necessity of moulding language to fit a more and more subtle subject-matter, become the master – the still rather uncertain master – of an easy, delicate, often sweet and, without extravagance, luxuriant style. It was not, I think, developed

People and Places

by much conscious effort, but grew to his use like the handle of a walking stick.

Thomas goes on:

> He was now in the main a poet... the old world of 'Fear God, Honour the Pheasant and Damn the Rest' became dim to him. Something he may have lost but the neighbourhood of pheasants, at least, does little good. I knew a parish of 10,397 souls, of which ten thousand were pheasants and the rest human beings, so miserable – except 17 of them at the big house and the rectory – that they were not even worth shooting, or, as far as was known, eating.

Of *The Story of my Heart*, about which he might have been expected to have reservations, he says much, all in praise: 'Its movement, its parallel to Shelley's "Be thou with me, impetuous one!" places it beyond criticism, far within the realms of joy.'

Still he yields no inch falsely to his idol – he admits, in another place, what has to be admitted: 'Something there was in him, perhaps, akin to his uncomfortable humour, which unconsciously repelled – something that creeps into his writings, particularly in the more emphatic parts, and gives us a twinge as at an unpleasant voice.'

Elsewhere, Thomas says something interesting about humour, which is reminiscent of Yeats's contempt for the spirit of comedy. He says: 'It was not twisted inextricably into the strands of [Jefferies's] nature, it was often invisible, and let us be thankful for it, that yet another man of genius has been denied this heaven-descended monkey as a lifelong inseparable companion.'

Of the last two marvellous novels of Jefferies, *The Dewy Morn* and *Amaryllis at the Fair*, Thomas gives a full analysis, huge quotations and their just deserts. At the end of the *Dewy Morn* chapter, he pays Jefferies his greatest compliment: 'There are several places where the easy omission of a phrase or two would have cleared away an awkward fault. It is deftness only that is wanting, and Jefferies was never deft.' That last phrase has stuck in my mind since I first read this book. Thomas is praising a writer for not being 'good' in the accepted sense, for not being good in the way that caused Thomas himself to be accepted – for, in prose, Thomas was deft in a way he refused to be in his poetry.

Edward Thomas and Richard Jefferies

He quotes a short passage from the essay, 'Hours of Spring', written by a man, not yet forty years old, who would not see another spring; and after the quotation, Thomas rises to one of his highest flights of eloquence. He is defining and defending the kind of writer Jefferies was and, surely, in the process, defining the kind of writer he himself wanted to be, and the kind of writer he became.

> Is it not a triumph of beauty and life? It makes for goodness, joy, and beauty in its proclamation that life can endure most dog-like things and yet flourish exceedingly. Always these two truths – the exuberance of nature and the divinity of man. Even if it were all a nightmare, the very truthfulness of the agitated voice, rising and falling in honest contemplation of common sorrows, would preserve it, since it is rarely given to the best of men to speak the truth. Its shape is the shape of an emotional mood, and it ends because the emotion ends. It is music, and above, or independent of, logic. It obeys some deeper law than that which any model could teach. It really has the effect of music, with its succession of thoughts and images wrought into as real a unity as there is in the 'Ode to a Nightingale'. Some would say the effect is that of religious music, but it rebels against all the gods, against all things except life.

1978

In Pursuit of Spring

——— o ———

IN THE YEARS before the First World War, perhaps because of an unconscious sense of impending change, there was a vogue for country books, for celebrations of the unchanging state of rural England. It sometimes seems that no journey was too slight, no observation too trivial – so long as it contained observations of apparent permanence, descriptions of wild flowers, hills, country inns, preferably near London – but it could generate a fee for some literary man prepared to pad out the requisite number of pages. Edward Thomas was swept into the trade before he left Oxford – he called it 'the Norfolk-jacket school of writing' – and his groans to his friends, his increasing desperation at the treadmill it became, form the saddest part of his biography.

Nevertheless, he was the same Edward Thomas who, soon after writing *In Pursuit of Spring*, was to discover himself as a poet; and although he despised, or affected to despise, most of his prose, when writing at his best he was incapable of not giving a special flavour to even his bleakest pages; perhaps especially to those (which are the ones usually left out of anthologies of his prose writings). Also, it is hard for a writer of the present day not to envy him the space he was given and be glad he was forced to fill it. Nowadays we must hurry up with our descriptions, catch the reader's attention quickly or he will pass on, but it is the unexciting small things, the apparently insignificant detail, that touches a picture to life.

In this case, for example, Thomas is commissioned to take a bicycle ride from London to the Quantocks and write (in the original edition) a three-hundred-page book about it. Faced with such a task he takes up the first thirty-three pages describing his hesitations about setting off. But what do we get? Word-spinning, space-filling, he gives us an Impressionist London of shadows

In Pursuit of Spring

and glimmers that is reminiscent of Sickert.

Once in the intense bright of a jeweller's shop, spangled with pearls, diamonds, and gold, a large red hand, cold and not quite clean, appeared from within, holding in three fearful, careful fingers a brooch of gold and diamonds, which it placed among the others, tremulously, lest it should work harm to those dazzling cressets...[A tramp passes, not making a sound] save the flap of rotten leather against feet which he scarcely raised lest the shoes should fall off... Around this figure, clad in complete hue of poverty, the dance of women in violet and black, cinnamon and green, tawny and grey, scarlet and slate, and the browns and golden browns of animal's fur, wove itself fantastically.

All this is seen under changing light-effects, lovingly detailed skyscapes, that make the picture of 1913 London, interesting enough in itself, also a picture of impermanence, insignificance, in the face of the permanence and indifferent splendour of the natural world. It is surprising that Thomas did not make his readers uncomfortable. Presumably he did not, or he would not have received so many commissions to write this sort of book. Yet he is uncomfortable, as he is in his poems. He looks on English things impatiently, but also as a lover might look on his beloved for the last time. He seems always conscious that a world is coming to an end, though he never says so, it is in his tone and it is the tone of his poems; which it has taken us fifty years to hear.

It is not inappropriate to talk of his poetry in connection with *In Pursuit of Spring* because it is the piece of prose that marks his last step towards his poet-hood. He heartily disliked his own tendency to over-write and in this book he believed he had nearly cured himself. 'This isn't rhetoric,' he wrote to Gordon Bottomley, 'tho' I haven't wrung the beast's neck yet.' Very soon he was to meet Robert Frost. The friendship between Thomas and the older American poet has been well-chronicled; it has even sometimes been believed that Thomas became a poet by imitating Frost. Frost himself always denied this.

> I don't know what he looked for from me in his black days when I first met him. All he ever got was admiration for the

poet in him before he had written a line of poetry... Right at that moment he was writing as good poetry as anybody alive, but in prose form where it did not declare itself and gain him recognition, I referred him to paragraphs in his book *In Pursuit of Spring* and told him to write it in verse form in exactly the same cadence. That's all there was to it.

'His black days', his impatience with the kind of book he is writing, accompanies him throughout *In Pursuit of Spring* in the person of The Other Man. (Soon he was to write a strange poem called 'The Other'.) Slowly the reader begins to comprehend that this phantom-like companion who keeps popping up on the trip is Thomas's device for throwing derision at himself. He takes shelter in a bird-shop and watches The Other Man buy a chaffinch, put it in a paper bag 'and with an awkward air, as if he knew how many great men had done it before, release the flutterer'. His relations with The Other (seen as a fellow cyclist) are ambiguous. The Other bores Thomas with a disquisition on clay pipes to which Thomas adjoins *his* views on the matter, lengthily and informatively; The Other does not listen. Then The Other bores Thomas with a series of obsessive questions about Inn signs. 'Did you see that weather-vane at Albury in the shape of a pheasant? or the fox-shaped one by the ford at Butts Green? or the pub with the red shield and the three tuns and three pairs of wheatsheaves for a sign?' And so on. 'And not long after this I was asleep' is how the chapter ends.

It is very odd; as though Thomas felt his own interest in such things, or at least his professional need to record them, driving him mad; as though he is publicly tearing up his own notes and throwing them in the reader's face. Indeed, The Other later inveighs against just such note-taking: 'He rambled on about himself, his past, his writing, his digestion; his main point being he did not like writing. He had been attempting the impossible task of reducing undigested notes about all sorts of details to a grammatical, continuous narrative. He abused notebooks violently. He said they blinded him to nearly everything that would not go into the form of notes; or, at any rate, he could never afterwards reproduce the great effects of Nature and fill in the interstices merely – which was all they were good for – from the

In Pursuit of Spring

notes.' This is fascinating; briefly bursting the corset of his time and the kind of book he is writing, Thomas is publicly debating in front of the reader his doubts about whether he can write it at all.

Another theme, constantly recurring, is Thomas's bitterness against Christianity, perhaps against any organized religion. The venom jets up in the most unlikely places. It is important to remember the cant and oppressiveness of conventional Christianity in his day, yet it seems disproportionate, as though he is settling a private score – perhaps with his father? Or (if this is not to take advantage of Thomas's unanswering Shade) is it evidence of his exasperation with a continuing and painful debate that was going on inside him? At all events, his sneers are uncharacteristic. 'The cows made an excellent congregation, free from all the disadvantages of believing or wanting to believe in the immortality of the soul.' After describing a piece of weather that greatly moved him ('What was done under cover of that deliberate, irresistible raid, only a poet can tell...') he finds himself repeating 'with an inexplicable and novel fervour the words: "Glory be to the Father, and to the Son, and to the Holy Ghost, as it was in the beginning, is now, and ever shall be, world without end, Amen." No possible supplication to "Earth, Ocean, Air – Eternal Brotherhood" could have been more satisfying.' But he immediately counters with a piece of doggerel which 'also seemed appropriate'. This could be tiresome but there is ambiguity here too. It is into the despised Other Man's mouth that he puts his fiercest denunciation, when The Other recites 'with unction exaggerated to an incredibly ludicrous degree' George Herbert's sonnet on sin. 'At the conclusion of this, without pause or change of tone, he continued: "From Parents, Schoolmasters, and Parsons, from Sundays and Bibles, from the Sound of Glory ringing in our ears, from Shame and Conscience, from Angels, Grace, and Eternal Hopes and Fears, Good Lord, or whatever Gods there be, deliver us." This so elated him that he rode on at a great pace, and I lost him.'

Here, surely, is the Thomas who, disliking and distrusting so much of the England of his time, when asked by a friend why he then volunteered to fight for it, stooped, and scooping some earth into his hand said: 'Literally, for this.'

People and Places

But none of these quotations are to suggest this book is merely a psychological curiosity. On the contrary, it is the presence of the writer, in such a book, that gives it its greatest value. As Thomas says of W.H. Hudson, of whom he writes here with penetration born of love, 'the reason of (his book's) power is that it never paints a bird without showing the hand and the heart that paints it. It reveals the author in the presence of birds just as much as birds in the presence, visible or invisible, of the author.' This is equally true of Thomas, at his best, as it is true of all writing that moves us.

Of course, most of the exactly noted topography of this book will be out of date now – it would be interesting to go to some of the places so exactly described and find out if they are recognizable. But the book is pleasing for two reasons: the pleasure of feeling that one is actually in the presence of Thomas, and the pleasure of hindsight. For we know now that the restlessness and anger, the pressure that is building up, will soon be released in the two marvellous years of verse that are to follow. The chains will be cast off, the notebooks thrown away, and we are not just following a good writer on a bicycle, we are following, through his twists and doubts and snarls and epiphanies, one of the great poets of his generation; who of course has no idea, yet, that he is any such thing.

1980

A Traveller in Little Things

———— o ————

WE ARE QUICK to put writers into boxes, to give them categories in terms of what they write *about*. This can be a relief. There are so many books, how are we to find our way among them unless we can say, for example: 'This man wrote about country matters of long ago; we're told he's good but we needn't, surely, bother about *him*.'

I doubt if I would have read W.H. Hudson if a collected edition of his works had not come into our family. That full yard of thick volumes stood on the shelves, rebuking me, until, opening one, cutting the pages, I found myself standing beside (for that is the effect of Hudson: you feel yourself standing beside him, holding your breath a little in case he turns on you, for he can be fierce) one of the strongest literary presences of the last hundred years. As he says himself: 'When we write we do, as the red man thought, impart something of our souls to the paper.'

Even the titles of his books are uninviting to our restless eyes: *Idle Days in Patagonia, Afoot in England, A Traveller in Little Things.* That last title, we discover, is certainly ironic; but even so they evoke a world of parody, of chatterbox book-making.

But what is behind the titles, although in their way they are descriptive enough, is unlike anything, and can only be shown by an example. I shall pick it more or less at random, because not the least remarkable thing about Hudson is that his words and anecdotes seem to reel out of him effortlessly; you can pick him up anywhere along the tape, as it were, and come to yourself five pages or fifty pages later, so easily and naturally does incident lead to reflection, to exemplifying story, and then to further incident. Much has been written about his style, but usually the attempt dissolves into incoherence. Joseph Conrad made the best comment about him; you can sense the professional in Conrad flinging up his hands in despair. 'How does this fellow get his effects?' he asked. 'He writes as the grass grows!' Here is a bit of Hudson, taken from a book called *Hampshire Days*:

> It happened that one day, a mile or two from Lyndhurst, going along the road, I caught sight of a pretty bit of heath through an opening in the wood, and, turning into it, I looked out a spot to rest in, and was just about to cast myself down when I noticed a small white spider disturbed by my step, drop from a cluster of bell-heath flowers to the ground. I stood still, and presently the spider, recovered from its alarm, drew itself up again by an invisible thread and settled on the bright-coloured blossoms. Seating myself close by, I began to watch the strangely shaped and coloured little creature. It was a *Thomisus* – a genus of spider distinguished by the extraordinary length of the two pairs of forelegs...
>
> I had observed this white spider before, but had always seen it sitting motionless on its flower; this one was curiously restless, and very soon after I had settled myself down by its side it began to throw itself into a variety of strange attitudes... Pretty soon I discovered the cause of these actions in the presence of a second spider... This small, active, white creature was the male, and though moving constantly about in the heath at a distance of half a foot from her, it was plain that they could see each other and also understand each other very well. As he moved round her, passing by means of the thread he kept throwing out from spray to spray, she moved round on her flower to keep him in sight: but though fascinated and drawn to her, he still dreaded, and was pulled by his fear and his desire in opposite ways. And so the queer wooing went on, and seemed no nearer to a conclusion, when, to my surprise, I found that I had been sitting and lying there, with eyes close to the female spider, for an hour and a half. Once only, feeling a little bored, I gently stroked her on the back, which appeared to please her as much as if she had been a pig and I had scratched her back with my walking-stick...
>
> I had not been watching alone all this time: when I had been about half an hour on the spot I had a visitor, a small miserable-looking New Forest boy... I told him sharply not to come

A Traveller in Little Things

too near as his steps would disturb a spider I was watching. It did not seem to surprise him that I was there by myself watching a spider, but, creeping up, he subsided gently on the heath by my side and began watching with me... At intervals when there was a lull in the excitement of the spiders I could spare time for a glance at my poor little companion. He was probably 11 or 12 years old, but his stature was that of a boy of eight – a small, stunted creature, meanly dressed, with light-coloured lustreless hair, pale blue eyes and a weary sad expression on his pale face. We talked a little at intervals and I found him curiously ignorant concerning the wild life of the Forest... Nevertheless he seemed to feel a dim sort of interest in the spiders we were watching, and at length our intermittent conversation ceased altogether. When at last, after a long silence, I spoke, he did not answer, and, glancing round, I found he had gone to sleep... Getting up, I placed a penny piece on the turf beside his little crooked stick, so that on awaking, he should have a gleam of happiness in his poor little soul, and went softly away...

For long hours afterwards, I saw the boy vaguely, almost like a boy of mist, and was hardly able to recall his features, so faintly had he impressed me: while the spider on her flower, and the small male that wooed and won her many times yet never ventured to take her, were stamped so vividly on my brain, that even if I had wished it I could not have got rid of that persistent image. It made me miserable to think that I had left, thousands of miles away, a world of spiders exceeding in size, variety of shape and beauty and richness of colouring those I found here...

There are many things to say about that passage but the first is to admit that it is abbreviated, to its great loss, so natural and unhurried is the stepping from detail to detail. The next is the picture it gives of Hudson, alone – always alone – sitting in a glade and becoming enwrapped in a drama that is happening in front of his nose; one that, very likely, we would not have noticed. Capable of losing himself so for an hour and a half, of accepting boredom as he might have accepted rain, capable also, not only of thinking of scratching the back of a spider but of

People and Places

doing so without making it scuttle away.

The adjectives put upon the boy – 'small, stunted, meanly dressed' and so on – are at first sight chilling, and although they could be counterbalanced by hundreds of expressions of sympathy for people he encountered, this is a side of Hudson that has to be faced. It is nothing to do with snobbery – as we shall see, he was quite outside the English caste system – it is more that he accepted no need to *force* sympathy. It has everything to do with Hudson the observer.

Then there is the mention of that world 'thousands of miles away'. Hudson, perhaps the greatest recorder of the face of rural England – though even that is to limit his claims as a writer by too much – was given strength and eye and distance by not being English at all. He was born in the Argentine, in 1841, to an Irish-American farming father, whom he remembered affectionately as a man of 'shining defects', and a New England mother, whom he loved. He was brought up, or allowed to bring himself up, on the wide pampa, with his brothers and sisters, enduring the occasional travelling tutor but never going to school. All his life he despised schools, calling them 'shoddy factories'. Indeed, he had little regard for most of the things we think of as improvements in our lives, though he seldom bothered to scold. He had never been broken, in the sense that a horse is broken, and in the sense that everyone in Europe is put between the shafts and taught to pull, from an early age. It is as though he breathed a wider air, the air of the pampas perhaps, and remembered in his blood, past denial, how life should and could be.

His father was unsuccessful, he became poor in that wild and lonely place. Hudson was happy, solitary and, after a boyhood fever, not strong. As a young man he earned a meagre living by sending skins of birds to the Smithsonian Institute in Washington. He became a Corresponding Fellow of the Zoological Society in London, who regretted the literary, though always accurate, nature of his descriptions. He was thirty-three when he decided to see in person some of the naturalists he had been in correspondence with. With barely more than his passage money in his pocket he left the Argentine pampas and sailed for England. He never saw his ferocious spiders, or South America, again.

It is a strange story. He was trapped at once, because of poverty, in what he called 'the stone forest' of London; this mature man who had spent all his life roaming, free as an animal, one of the wildest and freest places in the world. Within three years he had married a woman possibly twenty years older than himself, because, it appears, of her beautiful singing voice. (As he shows in his extraordinary romance *Green Mansions*, in which the hero is led through the forests of Venezuela by the calls of unseen Rima, half-woman, half-bird, Hudson was almost mystically enchanted by voices.) But soon his wife's voice went. They kept boarding-houses, in London, and were very poor, so poor that on one occasion they lived for a week on cocoa and milk. From time to time, though, he and his wife were able to set out into the countryside. Of these expeditions he wrote:

> The walks, at a time when life had little or no other pleasure for us on account of poverty and ill-health, were taken at pretty regular intervals two or three times a year. It all depended on our means: in very lean years there was but one outing. It was impossible to escape altogether from the immense, unfriendly wilderness of London simply because, albeit "unfriendly", it yet appeared to be the only place in the wide world where our poor little talents could earn us a few shillings a week to live on.

People who knew his work implored him to make a break for it; they could not bear to see this eagle confined among ugly, dark furniture, with a wife they considered unsuitable.

Long before, his brother had said to him: 'Of all the people I have known, you are the only one I don't know.' And there is something mysterious in those years, for there is no resignation, no defeat, in the books written then: his enviable freshness of eye never deserts him. And someone described him as 'a lonely, almost a tragically lonely man', but that is not precisely the note of his writings.

Success did come, slowly. At last, when he was sixty, in 1901, he was awarded a Civil List pension and could move about more freely. Though now an old man, it would be during the next twenty years that he was to write some of his best books: *Hampshire Days*; *A Shepherd's Life*; the novel *Green Mansions*; *Far Away and Long Ago*, the account of his childhood with its unforgettable, simple pictures of an almost savage life; the violent South American stories, *El Ombú, Marta Riquelme*; and much besides. He must have walked and worked incessantly but there is no sign of hurry or strain.

He gives the impression that he is purged of every preoccupation that is inessential. He never rhapsodises about nature, or becomes feverish, as Richard Jefferies sometimes does; he is not a 'nature mystic' in any usual sense; he does not address us, it is as though we overhear him. His reflections on life and death and history, though stark, do not surprise; in the context they seem such as might occur to anyone – always provided, that is, that the anyone happens to be W.H. Hudson. They are natural and suitable, as the steady march of his thinking always is. He writes not so much as a man talks but as a man walks, putting one foot surely in front of the other, so that the motion is continuous, without jerks, sure of its destination and the interest of the journey. One of the books of this later period is called *Afoot in England*, not his most famous, but extraordinary. How about this for a revealing, only apparently inconclusive, anecdote? Certainly I had to read it twice before I saw that one word more would have spoiled it. He meets a colourfully dressed tramp. Hudson likes tramps as a rule, but not this one, who had, he says, 'the stamp of a blackguard on his face'.

> Walking by the hedge-side he picked and devoured the late blackberries, which were still abundant. It was a beautiful unkempt hedge, with scarlet and purple fruit among the many-coloured fading leaves and the silver-grey down of old man's beard.
>
> I, too, picked and ate a few berries and made the remark that it was late to eat such fruit in November. The Devil in these parts, I told him, flies abroad in October to spit on the bramble bushes, and spoil the fruit. It was even worse farther north, in Norfolk and Suffolk, where they say the Devil goes out at Michaelmas and shakes his verminous trousers over the bushes.
>
> He didn't smile; he went on sternly eating blackberries, and then remarked in a bitter tone, 'That Devil they talk about must have a busy time, to go messing about blackberry bushes

A Traveller in Little Things

in addition to all his other important work.'

I was silent, and presently, after swallowing a few more berries, he resumed in the same tone: 'Very fine, very beautiful all this' – waving his hand to indicate the hedge, its rich tangle of purple-red stems and coloured leaves, and scarlet fruit and silvery old man's beard. 'An artist enjoys seeing this sort of thing, and it's nice for all those who go about just for the pleasure of seeing things. But when it comes to a man tramping 20 or 30 miles a day on an empty belly, looking for work which he can't find, he doesn't see it in quite the same way.'

'True,' I returned, with indifference.

But he was not to be put off by my sudden coldness, and he proceeded to inform me that he had just returned from Salisbury Plain, that it had been noised abroad that 10,000 men were wanted by the War Office to work in forming new camps. On arrival he had found it was not so – it was all a lie – men were not wanted – and he was now on his way to Andover, penniless and hungry and...

By the time he had got to that part of his story we were some distance apart, as I had remained standing still while he, thinking me still close behind, had gone on picking blackberries and talking. He was soon out of sight.

That is how the little story ends. No more. The dismissal is complete. Hudson simply remains standing while the other goes on, talking to air. It is an indifference more scathing than contempt. He doesn't concern himself with the hard-luck story as guilt might constrain us to do, however we mistrusted the teller. In South America, survival had been a much tougher business. Nor does he appeal to the memory of his own poverty, hard work, illness, neglect. The man's determination not to see and enjoy is enough for him. 'It's all right for some!' Is not that what the tramp is saying? 'It's all right for some to enjoy beautiful things!' There are times when that seems the authentic note of contemporary England. And what does Hudson say, confronted by that 'All right for some'? '"True," I returned, with indifference.' He had made the natural world his own, his life. It was the tramp's world too. If he chose not to notice, that was no concern of Hudson's.

Yet it was. Hudson opened the eyes of so many. T.S. Eliot somewhere chafes at the idea that art, that literature, is meant to do us good, like, he says, a spiritual dose of Kruschen salts. He may have had reason at the time to say this but I cannot see what else art is meant to do. I agree with Leopardi, who praised a poem by saying that after reading it a man was incapable, for half an hour, of an ignoble thought. Hudson does that for me. His bony, tough philosophy fortifies me, his method delights me, his observations enlarge me. He makes me want to be tougher, less blind and deaf, and more myself.

It is an odd thought that a writer who can do this, who requires no special information in the reader, or any particular effort, who is even easily skippable, for if he doesn't take your interest in one place he is sure to in another, is unlikely ever again to be generally read. What he wrote about is still all round us. He lived no privileged life as a countrified dandy – not in Ravenscourt Park. His matter is the stuff of our lives and his manner is as natural as grass.

1980

Still Companion of the Dew

———— o ————

ABOUT FIFTEEN YEARS ago a London friend visited us in the country and became almost hysterical with delight when she saw a glow-worm. So great was her excitement that she appeared drunk and I am afraid I teased her. Just as I teased her, years later, when she took to tiptoeing round the house in case she put off the swallows who were prospecting us for possible nesting-sites. I wanted them to stay too but it seemed better for them to know what the place was really like. In the event they did stay, as she did not, alas. Shortly afterwards, suddenly, she 'went away', as they say in the west of Ireland, and I seldom see the swallows, which came back each year, and multiplied, without thinking of her, and regretting that I teased her. The intensity of her reaction to the small and vulnerable existences near where we live still lingers there, like a scent. But when I say that the swallows she whispered under came back each year, I mean they did each year until this one. Last summer there were seven nests, and twenty-eight swallows lined up on the electricity wire to ponder the long journey south; but not one has returned. Their absence reminds me of her too, as does the fact that since the night she went on about it I have never seen a glow-worm.

> Ye country comets, that portend
> No war, nor prince's funeral,
> Shining unto no higher end
> Than to presage the grass's fall;

Marvell got the season right but spoils the poem by turning it into a compliment to 'Juliana'. Beddoes, in a stout, English fashion, preferred glow-worms to Italian fireflies, which were beautiful – 'as if the swift whirling of the earth struck fire out of the black atmosphere... but not nearly so beautiful and poetical as our still companion of the dew, the glow-worm, with his drop of moonlight.' A lovely cadence, but W.H. Hudson, who quotes him, also checked up on his colour-sense: 'The light of the suspended glow-worm was of an exquisite golden green, and, side by side with it, the moonlight on the wet surface of a polished leaf was shining silver-white.' What a spellbinder Hudson is. He should be a bore, droning on about not very much, but when you open him, as I did, to see if he had anything to say about glow-worms, it is almost impossible to shut him up again, his sentences unwind like tape, and you are embarked on the next one before you notice. He ought to be set as an example in schools.

But what of glow-worms? Have they gone? The naturalist Anthony Wootton has made a survey of them and is reassuring. They take three, sometimes four, years to mature so any disturbance of their habitat (of the kind that has been going on in England for years) is long-lasting. But they still exist and seem to enjoy railway cuttings. It is the female that glows more brightly; she has no wings and lights her lamp to attract the flying male. There is a suggestion that mercury-vapour streetlighting is set at the same frequency as the glow-worm's lamp and there have been recordings of wretched males helplessly seduced towards the High Street. But Wootton himself puts forward an interesting idea, that it is not the glow-worms that have changed their habits, it is us. They don't light up much before 11 p.m. and nowadays, he says, few people are outside at that time.

Certainly intensive farming has reduced the number of places where they can live; the number of snails, too, on which they feed. They anaesthetise them first. Fabre, the French naturalist, watched them doing it: 'It all happens with such gentleness as to suggest kisses rather than bites.' Then, by some pepsine, the snail is turned into a kind of soup in the bowl of its own shell.

The female's glow is meant to have a sexual purpose, which Marvell doesn't mention and Hudson doubts. He suspects the males are attracted by scent and has seen them put off, scared, by the brightness of the light. Why, then, does she glow? Hudson has his usually sage, cool comment: 'We always find it exceedingly hard to believe that anything in nature is without a use; but we need not go very far – not farther than our bodies, to say nothing of our minds – before we are compelled to believe that it is so.' Good, heretical Hudson.   1986

Gone Before

I

THERE USED to be a feature in the *Reader's Digest* called 'The Most Unforgettable Character I Have Met'. Perhaps there still is. The poet Jonathan Price always behaved as though he was trying to be the Most Forgettable, and was failing because of a curious and attractive laughter that never found expression in sound but was nearly always in his eyes. There was no offence in it: he was laughing at you and with you, and at and with himself. It gave the impression of great intelligence, or, at least, of wisdom arrived at early.

We were contemporaries at university, the same age, and of all of us he was, I think, the first to be published nationally, and anthologized. Whereas our poems were carpentered from hope, bluff, half-understood emotion, his were those of a cabinet-maker who knew how to get the best from his materials; we put ours together with nails and glue and his were dowelled and mortised, his ideas slid in and out noiselessly, and hung true on their hinges. His poems were small in scale and few in number but the accuracy of their making gave them a force which shamed us in our windier attempts, or should have done.

It was a drab time, the early 1950s. Sometimes I think it may have been the drabbest time that ever was or will be. All of us, in our different ways, longed for a time that was warmer, more coloured, more glamorous even; not Jonathan. He wore the time's drabness like a cloak, a cloak of invisibility almost. He listened to our aspirations, dreams, boasts, and said nothing, always with the warming, quizzical look in his eyes. I once asked him, possibly with irritation, whether he did not plan to be a poet. 'Only a *little* one,' he said, grinning. It seemed not that his ambition was modest, but that he was ambitious for modesty itself. He appeared to embrace mediocrity like a bride.

I never knew him well, we lost touch, and from time to time I heard he had drifted into various not very good jobs, that led him nowhere, which doubtless was what he wanted them to do. Also, very occasionally indeed, I came across a poem of his that showed he was writing as well as ever, and in the same way.

Then we met again, after perhaps twenty years, and he was unchanged, the same look was in his eyes. He was working for a publisher, in some unstartling way. When I asked his colleagues about him afterwards they seemed barely to have noticed him. He was certainly being wasted, but that too, he may have preferred.

A year or so later we met again by chance. He looked a little gaunt perhaps but we become used to the changes in the appearance of contemporaries, as doubtless they recover from their shock at the change in us. He said that his poems were to be collected into a book, and seemed reasonably pleased, as I was. Not long afterwards I heard that he was dead. 'Did you not *know* that he was ill?' said the person who told me. But how could I have done? I probably blurted, at our last meeting, 'How are you?' but he was hardly likely to tell me, at a chance meeting in an Oxford street. But I wish I had known. As I say, we were contemporaries, and among these a sudden disappearance is always a shock.

He was dead before his book came out, which is somehow typical of him. It is a modestly sized volume, modestly received, yet I have wondered, as I have wondered in the past, whether he was not right all along; that the patient, disappointed and disappointing life he seemed to choose, and made his subject, is not nearer to the lives of most of us than we care to admit; that, in the least dashing way possible, he had stationed himself in the firing-line and was reporting clearly back to us; that

> Manner of speech depends in part on choice,
> In part on circumstance: when values quake –
> Black, white; right, wrong; on purpose; by mistake –
> One shuns the shouting, trusts the speaking voice.

It was a poet, Anthony Thwaite, who made him collect his

Gone Before

poems for Secker and Warburg and who had them published, recently, under the title *Everything Must Go*. And it is always poets who say the most significant thing about other poets. All of his poems were scattered in various magazines and (could any poet hope for a better remark?) 'this book', says Philip Larkin, 'will enable us to throw away the tattered cuttings we have kept so long.'

1985

II

I first got to know Geoffrey Grigson – who died at the end of November, aged eighty – when he was over sixty, which I regret, because he would have been an excellent man to accompany on long walks. He would know a lot, wouldn't overburden you with information, would notice everything, and always be capable of saying something surprising. Come to think of it, at a brisk walking pace, that nearly sums up his literary and poetic career.

But I knew him long before I met him, from some poems, from his account of his Cornish childhood and, above all, from his articles and reviews, which in the 1950s were like nothing I had ever come across. They were written by a man who belonged to no clique or trend and never looked over his shoulder, fearful of fashion or of losing his stipend (which he did not have). Then I became aware of his anthologies, which are so original and appetising they are the best form of criticism, and his country books which are so informative and unsentimental.

In fact – it must have been in 1956 – I remember a moment when I consciously joined his party, which I already knew was a party of one and likely to remain so, in practical terms, for he flew no banner. I saluted him; a difficult thing to do at the time because I was lying in a bath. On the walls of the bathroom were two charts of the kind that used to be published by Shell, the oil company. The one facing me was of different kinds of molluscs (drawn, I think, by Tristram Hillier) and below the drawings the information was useful and, although in his own phrase 'unencumbered with the waste products of personality', unmistakably by Grigson. I recall that I thought, as I lay back and contemplated the shells and Grigson, that I should not at all mind being such a man. I never would be, for all sorts of reasons, but I had never thought that way about another person, nor have I since. It affected my life. Ever after, when confronted by a confusion of loyalties, a pressure of fashion, or a disinclination to say what I really felt, I realize that I consciously or unconsciously consulted my idea of Grigson and was fortified.

He could be very fierce in his reviews. Sometimes the energy used in his demolishments was excessive, too deliberately personal and wounding. A son of the manse, he could go in for some hearty paganism – 'O to dry never, / To lay bright girls forever' and he could (a serious black mark) pursue vendettas. But it was as though, in a fearless man, one was not being told the whole story, that some inconsolable loss or hurt maddened him, not just the fool he chastised. (Indeed, I have a private thought that the early loss of five brothers had something to do with making him feel an embattled party of one.)

To meet him was a surprise. He was gentle, friendly, a little withdrawn but very sociable. Above all, as his poems show, especially the later ones which poured from him, he was an enjoyer. I had not chosen badly in my bath. It was a delight to see him and his wife together, they got on so unusually well. Jane was at that time beginning to make her name as a cookery writer and this, as well as helping (Geoffrey for years had kept them dangerously afloat on his unbribably freelance pen), had an effect on Geoffrey's skin texture and, to a discreet degree, on his shape. The freelance was being well fed. Her job would sometimes provide expenses-paid trips to famous restaurants abroad and Geoffrey would return looking well pleased, plumper, with tales of mediaeval alleys, and carved roofs, and little-known churches, as well as of old, little-known French poets. For it was not only writers that interested him, or long-barrows, or stars, or mushrooms, there was also architecture, and painting. He was one of those responsible for the revival of interest in Samuel Palmer, for example. He was so long and usefully devoted to pointing out the emptiness of the merely fashionable it is unlikely

Gone Before

he will ever become so. This would be a pity if it prevented him being read, for the enjoyment he transmits, and the sudden sense of freedom. He was very English, and unconstrains us English, who are more constrained than we know.

1985

III

Someone here remarked the other day that at least one good thing about the Roman Catholic Church was that it had 'conquered the embarrassment barrier'. By which presumably they meant that although it was keen on rules (which are more important to some than to others) it had kept its eye on the heart of the matter and could occasionally mention God. But I had a spasm of sympathy for the Church of England. Embarrassment can certainly be noticed in some of its pronouncements but surely this is because much of the time – birth, marriages, deaths – it is dealing with people who don't believe, or sometimes even know, a word of it.

The difficulty is particularly noticeable at funerals. The Church of England can hardly go the whole hog over someone who would have violently resisted such a thing while alive, yet something is often required of it. A member of our family, dying, requested that there be 'no fuss' after her death, and this threw her friends into more botheration, when the time came, than any other instruction could have created. We all wanted to do something, and there were as many ideas as to what this should be as there were people involved. Yet to do nothing at all (so far as that is possible) would be a chill business; and the Church of England clergyman involved, in the village where she died, was remarkably sensitive and understanding.

We need rituals, commemorations, memorials, if only for our own sake. They bring us together while we think roughly the same thoughts, and they satisfy a vague but decent desire to honour someone's life. At least, it seems as if most of us need these things, if the vast crowd that turned up at Philip Larkin's

People and Places

memorial service in Westminster Abbey is anything to go by. And what was especially good about that service, I thought, was the way it met the central difficulty head-on. It was only a few minutes old when this was said:

> ... In particular on this day we commemorate with thanksgiving Philip Larkin, who, possessing outstanding literary gifts, combined distinction with rare humility. We give thanks for his intellectual integrity which would not allow him to accept the consolations of faith which he could not share and which would have delivered him from a fear of dying by which all his life he was haunted. Of this he frequently wrote or spoke and never more movingly than in the lines:
>
>> This is a special way of being afraid
>> No trick dispels. Religion used to try
>> That vast moth-eaten musical brocade
>> Created to pretend we never die.

Putting aside the momentary incursion of Mr Blurb ('never more movingly') it is well phrased, and it was brave, in the midst of such a vast musical brocade, to quote those lines. Outside, afterwards, there were a few who were amused at the Church of England 'as usual' having it both ways and thanking God for Larkin's atheism. But perhaps these had not had a chance to re-read the text.

Inside the church there was Psalm 39, there was music of Sidney Bechet and Bix Beiderbecke and there was Ecclesiasticus, 'Let us now praise famous men', superbly read by the Laureate, Ted Hughes, whose slight regional accent made it (paradoxically, I suppose) timeless and universal. Jill Balcon read 'Church Going', the famous poem in which Larkin takes off his cycle-clips 'in awkward reverence' and stares round the church, the 'accoutred frowsty barn', much as the Anglo-Saxon Wanderer had gazed, uncomprehending, at Roman ruins, and then, as he leaves, donates 'an Irish sixpence'. Someone called even the reading of that poem, on such an occasion, 'an irreverence', which shows again the difficulty the Church of England is in, and which also forgets the last stanza that Larkin, always honest, begins, 'A serious house on serious earth it is, ...'

Larkin gains much of his Silver Classical feel from his reticence,

Gone Before

his obvious dread of embarrassment, which ought to have made him a Church of England man. What he would have made of this no one can tell. Most of us, I think, were glad it happened. It was finely done, and all the better for the central difficulty having been faced at the outset.

1986

Brotherhood

———o———

LONG AFTERWARDS, what I most clearly remember about a trip to Russia – to Leningrad – is two visits to a Russian Orthodox service. One tires, in the end, of trailing through all those gilded, rococo palaces so expensively redecorated (in some cases almost entirely rebuilt) since the war. So much pointless ostentation then, so much pointlessness reconstructed at ten times the expense now. Why? The pavements of the streets are broken, the shops are empty, and one easily forgets how many hundreds of pounds of gold went into the gilding of a single room in the Winter Palace.

Lenin stopped the looting after the Revolution and declared the palaces protected places: 'What was made by the Russian people belongs to the Russian people'. But even the first part of that is only partly true. The palaces were designed for a German queen (Catherine) by Italians, Germans, Scots; decorated by foreign craftsmen and furnished almost wholly with foreign treasures. One longs to see something specifically Russian in them. Besides, there are so many. Catherine the Great herself confessed that her passion for building amounted almost to a disease.

The only unrefurbished room on view in the Winter Palace is the Royal Chapel. It is now a gloomy, dusty place, paint peeling off the walls, gilding peeling off the pillars, revealing the rather crude woodwork. It is like being back-stage at a run-down pantomime, it punctures the illusion of the rest of the gleaming place.

But religion is now tolerated in Soviet Russia. Services were held in the town, we were told – but it was not possible for one to be fitted into our Intourist itinerary. So, one morning before dawn, we walked, a Russian-speaking companion and I, through sleeping Leningrad, to the Church of Saint Nicholas. Not quite sleeping; the cared-for squares near the palaces and official buildings were being washed by little carts, and along the narrow canals, their roadsides not washed, picking their way past piles of rubble, pipes, planks, evidence of roadworks that looked long abandoned, came files of Russian Army cadets, freshfaced boys, marching at ease like a school outing, led by an under-officer with a bicycle lamp.

At last we came to the church and that too was surrounded by puddles, rubble, upended paving stones; its outside was gilt, but dull, its paint swimming-pool blue (like the palaces) but flaking; a tolerated place, not an encouraged one.

We entered, rather diffidently, and under a low ceiling that gave the place the feeling of a candle-lit cave were about seventy people – this was a weekday morning, before dawn – and from behind the screen of the iconostasis (Russian altars are a series of screens that open at various points in the service, and are hung with icons) came beautiful singing from three or four voices, unaccompanied, unseen, half-chant, half-song, extraordinarily musical. A man with a crutch near us kept prostrating himself, wholly, his forehead touching the floor, and then, with difficulty, standing up again. Women with shawls over their heads standing about elsewhere, did the same, but at different times from him and from each other. There were public and private devotions, of great intensity, going on at the same time. Most of the people were old, or middle-aged. Then a priest emerged from a hidden part of the altar and many crowded round him, as though he were a salesman with much-valued goods. He was young and soft-bearded and spoke to them softly. Meanwhile the singing continued and peering round a corner, I saw that three rather well-dressed young people, a girl and two boys, were responsible for that sweet noise.

We resolved to come back, to a full-fig evening Mass, because here was something extraordinary going on, foreign and familiar at the same time. When we did so we found the place packed. Now there were young people also, not many, but some, and everyone crushing up to the altar, joining in the responses with fervour. We were interrupted by a man in a wig, some sort of church warden, who wanted to show us the rest of the church. Reluctantly we followed him up wooden stairs to the main church

People and Places

on the first floor, bedecked with icons of great antiquity in jewelled frames, the Czar's private pew (shielded on all sides by massive pillars) and the balcony where night after night during the war the Arch-priest walked alone, carrying the icon, praying for peace.

But this storey had the air of a museum, whereas on the ground floor some important communal emotion was being expressed, one that I recognized, and could share. I do not mean it was a sort of covert resistance to an atheist régime. I do not think anyone from England – surely the most pagan country in Europe – can crow on that score. And it would be miserable if this short description should be taken as political, an attempt to create further division. The experience was exactly the opposite of that. It was passionate and traditional, gentle too – that singing had no threat, no earthly triumph in it, was something beyond the material, beyond, far beyond, the political; an expression and partial fulfilment of a human need. None of the gleaming palaces expressed anything so important, or universal. There was a sense of brotherhood, and hope for us all.

1984

A Dry Time

———o———

THE ITALIAN WRITER Primo Levi was asked on television, rather surprisingly, whether his experience in the concentration camp had affected his belief in God. The question was surprising in the context because of the vastness of its implications, but almost simultaneously the surprise drained away because it became clear that the answer was expected: that it was not a question but a cue. Levi replied that life in a concentration camp did not encourage a belief in Providence: that he was not 'burdened' in that way. (The choice of verb was interesting: more often such belief is regarded as self-indulgent; 'burden' is accurate.)

It is obviously impossible to argue with a man's reactions to such circumstances, and certainly ludicrous to cite testimony of survivors whose reaction was different. Any mention of the camps, by one who has endured them, makes discussion impossible and in that sense is unfair. But in this case there is another unfairness, a surprisingly common one, and insidious because it is not logical: the implication that if a good God existed he would have interfered and as he did not, in any visible way, he either does not exist or is not good. Levi presumably plumps for the former view because a malevolent Providence ('beneficent care by God or nature', *Oxford Dictionary*) is a contradiction.

But where is the logic in that, or in other statements of that kind? The camps are useful here, for once (normally, as Coleridge said of Shakespeare, throwing up his hands, they are 'outside all analogy') because there is no other horror inflicted on humanity more specifically, politically, man-made. They were an insane political decision, not a visitation from on high. Therefore, why the premeditated question and why that form of answer? Why all such public questions – and they are frequent – if they are not a secular assault, not on a God that may be safely assumed by the

People and Places

questioner not to exist, but on the *idea* of deity that may still be lurking at the back of some timorous and suggestible minds which should have the true nature of reality presented to them. In other words, these questions are a form of propaganda, which ought to be examined because it is not logical and therefore, in its own terms, not true.

Sometimes the questions sound merely curious, as though from another planet. At the height of the Ethiopian famine some Irish missionaries were interviewed, one of whom was apparently holding a dying baby in his arms. He was asked if this did not affect his faith and he replied yes, it did (made it more of a 'burden' he might have said), and in the absence of an appropriate theological answer (if one exists) the question was left hanging, as though it had made its point.

But in a clearly argued paper by two scientists of the University of British Columbia, quoted in the *Times*, a case is made that the droughts in the Sahel are caused by man. It concerns migratory grazing and says the pattern has been disturbed, partly 'by well-intentioned aid programmes' and partly by 'new governments made uneasy by pastoralists' indifference to national boundaries', encouraging them to stay put and thus over-graze. This causes deserts which, because vegetation retains more warmth, reduce the power of thermal currents to take moisture 'provided by that very plant-cover, up to high altitudes, where it condenses as rain'. In other words, deserts create deserts, not 'Providence', and the Sahel droughts were caused by politics.

Perhaps the Western world will inevitably secularize itself, perhaps it is right that it should, although T.S. Eliot believed a culture without a religion was an impossibility, and it is difficult to think of one in the past. But, in the process, let us have some logic and some facts, and not have the blame laid at the wrong door, the existence of which door we are subtly bullied not to believe in anyway.

1985

The Fence

———o———

IT IS VERY MUDDY at Molesworth. As an increasing poundage of Cambridgeshire attached itself to each boot there was sympathy to be felt for the twenty thousand protesters who were expected at Easter.

Even on Palm Sunday there was tension in the air. At breakfast farmers were telephoned by police and asked to block off their lanes and tracks because an anti-Cruise convoy was said to be on the way. By midday the place looked like an open-air agricultural museum, brightly coloured trailers and harrows and seeders in nearly every gap; sometimes with doubtful legality, because they were blocking public rights of way, but there is much about the whole business that is doubtful.

The local pub is not in doubt. NO PEACE CAMPERS is on the door: 'Let them have as many bombs up there as they want, so long as they're ours,' comes from one side of the bar, and 'How would Bruce Kent like it if we protested at one of his Christian services?' comes from the other. The anxiety seems to be about the mess the protesters will make, that they will relieve themselves in public, and steal firewood. This is understandable. It was said elsewhere that the only bared buttocks glimpsed so far, and the only firewood filching, have been attributed to the unfortunate police, whose job is lonely, and has been extremely cold.

There is more in the air than fear of strangers; there is suspicion and dislike of neighbours. For example, some landowners, in no doubt where they stand, have torn up verges so that no one can park. Others, more hesitant, are regarded as 'unsound'. The fence has affected the world around it.

Stretching for miles across the handsome landscape, glinting in the spring sun, are intricate rolls of wire that does not have barbs on it but sharp little flanges like the ones that pluck the strings inside a musical-box. On the other side of this wire is a narrow

People and Places

gap then comes the high tightly meshed fence with more rolls of the wire on top of it. There are regularly spaced tall lights powered by generators whose pounding is heard in the village, and watch-towers round which, in an attempt to protect themselves from the wind, the wretched MoD police have draped polythene sheeting, much of it come adrift.

As we approached along the hedge a policeman leant out of his flapping tower, angled like a yachtsman tacking, to have a better look at us. There were larks above us, and a yellowhammer started up, but when we reached the fence the singing was drowned by the crackle of walkie-talkies.

The fence changed our mood. We had seen nothing in England like it. One of the effects of the mass of wire between us was that we felt we could not talk to the policemen who gathered on the other side of it. Nor did they speak to us, but to their radios. Behind them, what they were guarding was desolation, a muddy wilderness in which there was no shelter for them, that we could see. There has been much illness on the site.

It is said that the missile-base will take up about seventy acres, but six hundred acres have been fenced off, to which the public used to have access, and the fence is within an inch of the farming land around it. The zone of influence of the site has been extended to its physical maximum.

There is a tiny open patch by the main gate where what looked like a couple of families have set up camp; they have planted a flower garden, and coloured ribbons are attached to the wire, making it look almost festive. There is now a fine for attaching ribbons. One of the campers smiled and waved, they appeared eager to talk, but we were not allowed to stop.

There is certainly no room to camp where we went to look at the wire. We were there with my brother-in-law, who farms the field as far as the wire; we were with his son and our son and two galloping dogs. But we were stopped by the local police as we made our way back to his farmhouse. They had been radioed by the MoD police inside the wire.

The missiles have been given a *cordon sanitaire* of five hundred acres. But with relationships crumbling in the surrounding villages, and farmers questioned in their own fields, the fence is achieving a personality of its own, which spreads. 1985

Copper

———o———

YEARS AGO a solicitous and older friend was appalled to discover that I had not read a newspaper for several months. She regarded this as a sign of dangerous withdrawal from the world. In the circumstances she was probably right, and I have dutifully read newspapers, and listened to broadcasts, ever since.

Yet when I remarked in this column recently that listening to news bulletins is a 'lazy interest in the surface of the world' (a mysterious enough phrase, I admit) I realize I was to some extent defending my old position. When we hear, on the hour, by the hour, of destruction in the Lebanon, of murder in Northern Ireland (the list, of course, is endless) we are sorry, and horrified, are convinced that the world is a terrible place, and we turn back (as it is right that we should) to our personal lives distracted by shame and guilt. What we should do, of course, is turn back to them shamelessly, but with increasing concentration. What we are seeing, or hearing about, as shells crash into apartment blocks in the Lebanon, is all the tender associations and accumulations of individual private lives being smashed to pieces. Therefore we should the more fiercely appreciate our own – though not self-protectively, or selfishly. On the contrary, it is by our inattentiveness to the good, large or small, which momently surrounds us, by our refusals of insight offered, all the time, by things apparently trivial, that we shall be judged. It is our coarseness and obtuseness in this respect that makes the gunfire possible.

We all know this, but are frightened of being sentimental, or wet, or of seeming so. To be either of those things is a pity, but so is fear a pity, which is why I propose to write about the death, the other day, of our fifteen-year-old cat, Copper.

She was called Copper because she was brought to us, a stray kitten, by the local policeman. Also because, a tabby, she had a copper-tinged blaze on her forehead. She grew into a good-looking cat with a particularly beautiful face, but what was most remarkable about her, and knowledge of it settled on us over the years, was her gentleness. Voles, young rats and the occasional weasel would not agree; but about the house she padded in stately fashion, with a low murmur of greeting if anyone addressed her, and when she was hungry she never asked for food but sat patiently by her plate until somebody noticed. Unbidden, she used to accompany us on long walks across the fields, a camouflaged shadow along the bottoms of the hedges. I never saw her claws unsheathed in anger even when painfully manhandled by children; she just went limp and waited for it to pass. I took not much notice of her until one day I realized, so soothing was her presence, that I drank peace from her. I seriously tried to learn from that aware self-containment. However apparently asleep, you only had to whisper her name and one ear would twitch, the one nearest the noise (no wasted effort) and she would stretch and purr and settle herself again.

She stopped coming for walks. She, who had grown portly, now grew thin, her backbone discernible through her fur. The vet did all that was possible. The day before yesterday she followed me into the garden, which seemed a good sign, and then composed herself on the windowsill of my workroom. After a while she half rose and stretched and then fell from the windowsill. It is a shocking thing to see so sure an animal do that.

I took her in front of the main fire where she lay, looking healthy enough, eyes open, in her favourite sleeping position, and various members of the family lay beside her. She seemed content, and gentle as ever, and after some hours her breathing stopped.

In the morning we dug a hole for her in the garden and one of the burial party confessed he was almost ashamed, so deeply did he feel. I do not think he need have been. I found myself saying out loud to her, now stiff in that favourite position, 'Copper, for fifteen years you have given me nothing but pleasure.'

To speculate about the form of any after-life, that might happen to us, has always seemed to me futile; about what happens to animals even more so. But a thought struck me: if it is only human souls that survive, in the after-life there will be only us – which is a hellish thought, and therefore unlikely. 1983

Unpompous Circumstance

———o———

EDWARD FITZGERALD described marriage as 'standing at your work-table with a clear mind, and a big bonnet knocking at the door and asking to be taken for a walk'. Thereby he incurred the wrath of all right-thinking men, and women. (His marriage, it will be understood, was brief.)

Nevertheless, families can be powerful disturbers of trains of thought. To take a personal case. Not long ago I began the day with an idea for this column. I had left the writing to the last minute and had about three hours left in which to try and make sense of it. I had those three hours free, allotted, so I rose gaily, pondering my task. But during the course of the night, or at any rate when I was not around, a member of my family had caught his hand in a trap-door and while I was brushing my teeth he appeared, holding his swollen mitt towards me. Clearly a case for the doctor and I the only person to take him.

I read sometimes that the turnover of patients in the surgeries of city doctors is about two minutes a case. Deplorable; but it is possible to feel a pang of envy for such expedition while sitting in the club-like atmosphere of the waiting-room of our local and beloved quack. Everyone seems happily prepared for a long morning off. However, the wounded one was at last admitted and then he emerged, with the l and b doctor, who regretted having to say that there ought to be 'a photo'.

So, an hour later in the nearest town, an X-ray was taken and then presented, in a different place, to a doctor who rested her eyes on it and her bosom bleeped: an emergency in one of the wards. So we sat in the sun under a tree outside the mortuary and waited. It was a long wait, but even I could hardly resent an emergency that had made her run so fast. Even if I had been tempted, the presence of the mortuary would have clarified my thoughts.

People and Places

A man who would automatically be in any First XI of journalists, G.K. Chesterton, has much to say on the circumstances in which journalism is written (or in this case, it seemed, not written). He believes that these should be admitted because it would decrease pomposity and be a move in the direction of honesty if journalism 'dropped its tone of monastic meditation and Papal gravity, and talked a little more about the commonplace conditions of muddle and procrastination and flurry and scurry in which it is really produced'.

(Come to think of him in the First XI – Chesterton is the Ian Botham of journalism; capable of bowling some deceptively friendly overs that suddenly start to take wickets, and with the bat making the game look easy, dispatching to the boundary what are knotty problems to others, with a joyous heave. Come to think of it again – put a big black hat and a *pince-nez* on Botham and he could pass for the Chesterton of cricket.)

Chesterton's point is that the *dailyness* of journalism is its interest and this is precisely what the reader undervalues. So the journalist errs in the direction of bogus authoritativeness when real, confusing life is taking place round him which he feels forced to omit. Chesterton thinks that journalism is only vile when it misrepresents the journalist's own soul, and this is less likely to happen when a man writes hastily: 'The slapdash style is all on the side of morality.'

As usual he is on to something: journalism as an art-form – a performance-art, perhaps. Not as a form of egotism, 'for egotism is even more of a nuisance to the *ego* than it is to other people – I decline to know myself; he is not in my set.' But surely, he asks, matters would be improved if, under such a title as 'Will Australia adopt Bimetallism?' we could read in small letters 'Top of an Omnibus'?

'I state the circumstances in which the article was written because I am convinced that this is the only honest thing to do.' Thus he emboldens me – the boy has emerged, embarrassed, with an unbroken hand – to put at the end of this, 'The Cirencester Memorial Hospital, under a tree, outside the mortuary.'

1985

Zen

────o────

HAVING WRITTEN in the last two or three weeks about dislike of the month of August, and dislike of political obsessives, I have been set free to realize that I am really rather fond of August's blowsiness, and to remember that, like most people, I cherish many political views of my own; the trouble is the difficulty of fitting these into any available political package at voting time.

It is interesting the way writing about anything from one point of view immediately enables you to see it from another, as though there is some compensating force, always insisting on balance. It is the denial of this balance that is wrong with most political writing. But where does that leave two of my heroes, George Orwell and G.K. Chesterton? Orwell tells us that everything he wrote after 1936 was political in motive, and G.K. Chesterton spent his life thumping out his unchanging message. Of course they are different, Orwell and Chesterton. Orwell begins from a position of what he considers to be common-sense and coolly brings everything towards him, to fit it or fail to fit it. Chesterton is the opposite of cool; with outrageous playfulness he is always trying to show that it is only by standing on your head that you can appreciate what things are the right way up (which may be true).

It is the 'common-sense' of Orwell, and the cleansing effect it had on his prose-style, that is perhaps more to our taste at the moment. But when I think of Orwell's books, it is the descriptions of places and people and real-life experiences that I remember, not the political use he made of them. I am not sure many of his books will live because of their political content. I doubt, for example, that *Nineteen Eighty-Four* will long outlast the interest in the approach of that date.

I was recently in the house where he wrote *Nineteen Eighty-Four*.

People and Places

It is on the island of Jura, in the Hebrides, and the BBC were making a film about him there. With television's admirable passion for authenticity – even pedantry – they have refurnished his working-room with the sparse furniture he used. There is an iron bedstead, a worn rug, a suitcase, and a little writing-table (with its back to the magnificent view of the sea). It is the temporary billet of a minor staff-officer in the midst of a fast-moving campaign; it has an air of imminent abandonment, which I am sure is right; Orwell was a restless man.

When I poked about in it alone, while they were filming outside, it was the copy of *Tribune* that drew me, carefully placed on the shabby chest of drawers. It was (of course) of a correct date and contained one of the last of Orwell's free-wheeling columns which were called 'As I Please'. He wrote dozens, perhaps hundreds, of these for *Tribune*, about anything that came into his head: about *The Oxford Book of English Verse*, about house repairs, about planting roses cheaply. He even sometimes went in for nature notes. 'For the last five minutes I have been gazing out of the window into the square, keeping a sharp look-out for signs of spring' does not sound 'Orwellian' but it is Orwell. He then goes on to report a hawthorn bush in bud in Hyde Park (admittedly, it had been a terrible winter). These pieces would not have been remembered perhaps, and republished in Penguin, if he had not written his larger works, but I cannot help feeling that it is on these, and on some longer essays (like 'Shooting an Elephant') that his fame will ultimately rest. It is like a form of Zen; there must be a letting-go, a relaxation, even a suggestion of using only the left hand, before the writing can contain the real man. But of course there must be a real writer and a real man there in the first place.

Many good writers have come down to posterity in a form they barely took seriously themselves. At the moment (things can change) Hilaire Belloc is an example; there must be thousands who have enjoyed his 'Cautionary Tales' who are barely aware of his other work. I venture that D.H. Lawrence will be remembered for *Sea and Sardinia*. It would be a pity if Chesterton were remembered only for Father Brown. Those stories are not Chesterton at play but attempting to raise the wind, to pay for his *Weekly* (in which he printed Orwell). But Chesterton's time will

Zen

come, he is too good to go away.

It is not that a man's views are unimportant, it is what the views make of the man. It is this that comes down to us freshly, is contained in what he wrote when he was barely looking, able contentedly to accept the contradictions in himself without feeling the need to force them into a false coherence. It is possible to dislike August and like it at the same time.

1983

G.K.C., the Mob

———— ○ ————

G.K. CHESTERTON began as a Party Liberal. In fact he began as an art student, at the Slade, but as soon as he started to write as a journalist it was in Liberal newspapers and in what he considered to be the Liberal interest. He early became disillusioned with the Party, and then with the party system, because he did not believe it represented people's real needs. To him it was more like a share-out of jobs and privileges between several, often related, families on both sides of the House, with newcomers like Lloyd George heartily joining in.

For a man of his views, who wanted radical reform, the obvious course was to become a Socialist, like Bernard Shaw (who revered Chesterton) or, in some degree, like H.G. Wells. But Chesterton could not do this because, detesting the abuse of privilege, he also feared too great an increase in the power of the State and, even more important, he was haunted from the beginning by a sense of a broken historical continuity, which he wanted to help mend. This remained one of his central themes. Programmes of Socialist reform concerned themselves with social needs: Chesterton wanted something that satisfied the whole of a man, his spiritual needs as well as his material ones, and came to believe this balance had once been achieved in the past, and then was destroyed by the greed of a rising middle class. This led him eventually to be considered the advocate of a return to a sentimentalized 'Merrie England', which in a sense he was, but Chesterton was more intelligent than that and can be allowed to explain himself. (A chapter of *A Short History of England* is called 'The Meaning of Merry England'. He always delighted in meeting his critics head-on.)

This standing apart from his time, both from received opinion and from progressive ideas, had the advantage of keeping him clear of movements that were merely fashionable – which he called 'fads' – but it also kept him out of the general intellectual drift of his generation, which is something more powerful and significant than fashion, though of course it can be wrong. He became the odd man out among his peers (Belloc hardly counts in this respect because he was a professional odd man out, which Chesterton was not). This was dangerous for Chesterton, and still is, because he wanted his ideas listened to by the unconverted. There are two things to note about this isolation: one is that it never made him sound strident or angry, the other is that he was so popular and widely read it is extraordinary, looking back, to see how intellectually alone he was.

You would never guess it from his tone, which is confident and genially magisterial. He seems always to be addressing a large and friendly audience, past the heads of the 'moderns', the 'professors', the 'scientists' (or, worst of all, the 'modern scientific professors') and telling a receptive gathering what it half-knew already and would now, after his explanation, agree to be obviously true. Possibly these are 'the people of England, that never have spoken yet' and he is speaking for them, as well as to them. Very possibly: 'modernist' Ezra Pound was heard to sigh, despairingly, 'Chesterton *is* the mob!'

He would have appreciated Pound's remark because for him the mob – unintellectual, fundamentally decent, duped – was not a mindless thing, if it was given a chance. He uses the word in his peroration to a chapter ('The Return of the Barbarian') in *A Short History of England*, published in 1917; he is referring to the Great War: 'The English poor, broken in every revolt, bullied by every fashion, long despoiled of property, entered history with a noise of trumpets, and turned themselves in two years into one of the iron armies of the world. And when the critic of politics and literature, feeling that this war is after all heroic, looks around him to find the hero, he can point to nothing but a mob.'

It is possible that even now Chesterton's use of the word 'mob' could be misunderstood. He was frequently and astonishingly misunderstood by his opponents in his own day. He meant of course that the 'mob', the ordinary people, was the best thing about the nation. This was a belief he could not always find among Socialists.

His biographer, Maisie Ward, quotes from one of the many lengthy political exchanges in which Chesterton exulted, and it is worth reproducing because, apart from the continual pleasure to be derived from Chesterton's *tone*, it gives proof of the extraordinary difficulty some minds experienced, despite his patient clarity, in grasping what he was driving at.

He had written to the editor of the Liberal *Nation* pointing out, among other things, the illiberality of the new licensing laws. The editor, publishing the letter, had been unwise enough to add a brief comment of his own. Here is Chesterton's reply:

Jan 26 1911,

Sir,

In a note to my last week's letter you remark, "We must be stupid; but we have no idea what Mr Chesterton means." As an old friend I can assure you that you are by no means stupid; some other explanation of this unnatural darkness must be found; and I find it in the effect of that official party phraseology which I attack, and which I am by no means alone in attacking. If I had talked about "true Imperialism", or "our loyalty to our gallant leader", you might have thought you knew what I meant: because I meant nothing. But I do mean something; and I do want you to understand what I mean. I will, therefore, state it with total dullness, in separate paragraphs; and I will number them.

(1) I say a democracy means a State where the citizens first desire something and then get it. That is surely simple.

(2) I say that where this is deflected by the disadvantage of representation, it means that the citizens desire a thing and tell the representatives to get it. I trust I make myself clear.

(3) The representatives, in order to get it at all, must have some control over detail; but the design must come from the popular desire. Have we got that down?

(4) You, I understand, hold that English M.P.s today do thus obey the public in design, varying only in detail. That is a quite clear contention.

(5) I say they don't. Tell me if I am being too abstruse.

(6) I say our representatives accept designs and desires almost

entirely from the Cabinet class above them; and practically not at all from the constituents below them. I say the people does not wield a Parliament which wields a Cabinet. I say the Cabinet bullies a timid Parliament which bullies a bewildered people. Is that plain?

(7) If you ask why the people endure and play this game, I say they play it as they would play the official games of any despotism or aristocracy. The average Englishman puts his cross on a ballot-paper as he takes his hat off to the King – and would take it off if there were no ballot-papers. There is no democracy in the business. Is that definite?

(8) If you ask why we have thus lost democracy, I say from two causes; (a) The omnipotence of an unelected body, the Cabinet; (b) the Party system, which turns all politics into a game like the Boat Race. Is that all right?

(9) If you want examples I could give you scores. I say the people did not cry out that all children whose parents lunch on cheese and beer in an inn should be left out in the rain...' etc.

It is hard to see that much of what Chesterton complained of in our method of government has changed. This is perhaps unsurprising if the opacity of the editor is anything to go by. He still could not see what was worrying Chesterton. He now complained that Chesterton's criticisms only concerned 'small' things. Considering this was a large part of his meaning Chesterton is remarkably patient in his reply: 'What,' he asks with deceptive mildness, 'can be more fundamental than food and drink and children?'

On the particular point, anyone who has travelled about Britain with small children has had cause to curse the Children's Act of 1910. Only now is some small compromise being attempted, with gloomy 'Children's Rooms' in some public houses and hotels. The larger point, that it is precisely the 'small' and everyday that matters and to this our rulers pay too little attention, is Chesterton's constant theme. Indeed, again and again, with a thousand illustrations, he points out that we non-rulers cannot see the infinite significance of small things either, that we can barely see at all. This could be described, fundamentally, as a religious point of view; it is certainly that of a poet.

People and Places

Chesterton's poems are usually thoughts expressed in verse, or emotion expressed thoughtfully. He is as much a poet in his prose as in his verse, and this can be a useful way of approaching his work. It is certainly as a poet that he dislikes the way we prefer the general to the particular, because it is easier. He puts the point in verse (albeit light verse, but effectively) in a book – *New Poems*, 1932 – published twenty years after the letter just quoted:

>   *The World State*
> Oh, how I love Humanity,
>   With love so pure and pringlish,
> And how I hate the horrid French,
>   Who never will be English!
>
> The International Idea,
>   The largest and the clearest,
> Is welding all the nations now,
>   Except the one that's nearest.
>
> This compromise has long been known,
>   This scheme of partial pardons,
> In ethical societies
>   And small suburban gardens –
>
> The villas and the chapels where
>   I learned with little labour
> The way to love my fellow-man
>   And hate my next-door neighbour.

It is a simple criticism that Chesterton never tires of making but, if we look around fifty years later, there is little sign that it is too simple to be worth repeating.

Thus, among other things, it was the generalized nature of Socialist plans for amelioration that Chesterton did not like, though he was eager for change and, if necessary, revolution; although it is never quite clear how he envisaged such a thing. It seldom is, even in more practically-minded reformers. His political thinking took the form, roughly, of somehow giving back to the people what had been taken from them and this later came to be called 'Distributism', with *G.K.'s Weekly* as its mouthpiece. The idea attracted a following and, having established the idea, the way Chesterton interpreted his political rôle – apart from being badly out of pocket and dangerously overburdened with work because of it – is somewhere between the lines of this gentle, rather sad, rebuke to the more zealous of his followers, in 1929. There had been quarrelling among them:

> ...I could only manage to keep this paper in existence at all, by earning money in the open market; and more especially in that busy and happy market where corpses are sold in batches: I mean the mart of Murder and Mystery, the booth of the Detective Story. Many a squire has died in a dank garden arbour, transfixed by a mysterious dagger, many a millionaire has perished silently though surrounded by a ring of private secretaries, in order that Mr Belloc may have a paper... Many an imperial jewel has vanished from its golden setting, many a detective crawled about on the carpet for clues, before some of those little printers' bills could be settled which enabled the most distinguished and intelligent of the Distributists to denounce each other as Capitalists and Communists, in the columns of the "Cockpit" and elsewhere. This being my humble and even highly irrelevant contribution to the common team-work, it is obvious it could not be done at the same time as a close following of the various shades of thought in the Distributist debates. And, this ignorance of mine, though naturally very irritating to people better informed, has at least the advantage of giving some genuineness to my impartiality. I have never belonged distinctively to any of the different Distributist groups. I have never had time. (*Gilbert Keith Chesterton*, Maisie Ward)

It is important to recognize that it was his practical political concerns that led him to Roman Catholicism; it was not his increasingly dogmatic (in the true sense) Christianity that originally inspired his politics. In a way he *discovered* Christianity, found that for him it contained the solutions he sought, and he makes sure we can track him in this slow process from *Orthodoxy* in 1908, when he describes himself as hardly a Christian at all, but an enquirer, to *The Everlasting Man* in 1925, by which time he had become a Christian apologist. He was not received into the Roman Catholic Church until 1922, when he was nearly fifty.

He is always clear about the stages in his thought and then clear about his position; too clear for some. But the clarity is undeniable, though many still refused to believe that he meant what he said. In 1922 in *What I Saw in America* he puts it in a sentence: 'There is no basis for democracy except in a dogma about the divine origin of man.'

It is a challenge thrown down. It contains two words guaranteed to raise nearly every British hackle, 'divine' and 'dogma'. If the first doesn't do it the second certainly will. But Chesterton believed that dogma, willingly assented to, was the basis of intellectual and political liberty, because it was a shared premise. Perhaps he knew too little of what it was like to live in a Church-dominated country. Shaw tried to warn him, citing the example of Ireland. But that is perhaps not so relevant after all: he was writing in England. He would have had different targets in Ireland, or Spain – or for that matter in the Soviet Union. For him dogma was the frame within which man could move freely, with tolerance. Also, of course, he came to believe in the divine.

But he does not just leave it there, for the reader to agree or disagree. Even when apparently talking about something else, Chesterton is concerned to explain why he believes as he does, step by step, inviting the reader to argue with him. Any reader would have to be more in love with the secularized corporate state than he is likely to be, for him to turn away in disgust at the invitation, even if the writing itself were not so entertaining. However, it is possible that the entertainment Chesterton so prodigally provides can prevent an unwary reader (like the editor of the *Nation*) from hearing what he says. Chesterton disliked the way the world was going and tried to divert that progress: that he failed has caused him to be neglected, sometimes derided, but that does not prove him wrong.

He is, for example, frequently accused of being wilfully paradoxical, of standing ideas on their heads for fun. In fact he rarely does so. His gift is for brilliant analogies, often absurd ones. Belloc called it 'his genius for illustration by parallel...I can speak here with experience, for in these conversations with him or listening to his conversation with others I was always astonished at an ability in illustration which I not only have never seen equalled but cannot remember to have seen attempted. He never sought such things; they poured from him as easily as though they were not the hard forged products of intense vision, but spontaneous remarks.' Belloc also says it is the way Chesterton *'taught'* (he italicizes the word) and Chesterton certainly was a teacher, wanting to help us see, with our eyes as well as, figuratively, with our minds. For so speculative a man he is surprisingly visual. One remembers that he began as an art student, and drew all his life (frequently demons: behind his geniality, or rather at the root of it and of all his work, is a lively sense of the power of evil). But, although his mind was illustrative, he was myopic, and this may have affected his method; he preferred the broad sweep, both pictorially and intellectually, to the focused detail. Not that this led to any vagueness or evasiveness in argument, or blurring of outline; on the contrary, it added vigour to the forward march of his prose, as though it refused to be distracted by brief roadside glimpses. Nevertheless, though he seldom numbers the petals on a rose, his description of landscape (and townscape) and climatic *effects* in the Father Brown stories, for example, are often the best things in them; and they came from a man who was not only short-sighted but who could seldom bring himself even to go for a walk.

His work is filled with pictures, usually absurd ones; here are a couple (from A Short History of England):

> It is almost necessary to say nowadays that a saint means a very good man. The notion of eminence merely moral, consistent with complete stupidity or unsuccess, is a revolutionary image grown unfamiliar by its very familiarity, and needing, as do so many things of this older society, some almost preposterous modern parallel to give its original freshness and point. If we entered a foreign town and found a pillar like the Nelson Column, we should be surprised to learn that the hero on top of it had been famous for his politeness and hilarity during a chronic toothache. If a procession came down the street with a brass band and a hero on a white horse, we should think it odd to be told that he been very patient with a half-witted maiden aunt. Yet some such pantomime impossibility is the

only measure of the Christian idea of a popular and recognised saint. It must be especially realised that while this kind of glory was the highest, it was also in a sense the lowest. The materials of it were almost the same as those of labour and domesticity: it did not need the sword or sceptre, but rather the staff or spade. It was the ambition of poverty.

It is the 'preposterous' nature of these analogies that reinforce our surprise at being reminded of something we already knew: that great saints were sometimes spectacularly unsuccessful men, and yet were revered. It is in fact a paradox. But the analogies are also right in another way; it is of course the 'small' things which all of us know, which are without attendant drama – toothache, elderly relatives – that test our heroism. These are the same small things the importance of which was beyond the comprehension of the unfortunate editor of the *Nation*. Chesterton's work is all of a piece throughout. And the 'preposterous' can lead without strain to a noble and subtle sentence: 'It was the ambition of poverty.' This is only an apparent, not a genuine, paradox. The ambition to be poor we can understand, but now we understand afresh the spiritual poverty of our usual definition of ambition.

Chesterton's paradoxes are therefore not a form of play, they are literary devices, analogues to the paradoxical nature of history and truth. Even the Gospels are paradoxical – 'the meek shall inherit the earth,' and so on. The meek, in the form of monks (with the ambition of poverty) did indeed inherit the earth because by working it and putting it in good order their monasteries became rich. (One of the best chapters of *Orthodoxy* is called 'The Paradoxes of Christianity.')

It is not surprising, with his perception of the drama of the ordinary and gift for truth-bearing exaggeration, that he should feel kinship with Robert Browning and Charles Dickens. About each of them he wrote a book at the outset of his career, and on his chosen subjects he became, at once, an outstanding literary critic before there was such a thing as 'literary studies' and before Dickens, certainly, was fashionable.

In 1903, *Robert Browning* marked his commencement as a writer of books, as opposed to short pieces and poems. He was twenty-nine, and the book bursts with pent-up energy and ideas. He said of it later that it was really filled with themes of his own, 'a book in which the name of Browning was introduced from time to time, I might almost say with considerable art...' There ought to have been a law to prevent Chesterton saying things like that about his work because there were too many prepared to take him at his word. It is a brilliant book, illuminating about Chesterton (as it ought to be) and illuminating about Browning because Chesterton understood him.

But Chesterton always refused to speak seriously about himself and therefore there are those, bewilderingly, who cannot regard the work as serious. Because his touch is light they think his head is, whereas it would not be difficult to make a case that there is no more serious writer. Hardly a line of the enormous number he piled together is not concerned with the sort of questions liable to empty a room, such as 'the meaning of life', how we can best understand it, and live it. His touch was light because he was more interested in winning an audience than in status. He continued to work through Fleet Street because, doubtless, he enjoyed the fray and the companionship, but also because he cared more for his message than he cared for himself. Few men of genius have been so little interested in posthumous fame.

He probably did not care for himself enough. The size of his output was certainly bad for his health. Apart from commissioned books he wrote a long column in the *Illustrated London News* every week for thirty years (refusing to ask for an increased fee when he could have asked for anything he liked, because they had helped him with regular work when he needed it most). There was also, for years, the column in the *Daily News*, a multitude of regular or semi-regular contributions elsewhere, lectures all over the country, 'Father Brown' stories and novels and poems and long public controversies like the one quoted from the *Nation*; there were also public debates with people like Shaw. It was too much. In 1909 his wife managed to move them from London to Beaconsfield (which, contrary to the murmurs of disgruntled friends, who missed him, Chesterton makes clear he enjoyed) but the output continued as great. Between 1909 and 1915, apart from a quantity of journalism that would break any normal man, twenty-one books were published. Some of these were collections of newspaper pieces and stories, but the list includes three novels (*The Ball and the Cross, Manalive, The Flying Inn*), studies of Bernard Shaw and William Blake, *The Victorian Age in Literature*, a full-length epic poem *The Ballad of the White Horse* and a play, *Magic*. His absence of mind became legendary, but it was inevitable; he must have been composing sentences in his head, when he was not actually writing them, most of his waking hours. The jolly, bibulous journalist that Chesterton was happy to be considered had become almost pure mind.

But of course he kept that a secret, until in 1915 he collapsed and lay in a coma, or near-coma, for several months, his life despaired of.

After his recovery (when he immediately asked for newspapers; back numbers so that he could trace in detail the course of the War), Shaw wrote to tell him, 'You have carried out a theory of mine that every man of genius has a critical illness at 40, Nature's object being to make him go to bed for several months. Sometimes Nature overdoes it: Schiller and Mozart died.'

There is a lessening of élan after the recovery. There were many reasons for this: the war, of course; the misery of the Marconi Affair (in which his brother Cecil more or less took on the Government, accusing people connected with it of corruption). The malign atmosphere of this episode, in which he supported his brother, deeply distressed Chesterton; it seems he lost the last of his trust in public men. Then in 1918 Cecil died and, out of love for him, Chesterton continued his brother's political crusades; these involved him in burdensome editorships, culminating in *G.K.'s Weekly*, which were not only a drain on his pocket but also on his health.

But apart from these griefs and burdens that weighed down the wonderful springiness of his early style, there was also the natural disappointment, bound to come as the years pass, of a champion who sees that his causes will not triumph in his day, that for all his efforts the world goes on as before, or goes on worse. But Chesterton never became exasperated, as most men do. Although it is true that after the death of his brother he was guilty for the first and last time of violent language in public, it was to do with one of his dead brother's bitter battles, the Marconi Affair.

Yet, if one suspects a final diminution of energy, there comes *St Thomas Aquinas* (1933), a brilliant book on so tricky a subject that the Thomist philosopher Etienne Gilson threw up his hands in admiration and despair: 'The few readers who have spent twenty or thirty years studying St Thomas Aquinas and who, perhaps, have themselves published two or three volumes on the subject, cannot fail to perceive that the so-called "wit" of Chesterton has put their scholarship to shame.' Before that, in 1925, there had been *The Everlasting Man*, a massively ambitious work in which Chesterton attempts to pull together and in some sense systematise his whole view of the world. Its aim is to adjust an anti-Christendom imbalance in H.G. Wells's enormously successful *Outline of History* (which Chesterton admired) and so, despite its length, it can be considered yet another salvo in the continuous battle Chesterton conducted, more or less single-handed, with his time. Some have considered it his most important book. And there is the posthumously published *Autobiography* (1936) which is among his best books.

When he was received into the Church, thirteen years before he died, it was natural that the Church should use, and over-use, so notable a convert. His explicitly Roman Catholic work often suffers both from a too great sense of responsibility towards his subject, which is a form of humility, and a new sense of exclusiveness; for the first time he can sound too aggressively flippant to his opponents. The faltering in tone is only occasional but in a man whose tone is normally so exceptionally agreeable, it is audible. Also, his explicit Christianity, his view of 'Christendom' as a continuing imaginative and spiritual entity, could lead him not so much into mistakes as into mistaken emphases. He undervalued Oriental mysticisms, for example. He was much less than fair to the influence of Islam and, notoriously, was led to make some (but not many) regrettable remarks about the Jews.

The violent language mentioned earlier, after the death of his brother, was addressed to Jewish politicians and financiers such as Godfrey Isaacs, whom his brother had attacked. In an Open Letter to Sir Rufus Isaacs (by this time Lord Reading) he talks of the Isaacs 'tribe' and says: 'You are far more unhappy than I; for your brother is still alive.' Grief had unbalanced him, but he detested Imperialism and Capitalism anyway, and suspected some highly-placed Jews (it is important to remember that his criticisms were aimed at men of great power) of manipulating both of these to their own, supranational ends. He did not believe they could be loyal to his concept of Christendom because they did not belong to that tradition. He was not a racialist, he disbelieved in the existence of continuing racial characteristics in the displaced and frequently says so, scornful of the 'Teutonism' that was becoming fashionable in pre-War England. He did not object to these men on grounds of race but because of what he suspected about their personal behaviour, which he thought derived from their religion, whether they were religious or not. He was a Zionist because he believed a man could only be loyal to his own tradition. That Jews could become loyal Englishmen he appears not to have believed. If he did not do so he was wrong, but so would we be wrong, with our special and terrible hindsight, if we condemn him too much. Such views were a distasteful component of the atmosphere of his time and are almost the only example of Chesterton, consciously or unconsciously, breathing that atmosphere without caution. There are those who blame this on loyalty to his brother, and on the influence of his friend Belloc. But Chesterton can bear the responsibility himself. He early detected the threat of Hitler, and warned against him when hardly anyone else had noticed. He continued to do so when the Government began to parley with the Nazis. To say that some of Chesterton's best friends were Jews will only raise a sad smile, but it was true; however, financiers, and above all non-Christian financiers, clearly worried him to distraction.

But what is most remarkable about Chesterton, considering what a battler he was, is not his enmity but his lack of it. It is astonishing how few enemies he made, if he made any. It was always to be seen that it was the idea he hated, not the man. The man he enjoyed; and, if he could, liked. The more one reads Chesterton, and thinks about him, the more it becomes clear, quite apart from his views, how extraordinarily 'Christian' he was, in the everyday use of that word. He approaches most people's idea of a good man. His brother made many enemies, so did Belloc, who gloried in doing so: 'There is something sundering about Hilary's quarrels,' Chesterton was heard to murmur, sadly. His were not like that. Indeed, Belloc regarded this as a weakness in him, and was wrong, because Chesterton's lack of interest in drawing an individual's blood on particular issues keeps the issues clearer, makes them remain of interest to us.

If Chesterton was 'a genius who never wrote a masterpiece' a sense of masterpiece persists, though it is difficult to point at a book and confidently say, 'There, throughout, he is at his best.' Early in his career he was accused by outraged publishers of villainously misquoting Browning. He replied, rather grandly, 'I quote from memory both by temper and on principle. That is what literature is for; it ought to be a part of the man.' Perhaps that is where the impression of a masterpiece lies, in the part of the man that is his work. As his 'critic of politics and literature', looking for a hero of the Great War, could only point to the mob, so perhaps, looking for a masterpiece, we could point to the mob Ezra Pound called Chesterton.

1985

Beyond Hagiography

———— o ————

GRAHAM GREENE, in the Preface to *John Gerard: The Autobiography of an Elizabethan*, (Gerard was a Jesuit priest caught and tortured under Queen Elizabeth), remarks that one of Gerard's examiners in the Tower was Francis Bacon, and Greene is tempted to wish that Bacon had indeed been Shakespeare, because in Shakespeare's plays there is everything, except one thing: a character or passage throwing light on the religious confusions and persecutions of his time. Greene says: 'the martyrs are quite silent... One might have guessed from Shakespeare's plays that there was a vast vacuum where the Faith had been.'

There was no vacuum, there was a frenzy, too dangerous for Shakespeare to mention. It is difficult to make sense of it all even now, because of the prejudice that continues, on all sides. Also, if you try to do so it is difficult not to be sidetracked by interest in the characters involved, as I have been distracted by the personalities of the young English Jesuits who smuggled themselves into England, towards almost certain death, to give comfort to those who clung to proscribed religious ways.

At least, that was their stated intention, though no English government believed it at the time. It was thought that they planned to kill the excommunicated Queen. In fact the Jesuits were expressly forbidden to meddle in politics, by Rome, but the very source of this order would have been enough to make the government savage. England, rightly fearful of Spain, was introducing something national and new, and here were men taking orders from what was old, international and favoured by her enemies.

It comes as a surprise, therefore, to find that for a couple of years after they secretly landed, Henry Garnet and Robert Southwell were the only two Jesuits operating in the country. From the vigour with which they were pursued one would have thought

Beyond Hagiography

the place was black with them. They were both cultivated, intelligent men, Garnet an organiser, Southwell a poet, and they were both caught, tortured and executed. One of Southwell's examiners was Robert Cecil: 'They boast about the heroes of antiquity,' he said, years later, 'but we have a new torture which it is not possible for a man to bear. And yet I have seen Robert Southwell hanging by it, still as a tree-trunk, and none able to drag one word from his mouth.'

John Gerard was part of the next wave; he also was captured and tortured, but he lived to write an account of his experiences (translated from the Latin by Philip Caraman) which shows him to have been superstitious, practical, idealistic, and almost unbelievably brave.

After about three years of imprisonment he even managed to escape from the Tower. From his cell window he discovered that there was another Catholic, not a priest, and therefore in looser confinement, in the nearby Cradle Tower. He talked his warder into allowing him to visit this man. When in the Cradle Tower he was surprised to notice how near it was to the moat and the outer wall. So he wrote to his Superior (Garnet) asking if it would be all right to escape. (He wrote secretly, in orange juice – how odd that he should have oranges. All the details are surprising.) Permission was granted, more orange juice notes were passed to faithful laymen outside, arrangements were made to exonerate the innocent warder, the rescue party set out along the Thames, was delayed, caught by the tide, sank and nearly drowned. Gerard could hear their cries. To his astonishment (easy to imagine) the same party set out the next night, he drew up the rope, attached it to a cannon, sent his friend across first, whose passage made the rope sag nearly into the moat. Somehow, sticking, nearly fainting, he dragged himself down and up, this man who had undergone the torture to his arms described by Cecil. For a year he carried on as a priest a few streets away from the Tower. Then the hunt for him became dangerous to others and he escaped to Flanders. Did Shakespeare know of these extraordinary contemporaries? Ben Jonson knew of Southwell, said he would have sacrificed some of his own works to have written 'The Burning Babe'. There is more to be found in that passionate time, for too long obscured by prejudice.   1986

Credit Where Credit Is Due

———— o ————

SPARE A THOUGHT for Grosart, Alexander Balloch, 1827-99: 'All his literary work was marred by egotism, a want of taste, diffuseness, and clumsy arrangement of his materials. Yet by means of his elaborate series of reprints of Tudor and Jacobean writers, whose works were rare and almost inaccessible, he conspicuously advanced the thorough study of English literature.'

Handsome of the *Dictionary of National Biography* to add that last sentence, I must say, and I wonder whether the author of the entry had edited *one* 'rare and almost inaccessible' author, whereas Grosart tackled dozens. If you try and track down almost any old unfashionable poet, or a minor one (as well as some who have, since Grosart's day, become very famous indeed), you stumble across Grosart's work and are grateful. His scholarship has doubtless been superseded, but of the many who tidied the disordered sheaves of English verse, so that we can now have our annotated editions, and our clean texts in anthologies, Grosart stands out as a hero. The *DNB* does not even list all the authors whose texts he put in some sort of order in his *The Fuller's Worthies' Library*, at his own expense, but here are a few: John Davies (3 vols), Fulke Greville (4 vols), Henry Vaughan (4 vols), Andrew Marvell (4 vols), George Herbert (3 vols), 'besides the poems of Richard Crashaw, John Donne, Robert Southwell, Sir Philip Sidney, and others'. The 'others' included Quarles, Cowley, Daniel, Spenser... Why is there not a statue to this extraordinary man? We too often honour the wrong people. London is littered with memorials to obscure generals but there is none, I think, to Chadwick, who designed the drains which, in a sense, was what Grosart was doing, cleaning up for us the chaotic, 'rare and inaccessible texts'.

He was a Presbyterian minister in Blackburn (the membership

Credit Where Credit Is Due

of his church nearly tripled after his arrival) and this gives extra force to his description of the Jesuit poet Southwell's execution as 'judicial murder'. 'I should blush for my Protestantism if I did not hold in honour, yea reverence, his stainless and beautiful memory.'

The *DNB* has no right to be sniffy about such a man. True, in his introduction to his Southwell, he makes too much of 'the travesties on editing and mere carelessness of WALTER (1817) and TURNBULL later (1856) in their so-called editions' but that is only an advertisement for all the work he found he had to do, and is almost irresistible to an editor who now believes that he has the texts right.

He loves Southwell, 'the sweet singer', but, to my taste, Southwell seems often too much in love with easeful death, which, because of what we know of his fate, is worrying. Of course, a wish for death is natural if you believe the next life is better, but it does sound ungrateful to this one. Although not at all gloomy he is certainly short on praise of the joys of this world. I speak only of his poems, which were didactic in intention; he could take a secular lyric, gut it, and turn it into a religious poem, complaint to an unkind mistress becoming pleas to an elusive God. If his example had been followed we might have been saved some tiresome Cavalier addresses to *Chloe*. There are suggestions that Shakespeare listened to him and added depth to his *Rape of Lucrece*. In his dangerous work among men Southwell was tireless and, by every account, joyous. There are in his poems some sweet tunes:

> While pike doth range the silly tench doth fly,
> And crouch in privy creeks with smaller fish;
> Yet pikes are caught when little fish go by,
> These fleet afloat while those do fill the dish.
> There is a time even for the worm to creep,
> And suck the dew while all her foes do sleep.

Grosart has a long and useful note on the word 'silly', meaning 'innocent, harmless'. It is a favourite of Southwell's; Shakespeare and others use it in the same sense. All Grosart's work is useful, and it is pleasant to be able to give him credit for it. It is good too, remembering the particular horror of Southwell's last three years (most of them in solitary confinement after torture, lousy, maggot-ridden), to learn from his biographer, Christopher Devlin, that he spent a holiday, just before his betrayal and arrest, with his Copley cousins, one of whom had finally disgraced himself at the English College in Rome by attempting to preach a sermon with a rose between his teeth.

1986

September 1984

―――― o ――――

HAS ANY ENGLISH SUMMER, or English autumn, arrived so exactly as it should? Or as we imagine that it should, for presumably our usual complaints suggest our belief in the existence of some norm from which our weather is always departing?

This seems worthy of remark, and of celebration, and this is the place, because weather-talk goes on nowhere else, except as passing exchanges when we can think of nothing else to talk about, but feel silence would be rude, or from weather-men on television and radio who speak with a pace and intonation so different in all ways from normal human speech (and sometimes with inexplicable sadness) that they are almost impossible to listen to.

But this year, 1984, summer began when it is meant to, but very seldom does, in May. From that time on it remained summery. There were occasionally what seemed to be changes of mood but these proved to be temporary, fretful changes of expression that soon passed. We woke up each morning, at least in this part of the nation, to clear or almost cloudless skies, and the promise of warmth.

Then, last month, and on time, there fell long periods of haze which was not quite that. It was a sensation, on the eye, of an air filled with undrifting blue smoke, or that one's eyesight was failing. Nothing was quite clear.

After that came September, and thoughts of autumn, but still little sign of it, in wind, or change of warmth. Swallows had already begun making fresh nests, as though they sensed there was time.

But today, prompt and unmistakable as a monsoon, there is the sudden need for a jersey and, at night, a fire in the grate. It was possible to observe the change happen, there was no declension into 'slow, sad Michaelmas', it happened yesterday afternoon, September the ninth, or at least it did here.

Suddenly, there was a wind, a great wind, the sky darkened and then thick, angled rain arrived with no preliminary warning spatters, it just fell, in shining ropes. The flowers and bushes leant right over in the wind, leaves flew off trees, in a near darkness, and the angle of rain and flowers and leaves was to the east. It was a west wind, come suddenly from the Atlantic, and so obviously and dramatically bringing autumn in its train that it seemed worthy of a poem, even of an ode, until it was remembered that it had been so celebrated, more than once or twice. Odd how observant those olden-times townees must have been.

Then the rain stopped and the sun shone, picking out fields bright against the blue-grey background, as so often happens in the West of Ireland, on the Atlantic itself; and then huge, gold cloud-banks grew and towered, 'an Atlantic high / Prince of vapour... Cloud royal' as Ivor Gurney said, the best of sky-men, looking up long ago not far from here.

This morning the swallows are toppling out of the new nests and sitting in lines on the barbed-wire fence, both bewildered and twitteringly excited, like a young human family when the Pickford's van has arrived.

Things may change again, a Saint Martin's summer on its way, or winter come freakishly early. But that was autumn arriving yesterday, brusquely announcing itself, both exciting and disturbing for us, as it is for the swallows. For the onset of autumn is a melancholy time, more perhaps with each passing year of our lives. It is the impersonality of the weather, of the seasons, that causes us to think. Which is why in the account of it the attempt has been made to avoid the first person singular, which is as tiresome sometimes to the writer as it is to the reader, for it gives an impression of self-involved twitterings; but the avoidance is difficult, as are some of the reflections that arrive with autumn.

1984

Mentioned in Dispatches

———o———

BECAUSE IT IS exciting and coloured and will be forgotten next week, and because it happens so rarely – about once every ten years – and because it is going on now, at this minute, it is worth describing the brilliant turbulence that has struck this part of the world, which has been, until last night, almost weirdly still for weeks.

Today trees are making sea-sounds, birds hurtle at twice their normal speeds, yellow leaves leap everywhere like mice and just now gnats, or gnat-like creatures – they seemed too small for gnats, almost like grains of powder – were being blown about in such great clouds, in bright yellow light, that it seemed a sudden dust-storm, or some inexplicable sea-fret, or Scotch mist. But there is nothing whatsoever misty about the day, which is theatrical in its clarity and movement and assertion. Theatrical, too, in its lighting, because whorled clouds are moving almost as fast as the birds, sometimes covering the low sun and everything goes grey for a moment. Then they move on, and it is as though a galloping team has dragged the vast grey tarpaulin away at great speed, the fields are revealed as lime green again, or yellow brown and the shadow over them disappears, in a straight line. Along dulled hedges it is as though someone runs, sweeping them with an enormous yellow brush.

It all began last night. For days, for weeks, there had been no wind, and this is the first ingredient for a coloured Fall, because leaves have time to change colour. Round here they are usually torn off still green. But not this year, which has been like the one remembered from the 1960s when leaves stayed on almost unnaturally long and then there came a puff of wind and cars had to stop on country roads – at least they did on that day near Salisbury – because they were suddenly darkened with the fall of leaves, and then we continued between trees wholly bare, crunching through drifts up to our hubcaps.

Through last week's stillness came shafts of sun which made everything stand out so clear and brilliant, especially the field maples – an unsung tree, the autumn field maple – that however preoccupied you were you would have to be mad not to stop and stare.

It could not go on, the season had to change, things had to be stripped, but often this takes place almost imperceptibly, under wraps.

However, last night the wind began to blow, very hard. It was eerie, there were so many different kinds of noise after so long a silence. It whined in the window frames as if wasps or bluebottles were trapped there, it volleyed in the chimney like distant gunfire, even the stairs creaked, and it blew the coal-fired oven so hot that the cooking part of it began to glow white like something in a Spielberg film, and all the lids and oven doors and the flue-cover had to be opened, until the kitchen was like the hothouse at Kew, and this amid the gustings and buffetings and shrieks of the wind outside.

So this morning everything was expected to be bare, and winter on its way. But it was not bare at all. Gone a little thin on top, perhaps, some of the trees. The compact, toasted-cheese-on-broccoli effect of the field maples and beeches was rifted, their coloured wigs had wider partings, showed more sky-scalp. But they were still battling, losing leaves one by one that blew off almost horizontal. They are doing this now. We should be out in it, exulting, but the north wind has an edge to it and, besides, this dispatch has to be written; this review, rather, for here is drama, the whole place is roaring, swaying and counter-swaying under an intermittent floodlight that sometimes defines every contour and makes you see the Bersagliere shot-green colour in what usually appears as the black in magpies.

These progress across the field with their self-important standing-jumps, both feet together. The sheep have hulled-down, facing the wind, and do not impede the magpies, who jump on their backs. The sheep take no notice. But one has gone too far and landed on a sheep's forehead, and the sheep shakes it off with the impatient jerk of the chin a New York short-order cook uses to ask what you want.

1985

Looking for a Lane

———— o ————

WHEN I TOLD people in New York that I wanted to go in search of the American countryside – not awesome scenes to whoop at, like Utah, Colorado, Arizona, but muddy dairy farms, and dozy country towns – they looked politely anxious. A taste for such apparently mild explorations is not an American characteristic. This was one of the reasons why I wanted to do it, being fairly certain that not too many others had done it before. They even doubted whether such places still existed; they were literary people, they all loved their Thoreau, but none of them would have been tempted to imitate him, or thought it possible. In this they surely differ from their English counterparts, in the back of whose minds such a dream often persists. Without much conviction they mentioned Stockbridge as a good place to go, in upstate New York, and their unanimity gave me doubts.

I decided to follow my nose, their ignorance of their own hinterland making me feel I was doing something uniquely intrepid, and I also decided not to burden myself with a car. One experiences so much more without a car. Ah, the innocence of those first hours in the United States...

New York State stretches all the way up to Canada, and in a bus station big as an airport, ten dollars fifty bought me a ticket to the State capital, Albany, a hundred and fifty miles away, and that seemed a reasonable place to start.

The near-empty bus headed north through a part of New York as old-looking and messy as London, and with the same air of having been blitzed not long ago.

Every European remarks on the *size* of America, but I had not expected to see space so cheerfully wasted. The houses cling to the Highway, with nothing but space behind them, so do the shops and discount-stores that the houses depend on. There is

People and Places

sometimes miles between the houses, seldom less than a hundred yards. It makes Europe seem cosy by comparison. They are right at the edge of the road, among stands of old trees, with streams running past them; white-painted clapboard 'residences' – no other word seems suitable for such discreet elegancies – with lawns so neat they look artificial, in places with Indian names, like 'Mah Wah'. Except that they are not 'places' at all; the metal Township boards that declare their names seem to have been set up arbitrarily, measuring the long strip of houses into lengths. There is no centre, no church, pub, local shop. If the houses are discreet the occasional vast store has no such inhibition: 'Tom the Tent Renter', for example, proclaims his wares from a 'Tyrolean' mountain-hut not much smaller, or lower, than a Tyrolean mountain.

What is clear is that everyone clings to the road (however carefully separated from his fellows) because whatever life there is moves along that road, and if he wants to see a friend, or buy a can of beans, he has to move along it too, in a car, which I did not have.

Albany arrives with a plume of factories, a rotundity of oil tanks, and a burly cab-driver immediately offers himself, taking it for granted I want to move on. But I point to an old-looking hotel. He shakes his head: 'Taken over by the legislators,' he says bitterly. 'Round here is dead after five. All legislators. They go home.' So I ask him to drive me towards Life and we go through a series of what seem to me suburbs. 'Where's the town-centre?' I ask. 'This is it,' he says, and I look out through rain at a Shopping Precinct: supermarkets, cinemas, wet asphalt, and nothing else, not even people. You drive in to the drive-in shop, sit in your car to watch a movie and then drive back to your distant house, distant from other houses. I had no house, and all six motels, a mile apart with nothing in between, were full. 'Must be those damned legislators,' muttered the taxi-driver.

In America, without a car, you are done for.

After a struggle I yielded, and found a car in Pittsfield, Massachusetts, where I heard the editor of the *Berkshire Eagle* deploring 'this damned automobile culture' on the telephone; to the BBC, of all people. I told him my tale, asked him where to go, and he suggested – Stockbridge. It seemed fated, so I gingerly pointed

Looking for a Lane

my newly-hired Toyota in that direction. ('You want a *small* car?' said Jake the hire-man, interested. Later in the trip a motel proprietor kicked my – rather large – vehicle, and grunted: 'I *hate* small cars!')

Stockbridge, Mass., of course, is a show-place. Every house is a perfectly preserved jewel. Even the filling-station looks as though George Washington comfortably Slept There. Each house has a classically-pillared veranda, a lacquered rocking-chair, and from the steps to the grass and on to the grass itself, is a *carpet*, as smooth and kempt as the grass. The people in the antique shops and the ante-bellum hotel (a pianist playing Noel Coward in the lobby) are like Occupying Forces. The place was only won from the Indians a couple of centuries ago, and they might come back. The Halloween pumpkins that line the perfect verandas are like trophies won from another culture, gained by barter from natives kept well out of sight.

Across the border, back in New York State, it is a psychologically more comfortable picture. The houses are mostly smaller, though large enough. (Later, calling on a carpenter who had looked after John Cowper Powys, I passed his house twice, unconsciously unable to believe that a carpenter should live in such a hacienda-like spread.) Some of the houses are even falling down, which is homely. Wooden frame houses take a long time to die. They hang in sections, drunkenly, looking ashamed of themselves, to be behaving so in front of the other houses. These, the undrunken ones, look as though dropped there that day by helicopter and just unwrapped.

But then, at last, there are cows up to their knees in muck, and a bald-headed man shovelling hay to them off the back of a truck. After Albany and Stockbridge that was a relief and reminded me that I had already spent too long in the car.

It is extremely difficult to leave it. In a country of such huge spaces you have to be helped to traverse them. Not only cars, but most of life, runs along the road. That is where most of the eating-places are, signalling 'Franks', 'Heroes', 'Subs', 'Grinders'. When you have risked a 'Sub' (no one has time to explain the others, and a Sub is a sandwich, submarine-shaped) you are back on the road again whether you like it or not, and it is designed to sweep you on to a Thruway to some far objective,

People and Places

like Canada. There are no signposts to small places off it, or these have a secretive air, as though to a private house. There are no maps and never a pedestrian to ask. That bald farmer was the only human being I had seen, unenclosed in a motor-car, all day. The road holds you comfortingly and will not let you go. It takes determination, and not a little courage, to decide to stay in one place.

Maddened, I pull in to a motel and am scrutinized by the limping proprietor. 'That'll be fifteen dollars. *In advance.*' I pay up and he softens, nearly imperceptibly. 'You alone? That'll be fourteen dollars eighty.' I puzzle over that twenty cents; you cannot buy the smallest glass of beer for less than thirty-five. In a bar in New York I was charged one dollar thirty-five for a tea-cupfull, and there was nothing special about the bar except that in the Gents you peed on ice-cubes.

At last, watched by the motel owner from behind slightly-parted curtains, as in a Raymond Chandler novel, I do the unthinkable. I set off *walking* along the nearly empty highway and turn up a side road called, invitingly, (tweely?) 'Whippoor-will Road'.

Slowly – it takes more to leave a car behind than merely to get out of it – I become aware that I am in a flawless autumn day, air stony-flavoured, like good white wine, a cleansing wind high overhead, and around me in apparently endless succession, the tree-covered Berkshire Hills.

English people who have settled here have compared it to Shropshire, but the hills appear to go on forever. In English terms you are in virgin territory, the roads between the trees are 'dirt' roads, roughly made up. Occasionally prim suburban signs say 'Wolf Road', 'Hickory Road', but on a rough hand-drawn map of fifteen years ago (the only one I could find, and its existence was news to the lady Town Clerk in her trim bungalow on the main road) the names are different and some roads have no names at all. They go to lonely farms, past old overgrown graveyards of the early settlers, and sometimes they go nowhere, just go on. These are probably old hunting-tracks, the woods are full of game. The Algonquin Indians lived peaceable lives here, and when you sit by one of the neat clear pools fringed by birches, with one smooth boulder placed perfectly in it, as in a Japanese temple, it is easy to imagine an Indian figure in soft buckskin standing quietly nearby, contemplating the distant line of the Catskill mountains.

The grass round the little lake sings as though it is full of small canaries, and when you move away green and brown grasshoppers jump from your feet like splashes.

'This is God's country, don't burn it and make it look like hell', says a notice pinned to a tree, and how like God's country this must have appeared to the first settlers. Not only in its peacefulness and abundance, but also in the astonishment of its autumns. No description or photograph can prepare anyone for the colours of the trees in October.

Sometimes cherries ripen unevenly, bright red on one side, light yellow on the other; some of the maple leaves are like that, on the same leaf. On the same tree the leaves can go from spring green to purple to the hot orange of a fox, and there is range after range of these hills, covered with this technicolour fur. The birds share in this exuberance of colour, even the sparrows have white throats and a neat centre parting, and American robins are bigger than thrushes and have slate-blue backs. Apparently it is the seasonal extremes of temperature that colour the leaves and improve the maple-sugar, which the Mahawks taught the settlers how to tap. There are three kinds of maple, there are birches with trunks so white they look snow-blasted, there are oaks and beeches and hickory, which has a shaggy bark, upward-pointing, like a slow undersea growth.

What is daunting are the Keep Out notices pinned to nearly every brilliant tree. 'POSTED! PRIVATE PROPERTY. ALL PERSONS ARE WARNED AGAINST HUNTING FISHING TRAPPING OR TRESPASSING FOR SUCH PURPOSE OR ANY OTHER PURPOSE WHATEVER. UNDER PENALTY OF LAW.' And each notice is signed by the owner of that piece of land. The hypnotic repetition of these warnings kept me out of the woods for half a day. Then I dared, fearing a shotgun blast, and entered a coloured tunnel as brilliant as a transformation scene in a pantomime, a Cave of Aladdin whose floor was as brilliantly coloured as its ceiling and its walls, for the dropped leaves keep their colours. A wind blew through the tops of the trees as though airing them, and occasionally dislodged an enormous dried-out leaf, three-pointed, that squatted on its three

People and Places

points, so that when I saw my first chipmunk I began by thinking it was a slowly hopping leaf.

And I began, slowly, to meet people. Someone told me of an eccentric 'Book Barn', up a track. It was indeed isolated, a second-hand bookshop whose trade must have been wholly postal, run by an Englishwoman. She mentioned the name of a poet, Peter Kane Dufault, who lived nearby, and pronounced it tentatively, as though he might bite. I found him by his river, chopping wood, living secluded, as an English poet might, earning his living by odd jobs – playing the fiddle at weddings, refereeing soccer matches – a whole world removed from the Thruway and the fast-food diner. After that we went for walks together. I had a native for companion. Secret lanes existed, and secret people.

I met Mrs Yagonoff, whose father-in-law from Russia had bought the small farm from Mr Cleveland in 1910 and had worked on it for years before that. It is an unpainted clapboard house by a stream, a hundred and sixty acres, mostly grazing, twenty black and white Holstein cattle.

At last I am up a lane, though it is farther from other lanes than any lane would be in England, and in a stuffy farmhouse kitchen with a black iron stove and a snarl of yelping dogs under the littered table. What would my New Yorkers make of this, only a hundred and fifty miles away, and the first inside lavatory put in here last year? I confess to a small sense of triumph, I had found what they did not believe existed; and then, as I sat talking to Mrs Yagonoff in her pinafore, as she smoked cigarettes, glad of the company, I slowly began to realize, with the same awe that Americans might feel in Winchester Cathedral or the Tower of London, that I was sitting in the original log-cabin.

The old exterior logs had been replaced by clapboard, Mrs Yagonoff did not know why – I should guess for social reasons – but the inside walls were the original undressed logs. This was the first house, built by the first white man to come to this place, fell the trees to build it, and so create the small clearing outside. I felt a greater sense of the past in her kitchen than I have in Europe in places thousands of years older. This was the beginning, unchanged, hardly overlaid. That early courage, hope, hardness was still in the air. The underbrush returns; her son is outside now cutting it back.

Looking for a Lane

She will survive, but not many have. Round here it was nearly all cleared at one time. Among the roots of tall trees you find the remains of old stone walls. But farming moved to the mid-West and the forest came back and still creeps on. Old fields are now given over to sorrel and the cotton-like milkweed, and there are forgotten graveyards with English and German names on their headstones which sag into the burrows of woodchuck.

The local village is Philmont. Once it was prosperous too, but now it has that passed-over feeling so familiar and attractive to Europeans. It calls itself a village (pop. one thousand seven hundred) but it takes a couple of hours to walk round it, so spread-out, as always, are the houses. It was an old textile town, its factory now idle, and the locals commute to Hudson. It is quiet by day and even quieter by night. Life-size Halloween dummies sprawl on the porches, one hangs by the neck from a rafter as though there has been a lynching. It is eerily silent, at night-time, everywhere is shut, there is nowhere to eat. I am the only person in the street and the squad-car crawls slowly past, its occupants peering at me. Blue lights flicker from between closed curtains, and dogs bark. There is a feeling, stronger than in England, that here are people in (large) boxes, watching a box and possibly eating out of a box also. But Americans know about this. No visitor could match their own energetic self-criticism.

There is a dark saloon, that advertises a cheap room in chalk on the wall. After hesitation (it is very quiet and sleazy, and filled with dark, silent figures) I take the room, and share the place with long-distance truck-drivers. We do not raise hell. We watch television, and make a sombre picture, perched on our barstools, looking up at the screen. It is baseball, the World Series: 'This isn't just the championship of the *world*' exults the commentator, 'it's the championship of the universe!' He may be right, but it is difficult to discuss the matter, the place is so dark.

Philmont is the 'village' but nearby there is also a hamlet, English-size, called Hillsdale. It is where that particularly English novelist, John Cowper Powys, found a hideaway and wrote *A Glastonbury Romance* in a little, English-style cottage set in the side of a hill. It is still there, and one of the reasons why I came to this neighbourhood is to find it. He called it 'Phudd's Bottom'.

One can see why he liked Hillsdale. It is old, pretty, a one-time staging-post. The Post Office has a wall of Poste Restante boxes, with glass fronts set in ornamental brass, that must date from the early days of Wells Fargo. I try to buy some postcards of the place and am directed to the local printer. He is a kindly man in braces, very much out of an early *Saturday Evening Post* cover, and he leaves his little press (on which he is printing 'POSTED!' notices) shaking his head sadly: no postcards: 'They're a hard commodity.' No one stops long enough to want them, just sweeps past. These places, because they are ordinary, are barely known to anybody but their inhabitants. What riches, and how sensible Powys was!

The shining days I spend walking the tracks through the woods with Peter, calling on Albert Crick the carpenter who knew Powys and loved him; on people who remember Theodore Dreiser coming here to visit him.

Peter, who has discovered in his own house Powys's initialled walking-stick, and presents it to me, is sceptical about the Limey writer; 'the old cassowary', he calls him. 'This is *my* patch!'

Peter Kane Dufault, who lives as many poets do in England, but more or less ignored by his peers, is possibly more cut off here than an English poet. Far off, New York circles entranced in its own orbit. He drives me to his lecture at the State University of Albany, and is immediately in difficulty with external America, tangled in Thruways and underpasses. In New York at a cocktail party the talk was all of intending to drive to one State and finding yourself deep in another. Americans have problems with their own scale. The University does too, it looks as though built by Mussolini (those 'legislators', maybe) and its cobbled campus would suit a rally at Nuremberg.

I go for a last walk in the first rain. The rain mutes the colours, putting a greyish-green mist over them, and I climb to some rumoured Indian graves among the trees. At least, that is what Powys thought they were (they are behind his cottage) and he used to climb to them to apologize, to placate their spirits. I had been told that thirty years ago America was full of Indian echoes, but that now they seem to have gone, as though there is nowhere left for them to bounce off. It was Peter Kane Dufault who said

Looking for a Lane

this to me, and perhaps it is true.

At the saloon I had been warned not to go anywhere near the woods, because it was first day of the season for the Bow Clubs. I had seen them at the side of the road, head to foot in SAS-style camouflage-suits, setting the points of their arrows, stringing their shining laminated bows. They were after the white deer and were, I was told, more eager than skilful, apt to shoot anything that moved.

So as I climb through the dripping trees I sing, to give them warning. At first I find I'm singing 'We'll turn Manhattan / Into an isle of joy', but this seems inappropriate for the Indians, to whom that certainly did not happen. Feeling foolish – for how could I explain to anyone what this European was doing, soaked to the knees, staring down in apology at small round heaps of stones on a hilltop among tall trees? – I give voice to a tune from 'The Trout'. It is at least European, roughly in period, and I am as fearful of the hissing of a shaft between the coloured leaves, the plunk of an arrow in my backbone, as the first settler from the Old World must have been when he climbed this hill for the first time, such a short while ago.

The Secret People

———— o ————

'WHY CAN'T THE ENGLISH teach their children how to speak? / This verbal class-distinction by now should be antique', sang Professor Higgins in *My Fair Lady*, and so sing all of us, or let's hope that soon we all do, even footballers.

HM Inspectorate of Schools has brought out two pamphlets on this and related topics. Among other things they suggest the teaching of 'Standard Spoken English', which has raised some opposition as 'an unwelcome imposition of "middle-class" forms'.

That would indeed be unwelcome but HMI does not suggest it, merely that there should be taught some common form to pupils, 'for those outside their speech community to understand', which, as a proposition, sounds reasonable.

But back to Alan Jay Lerner, and footballers. Lerner and Shaw were accurate, it is the *English* who seem not to teach their children how to speak, and after years of patient research among the sports reports on BBC radio, I think I know why; and it has nothing, or very little, to do with teaching.

Which is not to say the situation cannot be changed. It is a question of the need being strong enough. Take the example of trade union leaders. In the early days of television they often seemed hopelessly ill-matched against the smooth-tongued employers. These tongue-tied fellows were gradually replaced by other Trade Unionists of such persuasive articulacy, who began to be seen so often on television, and heard so often on radio, that we longed for them to go away as much as in an earlier era we had longed (at least I did) for the complacent employers to be taken down a peg.

This eloquence has not become fashionable among English footballers however, who are linguistically stuck in an earlier groove. If, among them, verbal class-distinction has not become

The Secret People

antique, it is because the footballers, who speak for millions of their adorers, do not want it to be. When the hero of a match is interviewed he mutters something modest and says, 'the boys done great', on purpose. The modesty, the grammar and the dullness are all part of a formula that announces, 'nobody is going to call *me* stuck-up'. The formula can be modified by peer-group teasing, but not much. The English cricket captain, Gatting, was laughed at in a kindly fashion because he always described his team's successive victories as 'tremendous'. At his latest press conference he promised he would not say 'tremendous' again, (loud laughter); he changed it to 'terrific'. There is a subtle and historical antagonism in this. He is refusing, certainly to the approbation of a great part of the nation, to sound like one of 'them', like 'the middle-classes', 'the bosses', or however 'they' might be described. He is giving evidence of a reasonable tribal fear. The only other tribe or class as exclusive as this, which has other reasons for self-protection, is the gentry; among them, also, an unusual word or unexpected formula is a signal of danger, an indication that a stranger is among them.

Why the same is not also true of Irish, Welsh and (with exceptions, but that is another matter), Scottish footballers is nothing to do with 'Celtishness'. In my view it is because they were all at one time conquered peoples, who could not, through the gift of the gab, rise to lord it over their peers because their lords were all foreigners. This set them free to relish language for its own sake – even their own language, if they were allowed to speak it – without suspicion of being turncoats. An Irish player, asked to describe his goal, does so in a way that puts the commentators to shame, because he is sure it will not put him to shame among his fellow-Irishmen. (His English team-mates may think their own thoughts; that he is an ignorant Paddy, perhaps.)

It is not done, for too many English people, to speak more brightly than your least articulate neighbour. There is generosity in this. But it is not ignorance, it is a fear that to relish language is to leave your tribe, which teachers have to allay. In his poem 'The Secret People' G.K. Chesterton looks to the day when the English People speak, 'who have not spoken yet'. It will be a shame, when the day comes, if we have forgotten how.

1987

Index

———— o ————

accentor hedge-sparrow 172-3
A Glastonbury Romance (J.C. Powys) 83-90
Albany, N.Y. 254-5, 260
Algonquin Indians 256-7
Amis, Kingsley quoted 112
Aquinas GKC on 241
'Arab Love-Song' Thompson's poem 142-4
A Ray of Darkness (Margiad Evans) 24-31
A Short History of England (G.K. Chesterton) 230, 231, 237-8
Auden, W.H. quoted 165; Patrick Kavanagh on 152; on MacNeice 154, 157; MacNeice on 156
autumn 40-41, 249-50, 251-2; in New York State 257
Aveluy, France in Ivor Gurney's poems 9, 12; World War I graveyard at 12, 13

Bacon, Francis interrogating Elizabethan Jesuits 244
Bangor, North Wales ITMA rehearsal 106
Barker, George C.H. Sisson on 165-6, 168
Barlow, 'Stone-waller' cricketer 62, 67-8
Bate, Walter Jackson biographer of Johnson 182
BBC and ITMA 104; MacNeice and 159-60; Religious Affairs 173; on Jura 228; 254
Beddoes, T.L. on glow-worms 207

Bedford Square film colony in 119
Belloc, Hilaire 228; and GKC 231, 235, 236-7, 242
Bellow, Saul *Herzog* quoted 178
Benn, Tony and Civil War 170
Berkshire, USA Hills 256; *Berkshire Eagle*, Pittsfield 254
Betws-y-Coed 34-6, 37, 39
Bewdley, Glos Packhorse Inn 20
Birdlip, Glos 32-3
Blaenau Ffestiniog 34-5, 36-9
Blake, William in Poets' Corner 15; 80; quoted 177; 240
bore, Severn 18-19
Boswell, James in Corsica 124
Botham, Ian 75-7; the GKC of cricket 226
Bradman, Don 71
Breconshire and Henry Vaughan 53
briony 41
Bristol 104
Brontë, Emily and Margiad Evans 25, 31
Browning, Robert GKC on, 238-9, 243
Burrell Collection 185-7
Bystram, Karol 72, 73

Cadman unfortunate birdman, Shrewsbury 22-3
Caine, Michael film star 117, 119
Cap Corse, Corsica 123-4
Capra, Jean in ITMA 107
Capua Vetere, Italy 182
Caraman, Philip translator of Gerard 245

Caulaincourt, France   World War I, 11
Catherine the Great   and Leningrad 216
Catholicism   100, 168, 235, 241
Cecil, Robert   and Jesuits' torture 245
Celts   32-3; (British) against Saxons 17
Centuri-Port, Corsica   124
Cheltenham, Glos   view of 32; College cricket ground 62, 63
Chadwick   designer of drains, deserving statue 246
Cherington, Glos   war memorial 43
Chesterton, G.K.   71; converse of Sisson 168; the Botham of journalism 226; compared with Orwell 227; 228; on socialism 230, 234, on democracy 232-33, 'The World State' quoted 234, Distributism and *GK's Weekly* 235, and Cecil Chesterton 240, and Jews 241-2; 'The Secret People' 263
Christianity   J.C. Powys and 82, 87; MacNeice and 154; Sisson as Anglican 168; and the Burrell Collection 186; Johnson's piety 181, 183-4; Thomas's bitterness 197; Larkin's poem 214; in Leningrad 216-17; GKC's 235-6, 241, 242
'Church Going'   Larkin's poem 90, 214
cigarette cards   of cricketers 71
Cirencester   hospital as byline 226
Civil War   Vaughan and 52-4; Sisson and Orwell representing 170
Clark, Kenneth   on Blaenau 39; on Burrell's Collection 185
Coleridge, Samuel Taylor   24, 27; 109-10; 142, 147-8; 153;

Notebooks quoted 26-7, 176; 219
Connemara   137
Connor, Tony   poetry reading by 151
Conrad, Joseph   on Hudson 199
Constantine, Learie   in Victory Test Match 71
Coole Park   camping near 139
Copper   the author's cat 223-4
Corsica   123-32
Cotswold Hills   32
Cowdrey, Colin   batsman 74
Crashaw, Richard   contrasted with Sisson 170
Creagh, Patrick   in Corsica 123, 125, 126
cricket   62-3: rained off in Cheltenham 62, Francis Thompson and nostalgia 62, French translations of Thompson's poems on, 62-3; Thompson practising bowling 65-6; Thompson's poems, parodies and prose 67-9; PJK and 70-75; Middlesex v. Somerset at Lord's, 1983, 75-7; behind the scenes at Lord's 77-9
Crick, Albert   friend of Powys, Hillsdale 255, 260
Crickley Hill, Glos   32, 33
Cronin, Anthony   *Dead as Doornails*, on Irish writers 152
Crystal Palace   Duke of Wellington's legendary solution to problem of sparrows in 115
cuckoo   33
Cummings, e.e.   MacNeice on 157
Cup Final   played in mud 133

Daniel, Wayne   bowler 76
De la Mare, Walter   Sisson on, 164
De Quincey   and Francis Thompson 65; on children 109

Devlin, Christopher biographer of Southwell 248
Diamond, Jean theatrical agent 117
Dickens, Charles GKC and 238
Distributism GKC and 235
Djakarta cricket club 72
DNB sneering at Grosart 246
Donleavy, J.P. 137
Donne and Vaughan 52; Sisson on Yeats and 165
Douglas, Norman on Edward Thomas 189
Dreiser, Theodore visiting Powys 260
Dryden, John in Poets' Corner 15
Dufault, Peter Kane 40; 258, 260
dunnock 172
Dyrham, battle of 17

Eastwood, Clint sheep impersonating 140
Eliot, T.S. 164, 206, 220
Elstree film studios 121-2
elvers 18
Empson, William on lyrics 146-7; on MacNeice 157
English as taught and spoken 262
epilepsy in *A Ray of Darkness* 28
Evans, Godfrey wicket keeper's hands 71
Evans, Margiad (Peggy Williams) writer 24-31
Evans, Meurig slate quarrier 37-8

Fabre French naturalist, on glow-worms 208
Fall, The psychologically satisfying idea of, to poets 145
Farrell, J.G. 138
fathers Francis Thompson's 64-5; watching cricket 74; John Cowper Powys's 82; in Iceland 93-8; Ted Kavanagh 99-108; 109-13; at Walmer Castle 114; Louis MacNeice's 154-5, 'The Truisms' quoted 161-2; Edward Thomas defying his? 197; W.H. Hudson's 202
fences notional nature of 139; at Molesworth 221-2
Fenton, James on a starving man 180
Fitzgerald, Edward cricketing parody of 68; on marriage 225
footballers attitudes to language 262-3
Forestry Commission in Wales 36
France World War I battlefields, and Ivor Gurney 9-14
Fretherne on Severn 17
Freud, Sigmund 109
Frost, Robert on translation 63; punctuation of poems 150; and Edward Thomas 189, 195-6

Galvani, Dino in ITMA 106
Garnet, Henry Jesuit martyr 244-5
Gatting, Mike cricket captain 76, 263
Gerard, John Jesuit hero 244-5
Gilson, Etienne on GKC's *Thomas Aquinas* 241
GK's Weekly 235, 240
Glastonbury and Powys 85-6
Gloucester 9, 18, 32
Gloucestershire Ivor Gurney remembering 9, 11; – Regiment, in World War I, 9, 11; – cricket team 1878, 67; 'image of Heaven' 174
glow-worms 207-8
Goethe, J.W. 80, 89
Grace cricketers: W.G. in Francis Thompson poem 62; the brothers 67
Grail in *A Glastonbury Romance* 86

grass 60-61; 63
Graves, Robert 16, 40, 165
Greene, Graham 244
Gregory, Lady 139
Grigson, Geoffrey on 'old man's beard' 41; on MacNeice 158; on song of hedge sparrow 172; 211-13
Grigson, Jane 212
Grosart, Alexander 246-8
Gurney, Ivor 9-16; quoted 133, 250

Half Moon Street film 117-22
Hall, Donald on misguided editing of Frost 150
Hamlet true hero of 102
Hammond, Walter slip-catch 62; century at Lord's 1945, 71
Hampshire Days (W.H. Hudson) quoted 200-1
Hancox, Alan bookseller 62
Handley, Tommy in ITMA 105-108
Hardy, Thomas and Powys 89; Sisson on 164
Heaney, Seamus 151
hedge-sparrow 172-3
Herbert, George Vaughan and 52, 54; Sisson and 170; Edward Thomas's alter ego reciting 197
Heuser, Alan editor of MacNeice 158
Hillier, Tristram illustrator of Shell guides 211
Hillsdale, N.Y. home of John Cowper Powys 1930-36, 259-60
Hitler, Adolf 177, 242
Hokusai portrait in Burrell Collection 186
Holmes, E.R.T. cricketer, his neckerchief remembered 71
Homer and Powys 80, 84, 88
Horace, Quintus Flaccus MacNeice and 160-61

Hornby, 'Monkey' legendary batsman 62, 67-8
'Hound of Heaven, The' 65, 68
Hudson, W.H. Thomas on 198; 199-206: watching spiders and New Forest boy 200, with tramp eating blackberries 204; on glow-worms 208
Hughes, Ted 15, 151, 214
Hulme, T.E. Sisson on 164

Iceland 93-8
Illustrated London News GKC's gratitude to 239
Indians (American) Algonquin 256-7; Mahawk 257; Powys and graves of 260; echoes of, 260-61
In Pursuit of Spring (Edward Thomas) 194-8
Ireland 34, 124, 134, 135-8; camping in 139; Irishness of MacNeice 157, 159; of Yeats 165; Shaw warning GKC of theocracy 236
Ironbridge Severn walk 21, 23
ITMA 101, 104-08

Jack-in-the-hedge 134
James, Henry 83
Jarrell, Randall poets as critics 153
Java 72; colour of green in 174
Jeeves cricketer, possible inspiration to P.G. Wodehouse 62
Jefferies, Richard 102, 188-93; unlike Hudson 204
Jenyns, Soame Johnson's review of *A Free Inquiry into the Nature and Origin of Evil* 181
Jesuits in Elizabethan England 244-5, 247
John, Augustus 39
John, Gwen 172
Johnson, Lionel Sisson on 'purged rhetoric' of 164

Johnson, Samuel   MacNeice on 159; 'Sermon 5' on human pain, 181; counting paces 182, prayers of 183, death mask 184
Jones, Methusalem   and slate quarries 37
Jonson, Ben   245
journalism   GKC on circumstances of, 226; GKC's output 239-40
Joyce, James   83, 85-6
Jura, Hebrides   Orwell's house on 228

Kavanagh, Patrick (1906-67)   152
Kavanagh, Ted   99-103; and ITMA 104-8
Keith, Sidney   in ITMA 106
Kent, Bruce   invoked in Molesworth pub 221
Kipling, Rudyard   and war graves 13
Knight, Professor Wilson   on Powys 83
Kwintner, Jeff   publisher 81

lambs   in Aga 43-4
Landor   'dining with', Sisson's comment on Yeats 165
Larkin, Philip   90, 167; on Jonathan Price 211; memorial service for 213-15
Laventie, France   and Ivor Gurney 9, 11
Lawrence, D.H.   16, 25, 27, 83, 86, 228
'Leaving Barra'   MacNeice poem quoted 153
Leavis, Q.D.   on Thomas's biography of Jefferies 189
Legge, Ben   of Rendcomb, Glos. 46
Leningrad   114; 216-18
Leopardi   Patrick Creagh translating 125; on moral force in a poem 206
Levi, Primo   219
Llansanffraid, Breconshire   Vaughan family 54
Lloyd George   GKC's view of 230
Llyn Transfynndd   power station 39
Llugwy, River   at Betws-y-Coed 34
London   Thomas's impressionist description 195; Hudson trapped in 202; and outskirts of New York 253
Lord's Cricket Ground   Francis Thompson's poem 67; 70, 71, 75; behind the scenes at 77-8
Lucas, E.V.   essay on Thompson's cricketing poems 1908, 67, 68
Lyndhurst, Hants   Hudson observing spiders at 200

MacCaig, Norman   poetry reading 151
MacDiarmid, Hugh   Sisson on 166
MacNeice, Louis   153-62
Malvern Hills   32
Marvell, Andrew   53, 63; on glow-worms 207
Matisse, Henri   inspiring old age of 80
Maugham, Somerset   depressing old age of 80
mausoleum   at Caulaincourt 11
Meredith, George   child portrayed in *The Egoist* 111
Meynell, Everard   biographer of Francis Thompson 64
Meynell, Wilfred   and Thompson 64, 65; editor of Thompson's poems 67
Michelangelo   150
Michie, James   17, 67
Middlesex   v. Somerset at Lord's 1981, 75

Miller, Henry and Powys 83, 84, 85
Miller, Keith batsman 71
Molesworth, Cambs. 221-2
Morris, Jan *The Matter of Wales* 32-3
Moss Bros 118
Mr Weston's Good Wine (T.F. Powys) 91, 92
Muratu, Corsica 128
Mytton, 'Mad Jack' pub at Atcham, Glos. 22

Nation GKC letter to 232-3
National Gallery and Blaenau Ffestiniog 39
nature writing and Margiad Evans 25; and Henry Vaughan 59; and Edward Thomas 194, 198; and W.H. Hudson 198, 201-2, 205-6
Newnham on Severn 19
New York City 252, 253, 256, 258, 260; – State, 253-61
Nietzsche quoted by Powys 89
Niolo plateau, Corsica 130
nuclear waste at Blaenau 39

O'Brien, Kate quoted on Ireland and Anglo-Irish 136, 137
Old Trafford historic match inspiring Francis Thompson 67-8
Omar Khayyám Thompson's cricketing parody of Fitzgerald 68
Origo, Iris on parents' 'death in the heart' 113
Orwell, George compared with Sisson 169-70; on political writing 227-8
'Ossian' Johnson's suspicion of 182
Owen, Wilfred 13, 16, 146; Sisson on 164
Palmer, Samuel 212
Paoli, Pasquale de Corsican hero 124

Peralta de Espés crusader tomb in Burrell Collection 186
Percival, Horace in ITMA 106
Philmont, N.Y. 259
Pitman, Jenny language of horseracing 40
Pittsfield, Mass. 254
poaching 45-51
poetry 141-8; 151-2
Pope, Alexander Johnson on 181
Popplewell, Nigel batsman 75-6
Posidonius on Celts, quoted by Jan Morris 33
Pound, Ezra quoted by Sisson 163; on Chesterton 231, 243
Powys, John Cowper 27, 39; 80-2; *A Glastonbury Romance* 83-90; in Hillsdale, N.Y. 255, 259-60
Powys, T.F. 84, 91
Price, Jonathan 209-11
Priestland, Gerald of BBC Religious Affairs 173, 180, 181
Priestley, J.B. on Powys 83, 84-5
punctuation importance of poets' 149-50

Queen Elizabeth I and Jesuits 244

rain in Gloucestershire 40, 133; in Wales 37; in Corsica 130, 131; in Berkshire Hills 260
Richards, Vivian batsman 75
Riez Bailleul, France and Ivor Gurney 9, 10
Romans in Wales 32, 38
Rooker, K. on Francis Thompson, in French, 1913, 62
Rousseau and children 109
Royle cricketer, lush description of by Thompson 69
ruins of Irish houses 135-8: pleasures of children in 135
Rushton, William as cricket captain 73

270

Savage, D.S.   on Margiad Evans 25-7
sawdust message   91-2
Saxons   17, 32
scything   60-61
Seferis, George   MacNeice on 158-9
Severn, River   and Ivor Gurney 9; 17-23; view of plain 32
Shakespeare   not writing about religion 244-5; and Southwell 247
Shaw, G.B.   and GKC 230, 236, 239, 240; 262
sheep   peaceful influence of 43; challenge to wall-building 139-40
Shelley   64; Thompson's essay on 65; quoted by Thomas on Jefferies 192
Shrewsbury   21, 22
Sickert   Thomas prose passage like 195
Silex Scintillans   (Henry Vaughan) 57, 118
Silone, Ignazio   on Ireland, quoted by Kate O'Brien 137
singles night   at Mytton and Mermaid, Atcham 22
Sisson, C.H.   163-71
slate industry   in Blaenau Ffestiniog 34, 37
Smith, Stevie   poem on Powys 82; on Muse 146
Snowdonia   34-9
Somerset   v. Middlesex at Lord's, 1981, 75
Somme, France   9, 10, 11
Southwell, Robert   poet and martyr 244-5, 247-8
spelling   mis-, in *Times* 149-50
Spender, Stephen   MacNeice on 157
spider   *Thomisus* observed by Hudson 200; roasted in Corsica 131
spring   by Severn 17, 20; in praise of wet 133-4

St Florent, Corsica   126, 127
Steele, David   cricketer 73
Stephens, James   'Nothing is easy' quoted 141-2
Stockbridge, Mass.   253, 254-5
'Stopping By Woods on a Snowy Evening'   Frost's punctuation of 150
summer   249
Swedenborg   on spirits meeting, quoted by Yeats 176-7
Sylvester, David   cricketing incident 73
Swaim, Bob   film director 122
swallows   207, 249-50

The Art of Happiness   (J.C. Powys)80-82
'The Truisms'   MacNeice poem 161-2
'The Waterfall'   Vaughan poem 54-5
'The World State'   Chesterton poem 234
Thomas, Dylan   40; MacNeice and 157
Thomas, Edward   16, 102, 146; Sisson on 164; and Richard Jefferies 188-93; *In Pursuit of Spring* 194-8
Thomson, David   137
Thompson, Francis   and nostalgia in cricket 62; translated into French 62-3; and Meynell family 64-5, on over-writing 65; on cricket 67-9; discovery of 142; 'The hunched camels...' quoted 142-4
Thoreau, Henry David   253
Thucydides   MacNeice and 155
Thwaite, Anthony   and Jonathan Price 210-11
Tomen y Mur   Roman fort, Wales 38, 39
tourists   in Betwys-y-Coed 34-5; in Corsica 124, 126; in Iceland 93-6

Tower of London Gerard's escape from 245; 258
Train, Jack in ITMA 107
Tribune Orwell's column in 228

Usk, River Vaughan's poems on 53-4

Vaughan, Henry 52-9
Vikings 93, 94
Volpajola, Corsica 130

Wain, John on Johnson 183
Wales 32; 34-9; and Vaughan 52; and Dylan Thomas 157
walking by Severn 17-23; in Glos. 42-4; in Corsica 126-31; in New York State 251-61
Walmer Castle, Kent 114-16
Wanderer Anglo-Saxon poem 138, 214
Ward, Maisie biographer of GKC 232
Ware, Fabian founder of War Graves Commission 13
War, First World and Ivor Gurney, in northern France 9-16; village memorial 43; 105; GKC on 231, 243
War Graves Commission, Commonwealth 12-14
War Poets memorial to, in Westminster Abbey 15-16; Sisson on 164
Weaver, Sigourney film star 119-21
Wellington, Duke of 114-16
Wells, H.G. and GKC 230, 241
Westminster Abbey Poets' Corner 15; Philip Larkin's memorial service 214
White, Terence de Vere on Anglo-Irish 136
Whitfield, Laurence 19, 21-3

Williams, Gareth Lord's organiser 78
Wiltshire Downs Edward Thomas describing 190
wind on cricket ground, on grass, 63; on leaves 115; wild west 250; 251-2
Windrush, River 174
winter 42-4; 91-2
Woolmer cricketer 74
Wootton, Anthony on glow-worms 208
Worcester 20
Wordsworth, William 27, 56, 88; 'Immortality Ode' quoted 110-12; 179
Worsley, Francis producer of ITMA 106
Wright, Clarrie in ITMA 107
Wright, D.V.P. 71
'wrong' mystery message 91-2

Yagonoff, Mrs of Berkshire Hills, N.Y. 258
Yeats, W.B. MacNeice pro- 159; Sisson anti- 165, 168; quoting Swedenborg 176-7; contempt for spirit of comedy 192
Yorick true hero of *Hamlet* 102
Yule, Fred in ITMA 106

Zen and writing 228